ROMANS IN FULL CIRCLE

ROMANS IN FULL CIRCLE
A History of Interpretation

Mark Reasoner

WESTMINSTER
JOHN KNOX PRESS
LOUISVILLE · KENTUCKY

Book design by Sharon Adams
Cover design by Eric Handel, LMNOP

First edition
Published by Westminster John Knox Press
Louisville, Kentucky

This book is printed on acid-free paper that meets the American National Standards Institute Z39.48 standard. ∞

PRINTED IN THE UNITED STATES OF AMERICA

05 06 07 08 09 10 11 12 13 14—10 9 8 7 6 5 4 3 2 1

Library of Congress Cataloging-in-Publication Data is on file at the Library of Congress, Washington, D.C.

ISBN 0-664-22873-9

This book is dedicated to
Hans Dieter Betz
and
Robert M. Grant

Contents

Preface

For two millennia, readers of the Christian Scriptures have been fascinated and puzzled by Paul's letter to the Romans. The fascination continues unabated, and readers of the letter continue to approach the text as if it holds answers to some of their most profound questions about God, God's relation to humanity, humanity's place before God throughout all of human history, the church's relationship to society in general, and the meaning of justice. This book is written to help Romans readers hear how their questions about Romans have been framed, asked, and considered in interpretations of the letter since the year 240. This book therefore gives voice to past conversations on key texts of Romans while telling the story of how Romans has been read among the nations (*ethnē*).

I have written this book with an upper-level undergraduate class or a second-year seminary class on the book of Romans in mind. This book is meant to be a supplemental textbook to give historical perspective to the questions that students inevitably bring to Paul's text and to offer a plot regarding how the earth's peoples (*ethnē*) with whom the letter is so concerned have interpreted the letter. If you are not in a Romans class but are studying the letter on your own, this book will also work for you. Students do not need to know Greek to read this book, though some Greek terms have to be mentioned when considering certain questions in Romans. I am responsible for all translations whose translations are not otherwise documented by the word *trans.* in the corresponding endnotes.

While I have written this to serve as a classroom text, I have resisted the inclination to make the book safe reading for all perspectives on Romans. It is impossible to be neutral on Romans. While I have not matched the polemical rhetoric of some of the most influential commentaries on Romans, I have decided not to hide what I consider to be the best approaches through each locus of the letter. I consider those approaches best that take into account the whole letter of Romans, make most sense as something Paul would have written, and make most sense for the church who seeks to live in light of Scripture.

Behind the joyful project of reading there are always authors and readers who create and re-create texts in relation to their particular circumstances. If this was true for Paul's letter to the Romans, it is also true for this book. And since the book is for students who are tracking how the letter has been read among the *ethnē*, I have decided to write as the missionaries' kid who I am, born and raised in Japan, who first studied the whole text of Romans in a graduate class at the University of Chicago, and who now teaches Romans to undergraduates in the shrinking context of Western Christianity. This context is shrinking because the church in the West is being eclipsed by the church in Africa, Asia, and Latin America. While this book charts how Paul's letter has moved in full circle for the last two millennia, it does so with eyes open to the ways this circle is still spreading outward among the *ethnē*.

Acknowledgments

The idea for this book came first from my colleague Kevin Cragg, history professor at Bethel University in St. Paul, Minnesota. He remarked once that he would like to read a book that described how Romans has been interpreted through history. A year-long stay in 2001–2002 at the Center of Theological Inquiry in Princeton, New Jersey, allowed me to begin the research for this book. I thank Wallace Alston Jr. and Robert Jenson for making that center such a conducive place for study, and fellow members Gary Anderson, Larry Bouchard, John Chryssavgis, Richard Hays, Joel Kaminsky, Travis Kroeker, Joseph Mangina, Anne Marie Reijnen, A. J. Reimer, and Robin Darling Young for reading an early draft of part of this project.

Two friends in the publishing world provided formative suggestions along the way, Jim Kinney and Carey Newman. Donald McKim at Westminster John Knox Press has been a very responsive and supportive editor, and the entire production staff there under Dan Braden's able leadership have been wonderful partners in producing this book. I register profound thanks to all of them for their artful midwifery.

People who have read various chapters include: Jean-Noël Aletti, Donald Alexander, Daniel Bailey, Peter Brown, Arland Hultgren, Hermann Lichtenberger, Richard Nysse, Alan Padgett, Riemer Roukema, Thomas Scheck, Thomas Schreiner, Walter Sundberg, and Christian Collins Winn. I sincerely thank these scholars for their advice and attention to parts of the manuscript; of course the errors and weaknesses of this book are my own responsibility.

I thank my friends Joseph Anderson, John Doutre, Steven Enderlein, and Richard Pervo for their counsel and encouragement. I thank my former department chair, John Herzog, for first suggesting that I teach Romans, and my current department chair, Michael Holmes, for encouraging my ongoing study of the letter. I thank Jay Barnes, the provost of my school, for letting me take the

2001–2002 school year to work on this book. I thank my father, Rollin Reasoner, for his interest in this project. Heartfelt appreciation and thanks go to my wife Wendy and our children, Kaitlyn, Seth, Emma, Clara, and Noah, for our life together.

In my first two terms of graduate school, I studied Romans with a professor who knows Paul's world very well. In the second term I also participated in a seminar on Origen with a leading patristics scholar. Both professors modeled what it means to identify and pursue key questions in the interpretation of this letter. In ways I could not imagine then, these teachers opened windows onto Paul's letter to the Romans that I could never have opened alone and influenced the course of my study to this day. The former scholar has also graciously allowed me to tell anecdotes from that Romans seminar in this book, and I thank him for his generous spirit. This book is therefore dedicated with appreciation and gratitude to Hans Dieter Betz and Robert M. Grant.

Mark Reasoner
St. Paul, Minnesota
January 2005

Abbreviations

Augustine

Abbreviations and English titles for the works of Augustine follow those used in *Augustine through the Ages*, edited by Allan D. Fitzgerald, O.S.A. (Grand Rapids: Eerdmans, 1999).

c. ep. Pel.	*Against the Two Letters of the Pelagians* (*Contra duas epistulas Pelagianorum ad Bonifatium*)
civ. Dei	*The City of God* (*De civitate Dei*)
Conf.	*Confessions*
div. qu.	*On Eighty-three Varied Questions* (*De diversis quaestionibus octoginta tribus*)
ench.	*A Handbook on Faith, Hope, and Love* (*Enchiridion ad Laurentium de fide spe et caritate*)
ep.	epistle
ep. Rm. inch.	*Unfinished Commentary on the Letter to the Romans* (*Epistulae ad Romanos inchoata expositio*)
ex. prop. Rm.	*Commentary on Statements in the Letter to the Romans* (*Expositio quarundam propositionum ex epistula Apostoli ad Romanos*)
f. et op.	*On Faith and Works* (*De fide et operibus*)
gr. et lib. arb.	*On Grace and Free Will* (*De gratia et libero arbitrio*)
mor.	*On the Catholic and the Manichean Ways of Life* (*De moribus ecclesiae catholicae et de moribus Manichaeorum*)

pecc. mer.	*On the Merits and Forgiveness of Sins and on Infant Baptism* (*De peccatorum meritis et remissione et de baptismo parvulorum*)
Retract.	*Retractions*
s.	sermon
Simp.	*To Simplicianus*
spir. et litt.	*On the Spirit and the Letter* (*De spiritu et littera*)
BA	Bibliothèque Augustinienne
Barth	
Romans I	*Der Römerbrief* (Bern: Bäschlin, 1919)*
Romans II	*The Epistle to the Romans*, trans. Edwyn C. Hoskyns (London: Oxford University Press, 1933). Original: *Der Römerbrief*, 2nd ed. (Munich: Chr. Kaiser, 1922)
BBK	Bonner Beiträge zur Kirchengeschichte
BECNT	Baker Exegetical Commentary on the New Testament
BGPTM	Beiträge zur Geschichte der Philosophie und Theologie des Mittelalters
BNTC	Black's New Testament Commentaries
chap.	chapter
CBQ	*Catholic Biblical Quarterly*
CCL	Corpus christianorum, series Latina
CD	Karl Barth's *Church Dogmatics*
CF	Collectanea Friburgensia
CSEL	Corpus Scriptorum Ecclesiasticorum Latinorum
CWE	Collected Works of Erasmus
diss.	dissertation
EKK	Evangelisch-Katholischer Kommentar
ESEC	Emory Studies in Early Christianity
ExpT	*Expository Times*
FBES	Forschungen und Berichte der evangelischen Studiengemeinschaft
FC	Fathers of the Church
FES	Finnish Exegetical Society
frag.	fragment
HTKNT	Herders theologischer Kommentar zum Neuen Testament

---

*Page numbers for *Romans I* are given first according to this original edition of 1919 and then the page numbers from Schmidt's edition follow in parentheses: *Der Römerbrief* (*Erster Fassung*) *1919*, ed. Hermann Schmidt, Karl Barth Gesamtausgabe: Akademische Werke 2 (Zurich: Theologischer Verlag, 1985).

ICC	International Critical Commentary
IFAO	Institut Français d'Archéologie Orientale, Bibliothèque d'Étude
JBL	*Journal of Biblical Literature*
JJS	*Journal of Jewish Studies*
JTS	*Journal of Theological Studies*
KD	Karl Barth's *Kirchliche Dogmatik*
LCC	Library of Christian Classics
LW	*Luther's Works* (standard English translation of Luther's works)
LXX	Septuagint
NE	Aristotle, *Nichomachean Ethics*
NovT	*Novum Testamentum*
n.s.	new series
NSBT	New Studies in Biblical Theology
NTS	*New Testament Studies*
ODCC	*Oxford Dictionary of the Christian Church*
Origen	Abbreviations and English titles for the works of Origen follow those in *The Westminster Handbook to Origen*, edited by John Anthony McGuckin (Louisville: Westminster John Knox, 2004). Those used in this volume are:
CCels	*Against Celsus* (*Contra Celsum*)
ComRm	*Commentary on Romans* (Scheck's chapter numbers of Origen's commentary are listed first with the volume and page number from his translation, which are identical with those of Migne in PG 14.837–1291, then Hammond Bammel's chapter numbers and line numbers are listed; fragment numbers refer to Heither's numbering of the Greek fragments of the commentary.)
PArch	*On First Principles* or *De Principiis* (*Peri Archōn*)
PL	Patrologia cursus completus series Latina, ed. J. P. Migne (Paris: Migne, 1844–64)
RAC	*Reallexikon für Antike und Christentum*, ed. T. Klaucer (Stuttgart: Hiersemann, 1950)
repr.	reprint
s.	*sermon*
SMRT	Studies in Medieval and Reformation Thought
TB	Theologische Bücherei
TI	Theologie Interaktiv

WA	*Weimar Ausgabe* (standard critical edition of Luther's works)
WSA	Works of St. Augustine: A Translation for the 21st Century, ed. J. E. Rotelle (New York: New City Press, 1990–)
WUNT	Wissenschaftliche Untersuchungen zum Neuen Testament

ORIGEN

His sin was to speak first
Among mutes. Learning
Was heresy. A great Abbot
Flung his books in the Nile.
Philosophy destroyed him.
Yet when the smoke of fallen cities
Drifted over the Roman sea
From Gaul to Sicily, Rufinus,
Awake in his Italian room
Lit this mad lighthouse, *beatus*
Ignis amoris, for the whole West.

All who admired him gave him names
Of gems or metals:—"Adamant." Jerome
Said his guts were brass;
But having started with this pretty
Word he changed, another time,
To hatred.
And the Greeks destroyed their jewel
For "frightful blasphemy"
Since he had said hell-fire
Would at last go out,
And all the damned repent.

("Whores, heretics," said Bede,
Otherwise a gentle thinker.
"All the crowd of the wicked,
Even the devil with his regiments
Go free in his detestable opinion.")

To that same hell was Origen then sent
By various pontiffs
To try the truth of his own doctrine.
Yet saints had visions of him
Saying he "did not suffer so much":
He had "erred out of love."
Mechtilde of Magdeburg knew him altogether pardoned
(Though this was still secret
The Curia not having been informed).

As for his heroic mistake—the wild operation
Though brusque, was admitted practical
Fornicationem efficacissime fugiens.

In the end, the medieval West
Would not renounce him. All antagonists,
Bernards and Abelards together, met in this
One madness for the sweet poison
Of compassion in this man
Who thought he heard all beings
From stars to stones, angels to elements, alive
Crying for the Redeemer with a live grief.
                                        —Thomas Merton

Introduction

I have fulfilled the gospel of Christ in the circle from Jerusalem to Illyricum.
Romans 15:19

"Have you ever taken a Romans class before?" The question came from a small man with piercing eyes, asked in a measured, quiet voice that reverberated in my mind. Here I was, twenty-five years old, with a newly conferred seminary degree, and an undergraduate major in biblical and theological studies, about to begin doctoral studies. But I had never had a course on Romans. After I left the office, when I began to think clearly again, I realized that my Greek translation course in college was on Romans 9–11. We read the chapters in Greek and diagrammed the logical relationships of each "proposition" in these chapters to one another. But a course on the whole letter to the Romans? I felt woefully unprepared as I answered Hans Dieter Betz, my advisor and teacher of a seminar on Romans for my first two terms in graduate school, "No."

Everyone begins somewhere. We have little choice or wisdom to revise our beginning position until we have learned more. Maybe you, like me on that day at the end of the summer in 1985, have never taken a class on Romans before. Or maybe you have, and want to learn more. Perhaps you have studied Romans from one perspective, as I first encountered Romans 9–11 in an undergraduate course taught by a Calvinist's apprentice, and now wonder if that perspective is the only way to read the letter. This book is therefore for both beginning and returning students of Paul's Letter to the Romans. The term "students" includes everyone who struggles with this letter. Even the experts are sometimes rendered speechless when working with this letter or—as often happens—change their minds about some of the points Paul makes in this letter. So even if you have never taken a class in Romans before, take heart: in one sense there is plenty that even your teachers—if they are worth the tuition you are paying—will admit they do not know about Romans. Everyone who wishes to understand this letter more fully must recognize that it opens vistas that extend beyond the reach of human vision and generates tensions that defy easy resolution. The extent of those vistas and the power of those tensions make comparisons between students' abilities to read and understand Romans an empty enterprise. No one, standing on the top of Mount Fuji at sunrise, is concerned whether she can see better than others. Instead, everyone tries to see some of Fuji's five lakes, Hakone, or even the sea—as far as the morning's weather allows.

This is a letter in which the apostle Paul tries to give an account of his gospel that bridges the distance from his Scriptures and their testimony of God's election of the Jewish people to the *ethnē* (nations), who are the primary audience of Paul's missionary efforts. Near the end of his letter, Paul claims that through the power of God's Spirit, he has fully spread the gospel of Christ in a circular route from Jerusalem to Illyricum. It is this full circle, he asserts, that now impels him beyond Rome to Spain. In the two millennia that have followed this letter's composition, one could also say that it has had a full orbit among the *ethnē*. It is primarily the *ethnē*—non-Jews who name Jesus as their Christ—who read this letter. I first encountered this letter as a child of missionaries in Japan, for example.

The *ethnē* have found this letter challenging in scope and at times dangerous in the claims it makes. At least since the late fourth century when an old priest in Rome sent his questions regarding Romans 7 and Romans 9 to a newly ordained, well-educated priest in north Africa, the letter has prompted pointed questions. It has been my experience in teaching Romans that students also bring their own questions to the letter and expect that a better understanding of the letter will provide answers to their questions. They expect that their instructor or the "right" commentary will bring final closure to their questions, though the best strategy is to listen to the conversations that have occurred for two millennia over their very questions.

It is best to be aware of others' responses to the questions we have when reading Romans because reading and studying this letter necessarily involve joining a conversation. Many students of the letter imagine their readings of this letter to be direct exposure to the thought of the apostle Paul. But these confident students do not recognize that reading Romans is more like joining a conversation. They do not realize the spectacles with which they read the letter, spectacles formed through the two millennia of questions and responses raised in the ongoing conversations on Romans. For example, why is it that when someone reads Romans 7 the immediate question is, "Does this refer to a Christian or a non-Christian?" This is the interpretive template put on this chapter beginning in the late fourth and early fifth centuries, but it is not the template of all previous commentators on Romans. If the very questions we ask about Romans arise out of what we automatically assume or have heard of the letter, we have the best chance of learning about this text by consciously entering the conversation room and listening to how two millennia of Romans readers among the *ethnē* have discussed our questions. This book is therefore written to help students of Romans find themselves and their questions in the two millennia of conversations that have occurred on Paul's letter to the Romans.

Besides readers' specific questions regarding Paul's diction and point of reference in this letter, there are the driving questions of Western civilization, such as the nature of justice, the nature of law, the relation of people to law, and the relation of humans to divine will or fate, that Paul raises in this letter. The letter has indeed become a foundational text in Western civilization. By summarizing past conversations about Romans, I attempt to chart how the *ethnē* have read this letter and argue that after two millennia in which the nations have been reading this letter a circular pattern is now discernible. As readers, the *ethnē* have configured Paul's letter in full circle.

While others have attempted to offer the history of interpretation of the letter and without doubt know details of this history better than I, their narratives have not attempted to find a general pattern or plot.[1] The account I offer in the chapters that follow attempts to make sense of this history by describing the plot of this letter's circulation among the *ethnē*.

It is impossible to give a complete account of how every verse of this letter has been interpreted in the two millennia of its history. Nevertheless, debates have centered around controversial texts in Romans, texts that pull each generation of readers—like strong ocean currents pull even the best of swimmers—back out into the sea of past interpreters' debates. What is it about these particular verses or paragraphs in Romans that keeps them controversial? In a sense it is what is missing from these texts. There are ambiguities and holes in Paul's expression, perhaps ideas and perspectives now lost to us that he and his early audiences shared; in other cases the ambiguities and holes may be intentional.[2] In any case, these controversial texts that leave questions in readers' minds are the places from which major currents of interpretation—in some cases one could say storms of interpretation—over Romans occur. I have identified twelve controversial texts—twelve "loci"—that we will use to chart how various students of Romans have read this letter. As an express train stops only at major stations on a train line in order to transport the highest number of riders and reach its final destination in good time, so we will examine only the main loci in this letter in order to help as many students as possible understand how the whole letter of Romans has been interpreted in the last two millennia. The loci identified in Table 1 are statements, not just words like "grace" or "righteousness," since it is complete statements in texts that generate meaning for readers.[3]

You will notice that in loci 3 and 5 I have used "made righteous" where you are used to seeing "justify."[4] I do this to force you to face significant questions

Table 1. The Loci of Romans

Locus Reference and Number	Locus Title and Text
1:16–17 1	**To the Jew First and to the Greek**—"For I am not ashamed of the gospel, for it is the power of God to salvation for everyone who believes, to the Jew first and to the Greek. For in it the righteousness of God is revealed from faith to faith, just as it is written, 'The just shall live by faith'" (see also 15:7–13).
1:19–21 2	**Natural Theology**—"For what is known about God is evident among them, for God has made it evident to them. For his invisible attributes are perceived from the creation of the world, being known by the things that he has made, both his eternal power and divinity, so that they are without excuse, for knowing God they did not glorify him as God or give thanks, but became empty in their reasonings and their senseless heart became darkened."
3:21–28 3	**Made Righteous by Christ**—"But now apart from law the righteousness of God has become visible, testified to by the law and the prophets, a righteousness of God through the faith of Jesus Christ toward all who believe. . . . for the display of his righteousness in the present time, so that he may be righteous and the one who makes righteous the person who is on the basis of the faith of Jesus."
5:12 4	**All Sinned**—"Therefore, just as through one man sin entered the world and through sin death, and thus death passed to all, with the result that all sinned. . ." (see also 3:9–19).
5:18–21 5	**The All and the Many**—"So then, as through the one, transgression passed to all people for condemnation, so also through the one righteous act there resulted a making righteous of life for all people" (see also 11:32).
7:7–8:4 6	**Warring Laws**—"I find then the following law in me, the one who wants to do the good: that evil is at hand in me, for I wholly agree with the law of God that is in my inner person, but I see a different law in my members, fighting against the law in my mind and capturing me with the law of sin that exists in my members."
8:28–30 7	**Calling, Foreknowledge, Predestination**—"We know that all things work together for good for the ones who love God, for those who are intentionally called. For the ones he foreknew, he also decided beforehand to be conformed to the image of his son, so that he would be the firstborn among many brothers and sisters; those he decided beforehand, these he also called, these he also made righteous; those he made righteous, these he also glorified."
9:16–19 8	**Not Willing or Running**—"So therefore it is not of the one who wills nor of the one who runs, but rather of God who shows mercy."
9:20–23 9	**Potter and Clay**—"Or doesn't the potter have authority over the clay, to make from the same batch one vessel for honor and one for dishonor? What if God, wishing to show anger and make known his power endured with much patience vessels of wrath fit for destruction, even in order to make known the wealth of his glory on vessels of mercy which he prepared beforehand for glory?"

(continued)

Table 1. (continued)

Locus Reference and Number	Locus Title and Text
10:4 10	**Christ the *Telos* of the Law**—"For Christ is the *telos* of the law for righteousness to everyone who believes" (see also 3:31–4:3, 23–25).
11:25–27 11	**Israel's Salvation**—"And then all Israel shall be saved; as it is written, 'The deliverer will come from Zion, he will turn ungodliness away from Jacob; and this is my covenant with them, when I will forgive their sins'" (see also 3:1–4).
13:1–7 12	**Let Every *Psychē* Be Subject to the Authorities**—"Let every *psychē* be subject to the ruling authorities. For there is no authority except by God; those which exist are ordered by God. So the one who opposes authority has opposed the command of God; those who have resisted shall receive judgment on themselves."

that keep emerging among readers of Romans: What is the righteousness (or justice) of God and what does it mean to say that God grants righteousness to someone? Various forms of this question emerged in the early fifth-century contest between Pelagius and Augustine, returned in the sixteenth century and were answered in slightly different ways by Luther and Melanchthon, and returned again in the twentieth century in the academic debate over the righteousness of God between Rudolf Bultmann and Ernst Käsemann and in ecclesiastical discussions between Catholics and Protestants.

I use Paul's very word *telos* in locus 10, since the translation of this word affects how one understands the locus. *Telos* ambiguously carries senses of both "termination" and "fulfillment," so using the word in our translation allows us to confront the options Paul gave his first readers better than any word in a modern language.

While *telos* preserves Paul's ambiguity in Romans 10:4, it is possible that *psychē* carries a specificity not found in modern translations of Romans 13:1. I therefore retain Paul's word *psychē* in locus 12, since one interpreter we examine exempts many believers from the obligation to obey civil government because of a specific sense of this word.

You will also notice that after some of the loci other references are given. These loci are not simply the only places within the letter where the questions they prompt emerge. These twelve loci simply represent highly contested entry points into long-standing questions that emerge from the reading of Romans. Not all of these loci may seem controversial to you, but chances are high that most of them lead to questions you have about this letter. So rest assured that our path over these loci in various centuries of the church's engagement with this text will include repeated side trips to related paragraphs in Romans to which these loci lead.

When I began studying Romans in college, I had no idea how differently various scholars could interpret Romans. I remember talking with my father in a cabin at Lake Yamanaka one summer and trying to remember the name of the commentator—C. E. B. Cranfield—we had used in the Romans 9–11 class in my previous semester back in the States. Back then I thought that all commentators' works on a given book of the Bible were basically the same; they differed only in the level of language and degree of detail. But then on the first day of the Romans seminar in graduate school, Professor Betz began to describe various commentators. Cranfield? "Cranfield is part of the Anglo-American apologetic consensus. . . ."

Perhaps an analogy will help the reader understand the differences in commentators. Compare recordings of Pablo Casals, Anner Bylsma, and Yo-Yo Ma playing Bach's cello suites, and you will begin to understand what I began to learn that day I listened to Professor Betz compare commentators.

Within each chapter of this book, I attempt to familiarize the reader with the main elements of conversation on the locus being examined. Because this is the format, you might be tempted to choose which interpreter you like best on a given locus. Your own entrance into the conversation on a given locus might be something like, "Augustine (or in other cases, Luther) got this locus right; everyone else is off track." But I recommend that you delay such judgment and try instead to hear the long conversation about each locus, attempting to discern where the conversation about the letter as a whole is headed. In this process I just called a "long conversation," some exegetes employed theological models very different from others. If one exegete's theological model has been replaced by another, does that mean that the former's contributions to the Romans conversation are useless? The following analogy from Wittgenstein helps me to learn from every exegete mentioned in the following chapters here, and opens up the possibility that charting a history of interpretation where theological models are at stake is not simply a contest to find which contributor beat all the others in "getting it right."

> Imagine we had to arrange the books of a library. When we begin the books lie higgledy-piggledy on the floor. Now there would be many ways of sorting them and putting them in their places. One would be to take the books one by one and put each on the shelf in its right place. On the other hand we might take up several books from the floor and put them in a row on a shelf, merely in order to indicate that these books ought to go together in this order. In the course of arranging the library this whole row of books will have to change its place. But it would be wrong to say that therefore putting them together on a shelf was no step towards the final result. In this case, in fact, it is pretty obvious that having put together books which belong together was a definite achievement, even though the whole row of them had to be shifted.[5]

This book therefore has the best potential to inform readers who do not lose the forest for the trees. I hope that you will join me in paying attention to the whole process of how Romans has been interpreted in the Western church, a circular progression in which interpreters are returning to how the letter was approached in the third century. Here is the plot of this circular progression of Romans among the *ethnē*.

Origen reads Romans as a letter in which Paul is the arbiter between Jews and the *ethnē*.[6] According to Origen, Paul is focused in this letter to show how his gospel takes account of both Jews and *ethnē*. In some cases Origen specifies that Paul is in this letter an arbiter between Jewish and Gentile believers in Jesus.[7] In other places it is clear that Origen is applying this model to Israelites who do not believe in Jesus and to Gentile believers.[8] For Origen, this letter is centered around the way Paul's gospel addresses the Jewish people—with and without Christ—and the *ethnē*—primarily Christ-believers but occasionally the pagan *ethnē* as well. This thematic center is illustrated by the quotation at the beginning of the chapter on locus 1. Origen's expansive reading of the letter through the broad pairing of Jews and *ethnē* certainly includes issues that later interpreters considered the single focus of the letter, always situating these issues in the salvation-historical move from the law of Moses to the faith of Christ and the tension between Jews and Gentiles who have placed their faith in Christ.

There are other minor agenda in Origen's commentary. It is written against Gnostics, who had used the letter to teach that people are born with fixed natures and without free will. Origen also writes against Marcion, who taught that there was no continuity between the Jews and their Scriptures and the *ethnē* who followed the Jesus they knew from their "New Testament." These subsidiary agenda items will surface in this book, but the plot centers around how Romans as Paul's arbitration between Jews and the *ethnē* has been used, ignored, and recently recovered by readers of the last two millennia.

Augustine uses the letter in different ways, depending on his polemical audience—Manichean or Pelagian.[9] For an introductory summary, Augustine finds in this letter the pattern for how an individual Christian from among the *ethnē* reaches salvation, which for him is a favorable verdict at the final judgment and life eternal with God.

In a fruitful period of reconfiguration, the medieval exegetes attempt to soften the later Augustine's hard determinism and redefine grace in this letter. Medieval exegetes such as Cassiodorus, Sedulius Scottus, and Abelard use approaches from Origen alongside Augustine in this millennium of reconfiguration. In this book I have chosen to present Romans interpretations from Abelard and Thomas Aquinas for the medieval period. Detailed documentation of the medieval period's explicit censure of Origen and simultaneous dependence on his exegesis is readily accessible in the fine work of Henri de Lubac, and now we are well served by Thomas Scheck's focused study on the medieval reception of Origen's Romans exegesis.[10]

Luther complicates the return to Origen's reading (here is the tension in this book's plot) by radicalizing Augustine with a faith/works distinction not found in Origen and unlike Augustine's anti-Pelagian rhetoric. At the same time, Luther discovers the power of God's righteousness and helps generations of readers find their identity in Christ with the model of justification by faith.

But with Barth and post-Barthian readings of Romans we are getting back to reading Romans through the lens of the Jew-*ethnē* struggle over the nature of God's election. In diagram 1, you will notice that direct lines from Origen's central description of Romans and his openness to the salvation of Israel link these post-Barthian readings to Origen. The lines in the diagram represent only ideological continuity, not conscious dependence.

The post-Barthian readings this book highlights are those of the new perspective and approaches such as those of A. Katherine Grieb and N. T. Wright. The latter two authors both appeal to a narrative substructure in their exegesis of Romans. They do not wish to be linked together into a definable "school" or single approach.[11] For the purposes of this diagram, I group them together as "narrative-based approaches" to Romans, but there are significant differences between them. For example, N. T. Wright's general narrative includes the assertion that Jesus has replaced Israel as God's representative for the world, while Katherine Grieb disagrees with Wright on this point. Grieb acknowledges her approach as an "exegesis of Romans that appeals to a narrative substructure."[12] Wright defines his approach to Romans as "a theological reading of Israel's story as the focus of God's story with the world, both of which reach their climax in Jesus of Nazareth."[13] The new approaches to reading Romans continue to minimize the direction in which Luther took the letter and question Augustine's individualistic reading of Paul's gospel, calling readers instead to read the letter as an exploration of how Paul's gospel accounts for Jews and *ethnē* throughout all of time in light of God's display of Christ for the world.

So in each locus I try to present some key strategies used in the time periods of Origen, Augustine, the Middle Ages, Luther, Barth, and the later twentieth and early twenty-first centuries. I also discuss how Origen's influence was felt, suppressed, transmitted, or recovered in the conversations on Romans that occurred at these different moments.

We have much to cover in a survey like this. So let's jump in.

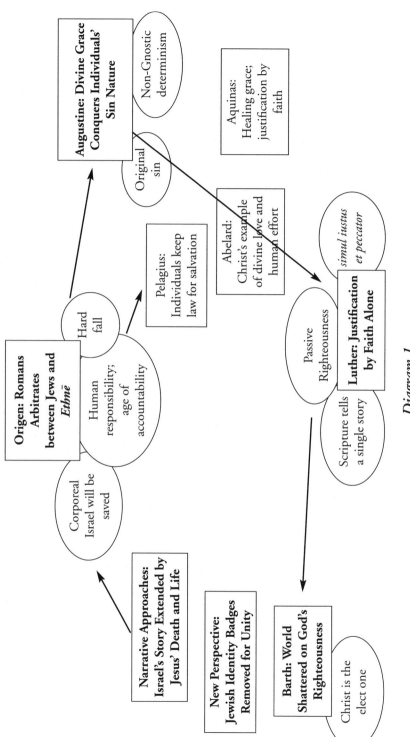

Diagram 1

Locus 1

To the Jew First and
to the Greek (1:16–17)

This letter yields no small difficulties in interpretation because many things are woven into this epistle concerning the law of Moses, about the calling of the Gentiles, about Israel according to the flesh and about Israel which is not according to the flesh, about the circumcision of the flesh and of the heart, about the spiritual law and the law of the letter, about the law of the flesh and the law of the members, about the law of the mind and the law of sin, about the inner and the outer man. It is enough to have mentioned these individual themes since in these it seems the contents of the letter are contained. But now let us hasten to his explanations as far as the Lord considers us worthy to disclose the way to us.

Origen[1]

All Romans readers need to consider: (1) whether this locus represents the "theme" or "primary topos" of the whole letter; (2) whether one phrase in this locus is to be emphasized as marking the theme of Romans; (3) what "the righteousness of God" means; and (4) what "from faith to faith" means.

ORIGEN

On Romans 1:16 Origen takes the "power to salvation" phrase to imply that God also has the power to destroy. This leads him to mention God's right hand of saving power and God's left hand of destroying power. Since Paul has equated the gospel with power, Origen suggests that Christ should be identified as "the power" here.[2]

His discussion of the next phrase, "to the Jew first and to the Greek," signals a sensitivity to Judaism that will be more apparent as the commentary progresses. Here he simply applauds Paul's division of humanity into Jew, Greek, and barbarian (as opposed to the Greeks' division simply into Greek and barbarian). Origen, perhaps inspired by Romans 3:2 and 9:4, says that Paul is right to place the Jews first, since they were the first people to live under laws, laws in their divine origin better than Greek laws.[3]

His comment here is significant for calling our attention to the wide horizon, both in terms of ethnicity and time, that Paul opens when discussing humanity in this letter. One gets the sense here and in Romans 5:12–14 that Paul would welcome a visit to the fossil beds in Tanzania known as Olduvai Gorge and a briefing on the remains of prehistoric humans found there, *Homo habilis* and *Paranthropus bosei*. Wherever humans can be found, Paul is eager to locate them in relation to his gospel.

Origen's literal reading of "Jews" here is not always followed. Origen glosses "Jews" at Romans 2:9 to mean believers in Jesus from every race, citing Paul's description of an inward Jew in 2:29.[4] His comment here at 1:16 also prepares us for one of his major contributions to our understanding of Romans. Origen's Romans commentary alerts readers to the different ways that Paul can use *nomos* ("law") in this letter. We shall come to these different ways as we progress through the loci of Romans, but notice here how even before Paul uses the word "law," Origen has introduced it.

Origen glosses "from faith to faith" to imply that Jews who had trusted in God under Moses were included in the faith of which Paul writes. In a move not unlike the Reformed tendency to see the gospel within the law, Origen says that to have life one must follow both law and gospel, though of course this assertion is prompted by Origen's anti-Marcionite attitude.[5]

This section of Origen's commentary as found in Rufinus is rather brief and shows no evidence that Origen or Rufinus considered these verses the thesis of the letter. The available Greek fragment on Romans 1:17 seeks to emphasize the continuity between Paul's gospel and the Mosaic covenant. Origen describes the righteousness of God coming to those who have newly come to the old faith and then explains, "For someone always had to believe in Moses in order that this one would believe in the Christ, and the one who believes in the Christ without believing in the prophets does not believe correctly."[6] Here we see Origen positioning himself early on in the commentary against Marcion, who taught that the God of the New Testament is a different god from the God of the Old Testament.

The Greek fragment goes on to exegete "the just shall live by faith" in a way that makes clear Origen never conceived of the faith/works distinction of the Reformation: "The phrase 'the just shall live by faith' teaches that if someone is righteous but does not have faith, or if he believes but is not righteous, he will not be saved."[7] With this exegesis Origen shows he is not rigidly distinguishing faith from works. He thinks a person must have faith and also have good works.

AUGUSTINE

Augustine's *Commentary on Statements in the Letter to the Romans* and his *Unfinished Commentary on the Letter to the Romans* make no mention of Romans 1:16–17. The omission of any comment especially in the former work fits with the general impression that in the patristic period these verses were not viewed as the thesis of the letter in the way they are often assumed to be now.

As we saw in the Origen section above, justification was not considered in this period to be exclusively by faith. Augustine is in continuity with Origen regarding the necessity of good works in the one who believes in Christ. He writes in *On Grace and Free Will* (dated to 427) that eternal life is given in response to good works and that we are saved by grace. His solution to this is to identify our good works as part of God's grace. But good works are most definitely necessary, according to Augustine's exegesis of Ephesians 2:8–9 in this text: "And the apostle himself, after saying, 'By grace are ye saved through faith; and that not of yourselves, it is the gift of God: not of works, lest any man should boast'; saw, of course the possibility that men would think from this statement that good works are not necessary to those who believe, but that faith alone suffices for them; and again, the possibility of men's boasting of their good works, as if they were of themselves capable of performing them. To meet, therefore, these opinions on both sides, he immediately added, 'For we are His workmanship, created in Christ Jesus unto good works, which God had before ordained that we should walk in them.'"[8]

ABELARD

Abelard gives no evidence of the later fixation on these verses as the thesis statement of Romans. He interprets the "to the Jew first" phrase in 1:16 primarily in a temporal sense, noting that it was from the Jews that the apostles were converted, and then later that through them the gospel was preached to the nations. He does not have a strong commitment to God's prior election of the Jews as something "first" in value, for he offers the possibility that "first" could mean "especially" to Jews and Greeks simultaneously, since now Paul was seeking to evangelize other peoples (e.g., the Romans).[9]

Abelard invests most of his words at this locus in a definition and explanation of righteousness. He interprets the righteousness of God primarily as God's just recompense of the elect to glory and the impious ones to punishment. Even the phrase "from faith to faith" is interpreted along these lines, so that it is on the basis of a faith in punishment that God directs us to a faith that results in rewards. To illustrate this definition of righteousness, Abelard turns to the Gospel of Matthew. The righteousness that Abelard finds is one that calls us to examine the root of our intentions (Matt. 6:22–23) and live with the conviction that all human action receives a divine recompense (7:2) culminating in a final judgment (25:34, 41). Abelard seems to gloss his explanation of righteousness as divine recompense with a doctrine of election, for it is the "elect," not the pious, whom Abelard identifies as those who receive a favorable judgment from God.[10]

AQUINAS

Aquinas is useful to read simply for his description of faith. Since faith depends on both the intellect and the will, faith is affected by the completion of the human will in the practice of love. Faith is thus much more than assent for Aquinas.[11]

The challenge of understanding whether "faith" in this locus means God's faithfulness, human faith in God, or both is also concisely laid out by Aquinas. While linguistically more handicapped than Erasmus, Aquinas knows of two versions of Habakkuk 2:4. He thinks Paul is quoting the translation, "My just one shall live by faith," while he admits that there is a translation based on the Hebrew that reads, "The just one shall live by his faith." Since he finds Pauline support for both senses of how one might live by faith, he accepts both senses here.[12]

LUTHER

We have already observed that these verses are not accorded special status by Origen, Augustine, or Abelard. Luther begins the trend to consider these verses as the thesis of Romans, a view that many people now accept as obvious. Once this locus is accepted as the thesis of the letter, then the stakes are raised very high in the exegesis of these two verses. Those who read Romans consciously or unconsciously through the eyeglasses of Luther, who taught that this letter is all about righteousness and being justified by faith, are prone to emphasize the "righteousness of God" phrase in 1:17a. Even those who do not think that righteousness is the theme of the letter are still indebted to Luther's identification of this locus as the letter's thesis if they try to outline the letter's argument based on these two verses.[13]

In Luther's lectures he describes the gospel as that message from God that reveals the righteousness of God, a righteousness that comes only by faith. This allows Luther to break with Aquinas and other scholastics. Luther's problem with Aquinas and even the Tübingen nominalists was that they relied on Aristotle, who taught that people become righteous by habitually acting in righteous ways.[14] Luther of course treats this as a humanistic tendency to ascribe to human agency what can only be done by God, through the cross of Christ. So we have a classic snapshot of Luther using Augustine against Aristotle in his first scholium on Romans 1:17.[15]

The actual identification of this locus as the thesis of Romans comes through Luther's autobiographical reflection on the righteousness of God that he penned for the 1545 edition of his Latin writings. But he had already described it as the "whole conclusion of the whole letter of blessed Paul to the Romans."[16] If it is such a "conclusion," then the exegete's choice of what phrase matters most in these verses, and how it is defined, influences the way the whole letter is read.

If, as one strand of Luther's legacy understood it, the phrase "the righteousness of God" matters most and is defined as the forensic status of "righteous" that God gives people irrespective of their behavior, then this locus and the letter into which it leads is all about the vertical relationship between an individual and God. Romans becomes a road to salvation for individuals and no more. But if "to the Jew first and to the Greek" is still emphasized within the locus, a window is left open to consider God's righteousness as concerned with humanity as a whole and therefore to be both vertically and horizontally understood. For centuries, based on one understanding of how Luther read Augustine, we have been led to believe that the righteousness of God as described in Romans is in the first place about an individual believer's legal status before God and does not primarily concern how God's people live out God's righteousness—or justice—on the earth.

ERASMUS

Erasmus follows Origen in paying close attention to the descriptors of all humanity in Romans 1:14 (Greeks and barbarians) and 1:16 (Jews as well as Greeks). He differs from Origen in glossing the "Jews" in the latter verse as physical Israel, rather than as the Christ-believing *ethnē*.[17]

Erasmus has a lengthy survey of the various meanings of "faith" in his efforts to exegete the phrase "from faith to faith." After stating that faith can carry both subjective (God is faithful) and objective (one places faith in God) significance, Erasmus explains the phrase "from faith to faith" by quoting two different Greek translations of Habakkuk 2:4, with which Paul ends Romans 1:17. Since the standard Septuagint translation is that "the just one shall live by my [God's] faith," and Symmachus's translation (known from Origen's Hexapla) is that "the just one shall live by his faith," Erasmus claims that Paul is tapping into both traditions by framing his quotation with "from [God's] faith to [human] faith."[18]

BARTH

This locus, which for Barth is the central locus in Romans, becomes a revolutionary leaven for theology in general because of Barth's insistence that one read "the righteousness of God" as a subjective genitive. In *Romans I* he describes "the righteousness of God" as follows: "God deals in consistency with his very self, when he extends his saving hand to the world in this unified way. Then it is that there appears in this unified way on the earth the original, direct, normal relationship of humanity to God, the relationship in which God himself is just, that corresponds to his character."[19] With this interpretation Barth beckons his readers outside their own *pro me* orientation, in which God's righteousness is primarily viewed as something God gives to the human subject, such as Luther's "alien" or "passive righteousness." With Barth we bracket the human who is reading Romans and consider first of all how God is true to himself.

In his survey of the history of exegesis of "the righteousness of God," Ulrich Wilckens credits Barth for providing a new approach to biblical discourse on the righteousness of God. The distinctives of this approach are its emphasis on God's righteousness as being completely true to himself, and the way in which Barth wants to treat God's righteousness as inseparable from his mercy. The righteousness of God is thus emphasized as God's thoroughgoing self-consistency and not so much as a quality that humans think of as appropriating for themselves. Wilckens faults the political outworking of Barth's understanding of the righteousness of God by contending that it leads to inconsistency in Barth. If, in Barth's understanding, the righteousness of God leads to concrete action on behalf of the poor, wretched, and helpless, then such action in the present becomes effectively indistinguishable from the coming kingdom of God. Yet Barth always wants to hold the coming kingdom of God as completely independent from human action in the present.[20] This criticism by Wilckens misses the significance of Barth's emphasis in *Romans I* on the organic growth of the kingdom of God: this kingdom could not be built through human agency.[21] The same point of significance was held in *Romans II* using the time-eternity dialectic; what humans did in time could never bring in the eternal kingdom of God.[22] The theological repercussions of Barth's Romans commentaries of 1919 and 1922 derive their driving force from this exegetical move: the righteousness of God is not in the first place our possession; it is rather God's characteristic way of being true to himself.

From where did Barth derive this reading of "the righteousness of God"? It does not come from any previous interpreter of Romans. J. T. Beck, a scholar with pietist roots and author of Barth's favorite commentary during his composition of *Romans I*, writes on the righteousness of God at Romans 1:17 with a focus on the human subject and a confidence in a mystical sense of revelation (captured in his use of *apokalyptein*, "to reveal"): "This is a place where it would be well for us to observe how it contains the correct concept, as in the gospel the righteousness of God comes to the believer through *apokalyptein*, that is, so that it allows one to know and to experience the righteousness of God with an inner, mental vigor, that consequently the evangelical justification as spiritual act from the divine Spirit, the principle of *apokalyptein*, might be fully evident from the spirit of the believer."[23] Barth avoids any appeal to the believer's experience, for human experience can get no purchase on God, according to Barth.

From where then did Barth derive his particular emphasis on the subjective genitive when exegeting "the righteousness of God"? The apostle writes in Romans 1:17 that this righteousness is revealed "from faith to faith," and it is in Barth's exegesis of this phrase that we can find an exegetical precedent for his interpretation of the righteousness of God. Barth understands the first "faith" as belonging to God and chooses to translate it as "faithfulness," based on input from a professor of New Testament in Basel, Rudolf Liechtenhan.[24] In the preface to *Romans II*, Barth credits a letter from Liechtenhan as first giving him the idea to use "the faithfulness of God" in the first edition, and observes that Liechtenhan had since published an argument in favor of this translation.[25] Barth admits to receiving considerable criticism for the subjective genitive ("faithfulness of God"), and says that he has reduced the number of places in the commentary where he uses it, while still keeping it prominent in his section on Romans 3.[26] It still appears conspicuously it *Romans II* at 1:17: "**From faithfulness** the righteousness of God reveals itself, that is to say, from His faithfulness to us. . . . **Unto faith** is revealed that which God reveals from His faithfulness. To those who have abandoned direct communication, the communication is made. To those willing to venture with God, He speaks."[27] In both editions Barth considers the righteousness of God to be "the consistency of God with Himself" that is brought to light in Christ and thus comes to be recognized and honored.[28] The starting point of God thus directly affects the exegesis of this thematic statement in Romans.

This is an interpretive point that Barth pioneered for Romans research. It remains a lasting legacy to Barth's God-centered starting point in *Romans I* and *Romans II* that virtually all commentators today understand the expression "from faith to faith" in Romans 1:17 to begin with God's faithfulness. Barth's insistence on the subjective genitive (the faithfulness of God) here also means that he takes *pistis Christou* in Romans 3:22 and 26 as the subjective genitive (faithfulness of Christ), as we will see in locus 3.

Barth says that the theme of Romans is found here, "where the faithfulness of God encounters the fidelity of men, there is manifested His righteousness. There shall the righteous man live."[29] Barth thus begins with God's faithfulness. For Barth, the letter is not about how humans reach God by deciding to trust in Christ or God; the letter is rather about how God, who is totally outside the realm of history as we know it, is completely consistent with himself and who while being faithful encounters humanity.

POST-BARTHIAN APPROACHES

In the twentieth century a storm broke out over the meaning of "the righteousness of God." Rudolf Bultmann represents one development of Lutheran tradition with his definition of this righteousness as the forensic gift of the label or status of righteous that God grants to believers. In this sense, the righteousness of God is understood from its human side; it is a status that humans have. The expression is labeled a "genitive of origin,"[30] since the genitive "of God" is the origin of the righteousness believers have.

Bultmann's student Ernst Käsemann struck out in a new direction that was still rooted in Luther but not as directly tied to the legacy of the Reformation as Bultmann's explanation was. For Käsemann, the righteousness of God must first be defined as God's power or control over the world that is shown explicitly in the incarnation, death, and resurrection of Jesus. The expression is labeled a "subjective genitive,"[31] since in this understanding God is always the subject of the righteousness.

Arland Hultgren provides a useful survey of these two positions and review of the texts in Paul's Scriptures that provide a background for it. Hultgren chooses not to decide between the two, finding both senses in Paul's Scriptures. Particularly in Isaiah 61, for example, the righteousness of God appears to have both "subjective genitive" and "genitive of origin" senses, for God's righteousness is displayed to the earth (61:1) while at the same time righteousness comes to flourish on the earth (61:2, 11).[32] Hultgren's wisdom seems confirmed by the last phrase of Romans 3:26, where God is identified as both "righteous" and the "one who makes righteous."

The new perspective on Paul designates "a broad family of related interpretive tendencies" that all arise from a negative starting point: Luther and his followers from the sixteenth century on misinterpreted Paul to be presenting a gospel of individual salvation from guilt by opposing grace available through justification by faith in Christ with legalism in the Judaism of his past.[33]

The new perspective regards the letter of Romans as primarily Paul's attempt at negotiating between Jewish and Gentile concerns. I am not arguing that E. P. Sanders and others who have pioneered the new perspective came to this view of Romans by reading Origen. It is rather their own exegesis playing out in a post-Holocaust context that has allowed them to see that Romans "is really concerned with the Jewish-Gentile problem and is not a summary of Paul's theology in the sense of a tract."[34] If this is what Romans is about, "faith" becomes a utility term for Paul to present his own gospel in response to a Jewish emphasis on the necessity of Torah observance. In Romans, according to Sanders, "Faith represents man's entire response to the salvation offered in Jesus Christ, *apart from law*; and *the argument for faith is really an argument against the law*."[35] Righteousness in Romans 1 fits Käsemann's definition of it as God's power, but elsewhere in Romans it can mean other things, according to Sanders.[36]

Influenced by the new perspective in locating Paul's letters as profoundly concerned with Israel, one narrative approach to Pauline theology finds a version of the story of God and Israel as the narrative substructure for Paul's writings. A central tenet of this narrative approach as Richard Hays has developed it in relation to Galatians is an emphasis on the faithfulness of God and of Christ in keeping promises for God's people, who then are to respond by living as an obediently faithful community that reflects God's love.[37] Katherine Grieb applies this approach to Romans and argues that in Romans 1:17 "Paul seems to have four meanings [of 'righteousness'] in mind: (1) God's righteousness as the Creator to the entire creation; (2) God's special covenant relationship with Israel; (3) God as the impartial judge who will put things right, especially for the poor and the oppressed; and (4) God's saving faithfulness that will restore all things to right relationship at the end time." Grieb goes on in this section to interpret "from faith to faith" as from God's faithfulness to humanity and Israel to the faithful obedience of Jesus Christ.[38] In this reading there is no sense in which the locus is calling for humanity's faith in God, a sense that Origen, Augustine, and Luther all shared. Grieb does seem to participate in Luther's demarcation of this locus as the fundamental thesis for the letter, for she is taking pains to pack the whole narrative structure she sees beneath Romans into these two verses.

N. T. Wright also locates the theme of Romans in this locus. His sensitivity to Israel's story is evident in his connection of the phrase "not ashamed" in 1:16 with the psalmist's repeated prayer for deliverance from shame and occasional observance of enemies being put to shame (Pss. 31:1–3; 71:1–2, 15–16, 19, 24; 143:1).[39] Wright also uses his understanding of Israel's story to exclude Bultmann's "genitive of origin" that views righteousness primarily as a human possession. Instead, because of "Paul's Jewish background" and the coherence this will bring to Romans 3 and Romans 9–11, Wright emphasizes that this is God's righteousness, which is displayed from God's faithfulness to human faithfulness.[40]

As this letter continues to move outward among the *ethnē*, new understandings of such key phrases as "from faith to faith" can emerge. For example, an understanding of faith through the cultural lens of the Philippines can certainly augment or improve other cultures' understandings of faith.[41]

CONCLUSION

Beginning with Luther's identification of this locus as "the whole conclusion" of the letter, the locus of Romans 1:16–17 has been helpfully used as a heuristic reference point or thesis statement for the letter. Commentators and readers are ready to assume without argument that this is the letter's thesis. Origen's emphasis on the ways that Paul describes humanity and his literal reading and attention to the "Jews" of 1:16 as ethnic Israel is now echoed positively by the new perspective and narrative-based reading of Romans.

Locus 2

Natural Theology (1:19–21)

A proved God is world, and a God of the world is an idol.

Karl Barth[1]

On this locus the primary question is whether emphasis should be placed on how much humanity can know about God from creation, or on how little humanity can know.

ORIGEN

Since the subject of what is revealed is "what is known of God" (*to gnōston tou theou*), Origen twice emphasizes that not everything about God can be known. "He says that what is known about God is manifest to them. This shows that there is something about God that may be known and something about him that may not be known."[2] Origen will return to this theme and specify that what cannot be known is God's substance and nature, which he thinks are hidden from every human being. While he is more optimistic than Barth about the possibility of learning from nature at least that God alone is to be worshiped and not idols made in the likeness of other creatures, Origen takes pains to limit what can be known of God from nature, since the law of nature is "rather insignificant" (*mikroteros*).[3] On 3:21 Origen is again visibly concerned to limit natural theology, for on the

11

clause, "apart from law the righteousness of God is revealed," he says that God's righteousness cannot be known from the law of nature, since nature's resources are not sufficient for understanding God's righteousness.[4] This statement is consistent with the last quotation from Calvin offered below, and its limitation on what can be known of God from nature is passionately argued by Barth in his 1922 Romans commentary and in his famous response in 1934 to Brunner's advocacy of natural revelation.[5]

The wrath of God is revealed because people should have known of God from nature and from the human activity of accepting or learning what can be known of God, all of which Origen assumes is included in the process of natural revelation: "But if toward all people God manifested truth and what is known of himself through the resources in the word of nature as each one took it in when he completed the word, clearly on account of all that has profanely happened and has been unjustly performed it will be necessary correspondingly to some more and to some less for the revelation of the wrath of God to come from heaven."[6] Thus for Origen what may be known of God is enough to render humans liable to God's wrath.

On this locus Origen's insistence on the freedom of the human will also emerges. For he especially singles out the philosophers as those people whom Paul is describing here, who should know something of God from nature and yet have suppressed the truth. Origen specifies that these intellectuals have suppressed divine truth by denying freedom in their view of the world or by performing wicked deeds.[7] Here we see the Jew-*ethnē* pairing that frames Origen's exegesis again coming to the fore. It is the philosophers among the *ethnē* who should have been able to recognize God from creation, but who have not done so and are thus blameworthy for not honoring God.

An exegetical distinction within this locus also begins with Origen. He understands "invisible things" in 1:20 as created beings, while "eternal power" and "Godhead" refer directly to God. The "invisible things" according to this approach are therefore assumed to be angelic powers, since Origen mentions Colossians 1:16 in his explanation.[8]

Origen's sense of how God speaks to humanity is not tied to natural phenomena of creation. He says on Romans 9:25–26 that God speaks through the mind, heart, and conscience of all people, informing them when they sin that they are not God's people.[9]

AUGUSTINE

Augustine exegetes Romans 1:18–23 in an Easter sermon on the resurrection of the body. With regard to our locus, Augustine says that the best philosophers among the nations "had investigated nature, and from the works had come to know the craftsman." That paragraph ends with the statement that these philosophers understood that the ongoing existence of heaven and earth implied "a prime cause."[10]

Without mentioning Origen, Augustine therefore follows him by identifying those who could come to a knowledge of God from nature as the philosophers.

While there is no explicit dependence on Origen in Augustine's treatment of this locus, when introducing what Porphyry taught about physical bodies, Augustine does mention that Porphyry was corrected by Christians. The editor and translator Edmund Hill suggests that Augustine might be referring to Origen here.[11]

Augustine goes on to argue in this sermon that the beauty of changeable nature points to an unchanging, beautiful creator. From this interpretation of the text as describing what philosophers have observed from sea, sky, stars, and sun, Augustine moves to the human being. He states that the best philosophers searched for something that does not change after considering how the human soul seems to leave its body at the time of death.[12] It is worth noting how Augustine does not try to prove that all the nations could know God from nature; he focuses on "outstanding" philosophers and does not try to prove that everyone among the nations should have been able to recognize God from nature. He is indebted to Aristotle with his mention of the prime cause, and his introduction of God as someone who does not change also sets a precedent, as we shall see in the selection from Aquinas below.

When Augustine introduces Porphyry's idea that every body should be avoided, he counteracts it by saying that this would involve eliminating the universe itself, whose "world-soul" is known as Jupiter or Hecate.[13] Augustine argues further against Porphyry by citing Plato's description of how God made the celestial gods such as stars, sun, and moon and assured them that they would not have to leave the bodies he made for them.[14] Aquinas probably got his comparison of the various bodies (celestial to earthly) from Augustine's discussion of this in *City of God* 13.16–18. He refutes Porphyry again in *City of God* 22.26.

Augustine began writing *City of God* about two years after giving the sermon mentioned above. In book 8 of *City of God* we see that there is now a known locus within the Latin church called "natural theology": "We now have need of a far greater effort of mind than was necessary in solving and explaining the questions raised in our previous books; for it is not with ordinary means that we are now to discuss the theology which the Romans call natural."[15] In his discussion of this theology, Augustine argues that Plato and his school are the best and only philosophers worth engaging in conversation, and he notes that from the natural world these philosophers saw that a "Primary Form" must exist and that it could not exist in changeable creation. This "Primary Form" could not be meaningfully compared with anything else and represented the uncreated "First Principle" by which all else had been created. After this summary of his understanding of Platonic theology, Augustine quotes Romans 1:19–20.[16]

In *On the Spirit and the Letter* Augustine also quotes Romans 1:18–23. He states that Paul includes the description of people coming to know God from nature to explain the source of the truth that people have suppressed (1:18b). While he begins by exegeting this as if it applies to all peoples among the nations, he describes the quest for knowledge of God from the natural world by saying that "great minds truly persisted in the search, and they were able to find him."[17] He is thus consistent in his tendency to explain this locus by pointing to the cosmological arguments of the Platonic philosophers; he does not imagine that all people have known God from the created order.

This locus is clearly related to the description of the righteous Gentiles in Romans 2:13–15. Augustine uses the link of the natural theology locus to bridge from 1:16–17 to the description of people being judged or rewarded in 2:8–14. Those judged are those who knew God from nature but did not worship God. The righteous Gentiles of 2:14–15 Augustine defines as those who have believed in Christ.[18]

PELAGIUS

Pelagius's view that creation is inherently good is shown by his comment on 1:19b–20—"For if he made the things which are visible so splendid that some considered them gods and tried to assert that they are eternal, how much the more were these people able to understand that the one who made these things is everlasting and almighty and boundless."[19] This positive view of creation feeds Pelagius's emphasis on the human's capacity for sinlessness. Even though Pelagius at one point ascribes the phrase "everyone is a liar" in Romans 3:4 not to Paul but to Paul's imagined Jewish interlocutors, still Pelagius goes on to argue that "everyone" means "most people," because he wants to preserve the possibility that humans can be sinless.[20]

AQUINAS

In the medieval period, Aquinas is also careful to emphasize that what can be known of God by reason contains many errors. He insists that wise guidance is needed for anyone seeking to understand God by reason, which guidance he seeks to provide in his *Summa contra Gentiles*.[21] Thus, while Aquinas cautions that neither reason nor nature is sufficient to bring one to an accurate knowledge of God, he does retain a positive use for natural theology, provided the right guidelines are offered for making rational inferences of what he understands to be self-evident or foundational.

In his Romans commentary, Aquinas is very balanced on this locus and is quite clear on the tension within this locus. The tension arises from the sense perception through which, according to this locus, people are to know something of God. For this sense perception is at once the way through which the knowledge comes, but it can only sense what is similar to the human and thus cannot accurately receive any representation of the divine essence. I include a section of Aquinas's commentary, since it illustrates this so well.

Rightly I say that they possessed the truth of God, for it was in them, to some degree, the true knowledge of God, since "that which is known of God," that is, what is knowable of God by humanity through reason is manifest in them, that is, it is manifest to them from that which is in them, that is, from an inner light. Therefore it must be known what about God is generally unknown by people in this life, that is to say, what God is. On this point Paul also found among the Athenians an altar inscription: To the unknown God [Acts 17:23]. And therefore that human knowledge begins from what is of natural affinity to it, that is to the senses of the creature, which do not match how the divine essence must be represented.

Nevertheless a human can, in the way of a creature, know God in three ways, as Dionysius says in his book *On the Divine Names* [chap. 7, lecture 4].

First indeed there is the way through causality. Since there are deficient and changeable things in this kind of creation, it is necessary to trace them back to something which in principle is immovable and perfect. And it follows that this is recognized to be from God.

Second, through the way of excellence. For everything is not traceable back to a first principle, as to its proper and single cause, according as human generates human, but instead it is to a shared and excelling cause. And by this is recognized what is above all things.

Third, through the way of negation. For if the cause excels, there is nothing of what is in creation that can compete with it, just as a heavenly body can never be properly said to be heavy or light, nor hot or cold. And it follows that we call this motionless and infinite entity God, even when some other kind of term is also spoken.

They have this kind of knowledge through the implanted light of reason. Psalm 4:6: "Many are saying, 'What good does he show us?' The sign is over us, the light of your will, Lord."[22]

It is significant that Aquinas ends his catalog of ways God is known from creation with "the way of negation."

LUTHER

Luther takes what will become Emil Brunner's side here, reading this locus as if the creation of the world testifies to God's nature. Luther also goes on to describe how even idolatry presupposes a knowledge of God. The fact that all people (here Luther is not following Origen and Augustine's limitation of the text to the Gentile philosophers) have clear knowledge of God available to them is shown by how some naturally make idols and worship them as divine.[23]

Already at this locus within Romans it is clear that Luther does not share the high assessment of human potential that Pelagius displays, an assessment now reemerging through Renaissance humanism among Luther's contemporaries. Luther objects to Peter Lombard's interpretation of "creation of the world" in Romans 1:20 as "creature of the world," that is, the human being. Luther uses the phrase *massa perditionis* to refer to humanity, a humanity that stands in its entirety before the law in need of the grace Christ can give; his scholium on 1:20 attacks Nicolas of Lyra's particularizing exegesis of referring to a specific Jew-*ethnē* problem in Rome, referring it instead to all the nations as "the whole mass of lost humanity."[24] In his scholium on 8:3 Luther writes that without grace, all are equally the lump of ruin as described in Genesis 8:21.[25] Luther quotes Augustine in his scholium on 9:21 to depict all of humanity as under God's righteous condemnation.[26] There is hardly a trace of the sixteenth-century's emerging humanism in Luther's exegesis of Romans on the human condition.

ERASMUS

Erasmus follows Origen's observation that "what is known of God" in 1:19 signals that some truths of God can be known from nature while other truths most definitely cannot be known from nature. Erasmus mentions Origen's interpretation of the "invisible things" as creatures created by God and respectfully disagrees, following Ambrosiaster and Chrysostom in stating that the eternal power and Godhead are really the definition of "invisible things" here, which thus has to refer to God. Erasmus does follow Origen in mentioning the philosophers as the people Paul really thinks can gain a knowledge of God from the natural world, using the anomalous "in them" of 1:19 as a clue that this must refer to a specific subset of humanity.[27]

CALVIN

Calvin follows in Origen's footsteps by calling attention to the "what is known" phrase in 1:19 (to gnōston), and just as Origen does he emphasizes that not all of God can be known: "Only fools, therefore, seek to know the essence of God."[28] He also follows Erasmus in calling attention to the unusual "in them" phrase at the end of the first half of the verse.

The heart of the limitation of natural theology is well stated by Calvin: "The manifestation of God by which He makes His glory known among His creatures is sufficiently clear as far as its own light is concerned. It is, however, inadequate on account of our blindness. But we are not so blind that we can plead ignorance without being convicted of perversity. . . . This knowledge of God, therefore, which avails only to prevent men from making excuses, differs greatly from the knowledge which brings salvation."[29] A similar approach is explicit in his *Institutes*.[30] The negative function of the witness of the natural world that we have already considered in the Aquinas section above is here spelled out in detail. It is humanity's sinful nature that keeps us from gaining a positive knowledge of God from nature. This analysis also explains why Pelagius has a much higher estimation of the potential of natural theology than the other interpreters surveyed in this chapter.

The negative use of natural theology, that is, that nature provides enough evidence to render humanity culpable but not enough to lead humanity to God, is thus characteristic of the Reformed understanding of this locus. Romans 1:19–21 is used negatively to show that humanity's understanding of God from nature functions as a ground for humanity's indictment rather than positively as claiming that all can come to an accurate faith in God from observing the natural world.

My missionary father does not consider himself Reformed in theology, but he also used this locus negatively when debating a Communist. Around 1965 in the town of Tsuru, between Otsuki and Fujiyoshida, my father's preaching was interrupted by a Communist from the local university yelling, "Only believe! You people have no intellectual capacity!" "What's your problem?" my father replied. The Communist then identified himself with science and claimed that the Bible's account of creation was untenable. My father replied that the Communist's theory of origins was only a theory and that they were in one sense both believers and should shake hands. But the Communist would not shake hands, so my father continued the debate by asking him where the earth came from. The Communist said he thought evolution taught that the earth came from the sun, but then admitted he did not know where the sun came from. At that point my father read Romans 1:19–21 aloud and identified his Communist interlocutor as without excuse. The Communist then walked away and my father continued his evangelistic message from the Bible.

BARTH

In *Romans I* Barth sounds both the theme that humanity should be able to recognize God from creation and the theme that this God is unknowable (*unsichtbar*) for us. This unknowable characteristic of God (*Unerforschlichkeit, Unsichtbarkeit*) is not the original condition of the relationship between God and humanity. The human person has repressed the knowledge of God, a knowledge for which she is fully capable. At the same time, Barth insists that God is totally outside the human and not to be placed as one among other authorities in our life. In other words, the knowledge of which the human is capable is a knowledge of difference. The human is not God.[31] The Kantian underpinnings to Barth's theology, which are generally traced to his teacher Wilhelm Herrmann, are surely evident in Barth's consistent rejection of the empirical world as a viable medium for people's knowledge of God.[32]

Barth glosses the refusal to give thanks in Romans 1:21 with a refusal to recognize our absolute dependence on God (with a footnote to Schleiermacher), which results in a clean separation from religion and morality so that God becomes an authority among others and ultimately vanishes in our own, human greatness. He appends to this stinging indictment an illustrative quotation from Goethe's poem "Prometheus."[33] We see in *Romans I* the picture of a human apostasy (the section on 1:18–21 is entitled "Der Abfall"), a posture that humanity has come to assume before God, in which God's eternal power and divinity are relativized, or placed alongside human consciousness and therefore denied their full due. This reappears in the commentary at 5:12. Barth describes sin there as the human "seizure of *the* truth, which God sees and is seen by God in the works of creation [1,18–20], the birth of objective humanity . . . that holds together God, the world, and humanity."[34] Thus Barth acknowledges that God sees the truth that is embedded in creation. But for a human to think that she can observe creation in an objective way and come to the truth about God is essentially sinful.

In *Romans II* Barth continues to emphasize the complete difference between God and humanity. By relating to God as if he were an entity within human experience, humans have confused eternity with time. This is the famous time-eternity dialectic that Barth employs in *Romans II*; explicit reference to it appears two times in his section on 1:18–21.[35] In *Romans II* a new element is an emphasis on the questionable and fragile nature of human existence as a testimony to God and the eternity that God inhabits. In both *Romans I* and *II*, clear statements are made as to the culpability of humanity. Humans are responsible and thus "inexcusable" (Paul's word in 1:20) for ignoring the true God.

Barth returns to his exegesis of this locus in *Church Dogmatics* I/2 in a section entitled "Religion As Unbelief." Here he emphasizes that this short paragraph in Romans is what Paul says of Gentiles *after* they have rejected the death and resurrection of Christ: "We cannot isolate what Paul says about the heathen in Rom. 1:19–20 from the context of the apostle's preaching, from the incarnation of the Word. We cannot understand it as an abstract statement about the heathen as such, or about a revelation which the heathen possess as such. Paul does not know either Jews or Gentiles in themselves and as such, but only as they are placed by the cross of Christ under the promise, but also under the commandment of God."[36] Barth then hammers home this exegesis relentlessly in the opening of his section on "The Knowledge of God" at the beginning of *Church Dogmatics* II/1.[37] Here he defends his exegesis by arguing that Paul's epistemological assertions in Romans 1:18–21 come in the context of the gospel; the judgment of God on humanity that is described in these verses is "the shadow side" of the good news, arising out of humanity's rejection of Jesus. Barth describes this paragraph as follows: "It is not the structure of an anthropology or philosophy of religion or apologetic. It cannot be separated even for a moment from the apostolic *kerygma*. On the contrary, it is all the shadow side, the judgment side, of the Gospel declared to the heathen. It is all the objective judgment upon men which is grounded only in the fact that the Jesus Christ who was rejected and crucified by the Jews and rose again on the third day has, in and with the truth of God, also brought to light the truth of man, namely, that he is directed towards God."[38]

This is a well-known locus in Barth's exegesis of Romans, for he takes what some see as a straightforward, epistemological flowchart in the text—that a human can look at the mountains, sea, and dry land around her and find qualities of God that this creation illustrates—and subverts the flowchart to insist that what nature and human experience testify, if one really listens to them, is that humanity has arrogantly ignored God and does not know God at all. Barth's exegesis arises out of a desire to avoid starting with the human and a simultaneous turn to emphasize the priority of God's action in Christ as the basis for all epistemological contact between God and humanity. By starting with God and emphasizing that this paragraph occurs in the context of a description of the gospel, Barth treats this locus not as a testimony for the way humans can know God via natural theology, but rather as a testimony to human culpability that becomes obvious after the Christ event. This is a clear case where Barth's decision to begin with God when he reads Romans overturns the exegesis of Romans in a revolutionary way.[39]

It is ironic that when asked to explain his relationship to Emil Brunner, which was strained by differences including natural theology, Barth's response centered on God's creation of the whale and elephant.[40] Barth's last communication to Brunner, through the medium of Brunner's pastor, included these warm words that put their difference over natural theology into perspective: "And tell him the time when I thought I should say No to him is long since past, and we all live only by the fact that a great and merciful God speaks his gracious Yes to all of us."[41]

POST-BARTHIAN APPROACHES

In the *ad fontes* tendency within the historical-critical approach to the New Testament, readings of this locus start with the recognition that Paul is using Stoic terminology. Vielhauer's brief treatment of this locus is a classic example of this approach. After stating that for both Paul and the Stoics, to acknowledge God as creator is also to come to know oneself, Vielhauer compares this locus to the Areopagus speech in Acts 17. He correctly finds their respective appeals to natural theology to differ greatly. Acts 17 has a positive regard for how humanity has related to the transcendent as discerned from nature. With no mention of sin or the grace that comes only through Christ, the preacher on the Aeropagus is only concerned to tweak his audience's appreciation for the Divine by focusing it in a single creator. Our locus, on the other hand, describes humanity's relation to the transcendent as discerned from nature only as the necessary evidence that humanity is guilty. Philipp Vielhauer locates the Aeropagus preacher as closer to Justin Martyr than to the apostle Paul, who does not write in the preacher's manner about humanity's natural relation to the Creator.[42]

As a proponent of the new perspective on Paul, J. D. G. Dunn is sensitive to the witness from Judaism and finds parallels from Hellenistic Judaism that claim that something can be known of God from nature. Within general parallels between this locus and Wisdom of Solomon 12–15, Dunn especially notes Wisdom 13:1–9 as an explanatory parallel.[43] In both texts blame is laid on people who can perceive the greatness of nature while not recognizing the Creator. In this regard, Dunn stands firmly on the side of positive natural theology at this locus.

On this locus Dunn is sensitive to the differences between Hellenistic Judaism and traditional Judaism. He observes that with Paul's Stoic terminology and nod toward the natural world as sufficient for a rational grasp of God's existence and nature, Paul is working outside "a traditional Jewish world-view."[44] This is because Judaism traditionally emphasizes that humanity cannot know God completely, and pictures the *ethnē* without Torah as reduced to guesswork about God's essence.[45]

The new perspective does not always sufficiently emphasize the apocalyptic worldview behind Paul's writings, but in this case Dunn makes sure to indicate that Paul's terminology takes Stoic terms and sets them in an apocalyptic construct that expects God's wrath to be shown on the earth.[46]

On this locus N. T. Wright is clear that Paul is retelling the creation narrative from Genesis.[47] Paul's following description of descent into sin mirrors *Wisdom of Solomon* 12–16, which describes how the Israelites escaped from judgment in the wilderness with God's warning while God judged the *ethnē*. Wright contends that this stereotyped narrative is already stretched by veiled references to Israel in Romans 1 that prepare us for the critique of the boastful Jew beginning in 2:17.[48] Already it is clear that a narrative-based approach shifts the reader's eyes from an individual's salvation to God's relationships with Israel and the *ethnē*.

The philosophical explanation for the Reformed rejection of a positive natural theology also deserves attention. Barth's exegesis of this locus in *Romans II* is fully consistent with his Reformed identity. Barth has influenced Romans commentator C. K. Barrett (not otherwise known as Reformed) to emphasize how God cannot be known from nature.[49] The Reformed philosopher Alvin Plantinga explains that the Reformed rejection of a positive natural theology is in essence a rejection of the classic foundationalism that such people as Aristotle and Aquinas held. Classic foundationalism demands that people work within a rational noetic structure in which rational implications are followed from a foundation that is defined as properly basic or self-evident to that person. Reformed theologians, on the other hand, insist that belief in God is something that is basic, part of one's foundation, and that God can be known without argument or proof. They might call themselves weak foundationalists, but they will reject classic foundationalism's demand that their belief in God satisfy prior logical or rational protocol. Plantinga's affirmation of this Reformed position is worth pondering while reading Romans 1:19–21—"I think [the Reformed theologians] were entirely correct; both ancient and modern foundationalism are self-referentially incoherent."[50]

CONCLUSION

This locus does not connect as directly to Origen's general perspective of Romans as a letter about the Jew-*ethnē* audiences of Paul's gospel as other loci in the letter do. However, we still see Origen's emphasis on the limitations of what can be known about God (1:19) alive and well through the Reformed interpreters of modernity, from Calvin through Barth. In light of the identification of the people who are able to understand God from the created world (1:19a) with Gentile philosophers, a position held by Origen, Augustine, and Erasmus, it is fitting that one of their number—philosopher Alvin Plantinga—recognizes exactly why it is inappropriate to attempt a rational argument from natural phenomena to God's existence.

Locus 3

Made Righteous by Christ (3:21–28)

> *The unity with Christ arising out of faith affirmed by [Paul] occurs nei-*
> *ther through our working, nor in our experience, but rather in the action*
> *of Christ, through this one who establishes us and gives to us. Accordingly*
> *the subjective side has its permanent place in faith.*
>
> Adolf Schlatter[1]

After locus 2 there is a section describing the descent of the *ethnē* into sin (1:21–32); an attack on an interlocutor who has self-righteously enjoyed reading about that descent (2:1–16); an attack on Jewish pride in possession of the name "Jew," Torah, and circumcision (2:17–29); an affirmation of Jewish advantage, even though Israel has been unfaithful (3:1–9); and a catena of Scriptures that emphasize how thoroughly humanity is implicated in sin and rendered silent before God's judgment (3:10–20).

Locus 3, 3:21–28, then describes how God's righteousness comes both to the Jews and to the *ethnē*. Three profound questions drive the exegesis of this locus: (1) What is the meaning of *pisteōs Iēsou Christou* (3:22, 26)? (2) How does Christ the *hilastērion* make people righteous (3:25)? (3) How do faith and works relate to each other in the salvation that God in Christ brings to believers (3:27–28)?

ORIGEN

Origen is worth reading at the beginning of this locus for how he distinguishes the senses of the word "law." In 3:20, where it appears that the whole world is under a law that indicts sin, Origen argues that Paul must mean a "natural law," since the *ethnē* are not under the law of Moses and since people such as Cain, Joseph's brothers, and Job all spoke of their sin without the benefit of possessing Torah.[2] At the beginning of this locus in 3:21 Origen then affirms that "law" in the opening phrase "apart from law" refers to natural law, but that the term's occurrence in "being witnessed by the law" refers to the Mosaic law. His theological argument is that the righteousness that comes in Christ cannot be known by natural law, as mentioned in the previous chapter on locus 2, so if it is witnessed by "the law and the prophets," "law" in this case must refer to the Mosaic law.[3] This pattern of finding natural law in one part of the verse and Mosaic law in the other fits with Origen's tendency to keep in mind that Paul is always working as an arbiter between the Jews and the *ethnē*.

In the fragments of Origen's Greek commentary on this section, he favors the objective genitive understanding of *pisteōs Iēsou Christou* while also mentioning the subjective genitive as a possibility. Enough of section 4 of the Tura Papyrus survives for us to see that both senses are included: "and those believing in Jesus Christ or those making room for faith, which Jesus Christ created for them, in the Father."[4] Origen returns to what he means by faith "which Jesus Christ created for them" in the conclusion of his comments on 3:25–26. While the objective genitive is clearly in view, a faith that is characterized by Jesus' faith in God is also in view: "And making righteous the one who is on the basis of faith, that is the one who *believes* in Jesus and *through Jesus in God*, and is not opposed to receive the 'making righteous the one on the basis of the faith of Jesus,' that is to say that just as 'Abraham believed God and it was reckoned to him for righteousness,' so for those who *believe* in Jesus or *in God through Jesus*, God reckons faith for righteousness, and so he will make righteous the one who is on the basis of the faith of Jesus."[5] In this second quotation the phrases I have emphasized leave open the subjective genitive reading. Origen draws an analogy between Jesus' faith in God and Abraham's faith in God, which is one argument used today for reading *pisteōs Iēsou Christou* as a subjective genitive.[6] If we keep both of the quoted sections in mind, we see that Origen primarily reads *pisteōs Iēsou Christou* here as an objective genitive, though he leaves open the sense of the subjective genitive as well.

Origen spends a significant amount of space on 3:25–26 exploring how the word *hilastērion* is used in the Pentateuch, in order to understand what it means here in Romans 3:25. Such careful scrutiny of the Torah shows that he is taking seriously Paul's signal that the righteousness of God is witnessed by the law (3:21). Origen takes the description of the *hilastērion* as the ark of the covenant to be an allegorical description of Christ. When "pure" and "gold" are used to describe the ark, it symbolizes the soul of Jesus. The dimensions of the *hilastērion* also show that Jesus' soul is between God and humanity, thus becoming the mediator.[7] Indeed, this human soul of Jesus, a created addition to Jesus' eternal deity, was "pre-determined and preordained" to be a *hilastērion*.[8] Origen comes to this idea from a careful reading of Romans 3:25a after reading *proetheto* as "pre-determined" and *hilastērion* as equivalent to the soul of Jesus.[9]

Origen includes various ideas when explaining how Jesus' death covers human sin. He notes that Jesus is called *hilastērion,* sacrifice, and priest, and sees no difference between Jesus as *hilastērion* or as "appeasement."[10] In today's categories, his explanation might be thus classified as an "expiation."

It would be a mistake simply to read the paragraphs in Origen's commentary on 3:21–28 and not examine what he says about justification by faith throughout his commentary and in other writings. In some places Origen sounds like a reformer, saying that faith alone is what saves.[11] Indeed, his *ek monēs pisteōs* or "sola fide" at 3:28 forms a precedent for a later translator of the New Testament who added the word "alone" in this verse, despite his insistence that he was completely independent from Origen.[12] Yet Origen also makes clear that faith and works are inseparable. For example, when explaining "faith reckoned as righteousness apart from works," Origen quotes Paul's maxims that faith without love is worthless and that love believes all things (1 Cor. 13:2, 7), and goes on to say that some who believe are not justified (Exod. 14:31), while those who have complete faith that includes love are credited with righteousness (Gen. 15:6).[13]

The contradiction that we see in Origen, based on viewing him through Reformation lenses, is resolved when we see that Origen defines being "in Christ" as being in the virtues, including righteousness. As Maurice Wiles has seen so well, for Origen, "faith in Christ does not need to be supplemented by the virtuous life, it *is* the adoption of the virtues. Thus the connection between faith and works is a logically necessary one."[14] Origen explains Paul's statement that God's righteousness comes by faith in Christ apart from works to mean primarily that this righteousness comes apart from the ritual aspects of the Mosaic law, such as circumcision, sacrifices, and observance of Sabbaths and new moons.[15] In this regard Origen is an early precedent for the new perspective, which argues that Paul's "apart from works" usually means apart from those works of the law that visibly separate the Jewish people from the nations. Origen does not separate faith from good works. Good works are necessary for salvation, but they are not grounds for boasting, for Origen is adamant that one can only boast in the cross of Christ.[16] "Justification by faith" in Paul and Origen does not have the juridical sense that it would later receive.[17]

A favorite case study for the question of justification, the repentant thief, appears in Origen's commentary three times. Origen first mentions this thief as an example of someone who cannot boast in works, since he was saved only by faith.[18] The thief reappears when Origen is exegeting 4:1–8 as an example of complete faith. Partial faith will not save, but only complete faith that renders a person godly, so that the thief on the cross who believed could not blaspheme any longer.[19] Here we see that faith is constituting the believer as righteous; Origen is not espousing Luther's passive righteousness here. The necessity of works alongside faith becomes clearer in the final reference to this thief. When exegeting what it means to be planted with Christ in his death in order to share in his resurrection (6:5), Origen cites the thief's confession to Jesus and rebuke of the blaspheming thief as evidence that he was planted with Christ in a death to sin.[20]

Origen originates the famous "sola fide" phrase at 3:28, but as his commentary continues, it is clear that he means by this that works in which one can boast do not save, but a full faith necessarily accompanied by works brings God's salvation. In this comparison it must be acknowledged that sometimes Origen views justification as a process. For example, when exegeting Paul's expression that God justifies the circumcision from faith and the uncircumcision through faith in 3:30, Origen writes that those whose justification begins with faith need perfection through completing good works, while those who begin with good works need perfection through faith.[21] Justification for Origen is therefore a process, not a momentary experience or singular transaction.

Origen does not specify the exact proportion of human action and divine grace received in faith. Camille Verfaillie is content to characterize Origen as affirming the necessity of our free cooperation with God's grace, without bringing the matter to a precise solution. He also notes Origen's famous statement on Psalm 120:3 that the beginning of faith is our necessary responsibility.[22]

AUGUSTINE

In Augustine's early *Commentary on Statements in the Letter to the Romans* he begins paragraphs 13–18 with a citation of Romans 3:20 regarding how the knowledge of sin comes through the law. Here he presents his four stages of human life: before the law, under the law, under grace, in peace. He seems to be using "law" (*lex*) here in the sense of a moral law from God incumbent on all humanity. Augustine goes on in this section to assert that the law is a good thing, but that it can be kept only through the grace made available in Christ. This section is also significant because it is an early assertion of Augustine's position on free will: Adam had free will in that he could refuse to sin; before we receive Christ's grace we cannot fully exercise free will, for we can freely desire not to sin, but we cannot freely choose not to sin. When grace comes, then our wills are strengthened so that we may act rightly.[23] It is noteworthy that at this point, still in his anti-Manichean stage, Augustine makes no comment on 3:21–28, which beginning with his anti-Pelagian writings would emerge as a central and contested locus, with the stakes of its interpretation rising considerably after the Reformation.

In his anti-Pelagian *On the Spirit and the Letter*, Augustine returns more than once to this locus. Here he finds the resources to argue that what people need is the righteousness of God, not that righteousness that comes from inside humans or from their will. Still, Augustine treats it as an objective genitive, stating that it is the righteousness with which God clothes people. Augustine's view of justification at this point is sanative: the law "indicates clearly enough that human beings are justified by the gift of God through the assistance of the Holy Spirit. . . . the believer is not helped by the law, since God shows human beings their weakness through the law in order that they might take refuge in his mercy through faith and be healed."[24]

In the next section of *On the Spirit and the Letter*, Augustine goes on to argue against the Pelagians that the law is meant to bring unrighteous people to grace. Once they have been made righteous by God's grace, these righteous people no longer need the law, for they receive grace through the law of faith.[25]

Augustine takes the objective genitive reading of *pisteōs Iēsou Christou* in 3:22. He rejects the possibility that the phrase refers to Christ's own faith and instead reads the phrase as the faith humans place in Christ. In a later paragraph of the same work he is clear that this faith in Christ is given to humans.[26] Thus, while Luther is usually credited with the influential innovation in the translation of 3:22 ("den glauben an Ihesum Christ" = faith in Jesus Christ), his departure point has precedents in the interpretations Origen and Augustine gave to the phrase.[27]

In the anti-Pelagian controversy this locus becomes foundational for Augustine. In explaining the identity of the Gentiles who have the law written in their hearts (2:14–15), Augustine goes to 3:22–24 and asserts that the righteousness has to come from grace, not from works.[28] In contrast to the way in which faith and works are viewed together in Origen, the Pelagian controversy begins a process that culminates in the sixteenth century's bifurcation of the origin of righteousness into a schema in which it must either be by grace coming through faith or by works.

ABELARD

Abelard's actual commentary on 3:21–26 moves efficiently over the main questions this locus raises. At 3:21 he explains that "But now" represents a division in time: before this time no one could be justified who refused to acknowledge natural law, "'but now,' that is, in the time of grace, 'the righteousness of God,' that is, what God approves and through which we are justified by God, that is, love, 'is manifested.'"[29]

Abelard follows Augustine in exegeting the *pisteōs Iēsou Christou* of 3:22 as faith in Jesus, though he offers Augustine's distinction of believing in Jesus' existence, believing in his word, and being bound to Jesus in faithful love.[30] Abelard makes a big point that divine love spreads through us as God in Christ unites with our nature. So while the word "love" does not appear in 3:21–28, Abelard mentions John 15:13 and Romans 8:35, 38 all as showing that love follows from faith in Christ. Abelard states that God's righteousness is found in the soul (*anima*) of Gentiles as well as Jews and not in their exterior works.[31] He almost sounds proto-Lutheran here.

On Romans 3:23 he simply explains that people have an obligation to glorify God; he does not emphasize universal sinfulness.[32] On 3:24 he emphasizes that the justification happens completely through grace and not from any merits that precede the believers' approach to God. He attributes the beginning of redemption completely as God's initiative.[33]

On 3:25 he glosses "propitiator" (Vulgate uses *propitiatorium*; Paul's word was *hilasmos*) with "reconciler." He specifies that the "through faith" phrase of this

verse limits the reconciliation that Christ's death has effected only to those who
believe. Abelard equates "the display of his righteousness" with God's love.
Abelard emphasizes that love is the driving force of the justification God effects,
so that his love is displayed to us or reaches out to us, bringing us into debt to
love God, who did not spare the Son for us. The forgiveness is described as a forgiveness of sins that have happened beforehand. This is a point Origen has made
in his commentary on 3:25 and again at 3:27–28.[34] Abelard does not comment
here on how sins to be committed in the future are to be forgiven.

In his explanation of 3:26, Abelard emphasizes that the phrase "in this time"
signifies the time of grace in which God's love is extended toward humanity. The
phrase "in the forbearance of God" is glossed as a time that God waited and even
delayed so that he might show his justice working in love, made available in Jesus
Christ. The forbearance also means that God did not punish sinners immediately, but gave them time to repent and return through penance to God, bringing an end to their sin and so gaining remission (*indulgentia*).[35]

Abelard treats 3:27 as directed to a Jew full of his own glory, to whom Paul is
saying that the law and its corporeal observance is now excluded and worth nothing for the Jew. Paul's "law of faith" that excludes the "law of works" is the love
that comes on the basis of our faith in salvation through Christ. Abelard spends
considerable space and energy answering the question of whether the external
rites of circumcision (before Christ) and baptism (after Christ) are necessary if
one can really be justified by a law of faith apart from any external works. He
answers that the truly justified will persevere in their righteousness and undergo
the rite of circumcision or baptism.[36] On 3:28 Abelard glosses "through faith" by
saying that this means without the observance of the law, or exterior and corporeal observance.[37]

In the Middle Ages this locus emerges as the primary arena for questions about
the nature of the atonement. How does the atonement work? Anselm's satisfaction theory portrays God as a feudal lord whose honor has been violated by his
vassals, who are sinful humanity. Humanity is in such debt to God that it can
never repay what is owed to God. God then sends his son to become human and
die in order that the debt might be repaid and the honor owed to God be paid
in full.[38] In the one instance in *Why God Became Man* that Anselm uses the term
justificatio, it simply means "justification from sin."[39]

Abelard writes shortly after Anselm and provides another interpretation of this
locus in his "Question" and "Solution" excursus that interrupts his commentary
at 3:26. Since there is no direct evidence that Abelard is answering Anselm, I follow Peppermüller's judgment that Abelard is simply writing on a question that
emerged as necessary to answer during the scholastic period.[40] By the time of
Abelard this locus is regarded as the definitive explanation of how Christ's death
intersects with human history. Anselm read the locus through the lens of a feudal honor code. Abelard reads the locus as a portrait of the divine love Jesus exemplified for humanity and evokes within humanity.

Abelard's excursus focuses the options regarding *hilastērion*, for he voices the questions lying just beneath this locus. He argues against the tradition that Christ's death brought redemption from the devil's power. If Christ's death really defeated Satan, why are only the elect freed from this power? How could Christ grant forgiveness of sins before his crucifixion, if this death was necessary to buy people out of the devil's power?[41] Against Origen, Abelard raises questions designed to eliminate expiation as a viable model for the atonement. If this death could expiate sins, what about the great sin of crucifying the innocent Son of God? Can this death expiate all later sins against Christ and those who follow him? And if redemption from God's own punishment is the model, why did God set the price of redemption to be the death of an innocent son? How could accepting this outrageous arrangement bring our redemption or righteousness?[42] From Abelard on, 3:21–28 becomes a locus begging for soteriological precision. Later readers of Romans, even if they have not read Abelard, feel a pressure to define exactly what happened in salvation history when God displayed Jesus as *hilastērion*.

Abelard's solution is that Christ exemplifies God's love for us. Note the language of pedagogy in the long thesis sentence (60 words in Abelard's text) of his "Solution" to the riddle of the atonement: "By this we have been justified by the blood of Christ and reconciled to God, that through this singular grace it was shown to us that his son took our nature and in it while instructing us as much by word as by example he endured to death, binding us more through love to himself, so that by such a favor, enlightened by divine grace, true love shrinks back and no longer submits to one's own concerns."[43] When focusing on the difficult question of how Christ's death makes us righteous, Abelard thus finds the ransom, expiation, and redemption models inadequate and introduces Christ's death as the supreme example for humanity. The binding love that arises out of Christ's supreme example of obedience is Abelard's extension of Augustine's doctrine of faith working through love, now emphasized in such a radical way that the forensic and sacramental dimensions of justification are eliminated.[44]

AQUINAS

Aquinas explains why the works of the law do not bring righteousness by connecting this locus with 15:8 and glossing the word "truth" there with "righteousness." So he claims that Christ's service toward the Jewish people is meant to bring righteousness. He also cites 10:3 to explain Paul's account of Jewish unbelief in Jesus—it is because they are ignorant of God's righteousness. Paul's "now" points to the "time of grace" that is revealed. Here Aquinas's phrase is similar to Abelard's.[45] Both interpret Paul's "now" to signify a new stage in God's working with humanity, called "the time of grace."[46] We thus note that they are pointing toward something Giorgio Agamben now calls "messianic time."[47]

Aquinas explains "faith of Jesus Christ" in 3:22 by citing Hebrews 12:2 and explaining that it is the faith that Jesus himself delivered. Since he quotes Romans 10:9 here as well, it is clear that he is not seriously entertaining any precursor to a reading of *pisteōs Iēsou Christou* exclusively as a subjective genitive. He does not mention Jesus' faithfulness and takes care to explain that his text (from the Clementine Vulgate) that has "who believes in him" at 3:22b helps to explain the form of the faith.[48]

Aquinas takes pains to emphasize that the faith associated with justification in 3:22 does not earn righteousness, naming the Pelagians as mistaken here. It is rather that the mind's first movement toward God is through faith. Faith is thus the first part of the righteousness that comes to us from God. Still, it is not an unformed faith. Aquinas cites James 2:26, Galatians 5:6, Ephesians 3:17, and 1 John 4:16 on his way to saying that love is the framework of this faith.[49] This is an emphasis from Augustine that the Protestant Reformers lost in their emphasis on faith alone: the faith in those made righteous by God is marked by love.[50] This is different from the passive righteousness that Wittenberg students would see in this locus three hundred years later.

Aquinas explains the phrase "justified freely" in 3:24 by saying that the righteousness comes apart from the merit of preceding works. The redemption effected by Christ is not redemption by example as Abelard suggested. Aquinas uses instead the language of health, as Origen frequently does. He says that only Christ could meet the infection that the whole human race gained from its first parents, since only Christ was immune from all sin.[51]

Aquinas describes "propitiation" with a sacrificial model, citing Exodus 25:17 and then saying that Christ placed the church on the tabernacle's ark. The death of Christ is seen as proportionate for expiating the sins of the world. This expiation works for both present and past sins. This power of the blood of Christ in expiating sins works through human faith. Sins committed before Christ can be covered and forgiven only by the blood of Christ.[52]

Aquinas seems to follow Origen in using both the law of nature and the Mosaic law to explain how God endured previously committed sins. He mentions that according to the law of nature, humanity fell into error and shameful sins; but after the law that brings the knowledge of sin was written, that is, the Mosaic law, humans sinned through their weakness.[53]

In God's righteousness God would destroy sins, but God is just because he forgave sins as promised when by Christ God led humanity back to God's righteousness. Aquinas explains the phrase, "the one who is on the basis of the faith of Jesus," at the end of 3:26 as referring to the one who through the faith of Jesus Christ (objective genitive) approaches God.[54]

On 3:27 Aquinas again follows Origen by emphasizing that Paul here introduces two laws, the law of works, which must signify "the old law" (Mosaic law), and the law of faith, which is the "new law" that makes the nations equal to the Jews. Aquinas admits that the old law required faith (Sir. 2:8a; Ps. 116:10), and that the new law requires works (Luke 22:19; Jas. 1:22). The difference lies in the old law's focus on the outer person and the new law's focus on the inner person, the heart (Rom. 8:2; 10:10).[55]

Aquinas takes pains to explicate the phrase "without the works of the law" in 3:28. He says that this phrase refers not only to the works of the ceremonial aspects of the law, but even to the moral commands of the law; he cites Titus 3:5 as proof that it is not the performance of the law that effects righteousness. But he goes on to say that Paul's phrase here in Romans 3:28 refers to works of the law that precede the grant of God's righteousness. It does not refer to works that follow, since James 2:26 says that faith without works is dead. Yet these following works are necessary and yet not able by themselves to bring righteousness, according to Aquinas.[56] For him, therefore, "justification itself is a life resulting from faith."[57] His more precise discussion of justification is to be found in his *Summa theologica*, which treats it as a process beginning with an infusion of grace, followed by the movement of the free will toward God, then the movement of the free will to detest sin (pointing here to the sacrament of penance), and finally the forgiveness of sin.[58]

LUTHER

Luther's most famous exegesis of this locus occurs in a verse of his hymn "From Trouble Deep I Cry to Thee": "With thee counts nothing but thy grace to cover all our failing." That stanza of the hymn goes on to assert that no life and no amount of good works can make one deserving before God, so the human must live only by grace.[59] To live by grace for Luther meant that one should not find one's Christian identity in good works or ascetic practices, but only in conscious dependence on divine grace made available in Christ.

Luther on *Pistis Christou*

It had to be conscious dependence, faith in Christ, according to Luther. His translation of Romans 3:22, *dikaiosynē de theou dia pisteōs Iēsou Christou eis pantas tous pisteuontas*, sets the stage for the objective genitive reading of *pistis Christou*, a reading that continues to haunt the church to this day. Luther's translation "faith in Christ" at 3:22 leads to an emphasis on the locus of faith in the human, which ultimately led through Schliermacher to the flawed enterprise of some twentieth-century theologians "to explore the religious subject as the focal point of theological inquiry, to understand faith in terms of a universal religious a priori . . . and to introduce Jesus as a modifying feature or directional motif within the basic structure of religion or faith."[60] My translation of 3:21–22—"But now apart from law the righteousness of God has become visible, testified to by the law and the prophets, a righteousness of God through the faith of Jesus Christ toward all who believe"—makes clear that I favor including both subjective and objective senses of the genitive here. What is at stake in the translation of *pistis*

Christou? The origination point of salvation is connoted much differently by these two ways of translating the phrase. Richard Hays, writing from the subjective side, has called the objective genitive reading of this Pauline phrase "anthropological" and the subjective genitive "christological."[61] Perhaps this is not entirely fair to Luther, who wanted people to locate their salvation in God's mercy rather than in themselves and so would resist any "anthropological" center for the grace that comes in Christ.

In Luther's gloss on 3:24 ("being justified freely by his grace") he notes that people are justified not by what they deserve or perform, but simply as a gift that is available through Christ's work of redemption. This grace involves "making satisfaction for us and freeing us."[62] Grace is the same as mercy and includes the idea that this mercy is not earned or merited.[63] As I mentioned toward the end of the Augustinian section in this chapter, Luther has less to say about grace than Augustine does. Romans 4:16b ("that it might be according to grace") is full of potential for an Augustinian exegete, but Luther glosses that phrase only with "that of God, who does not impute on the basis of the works of those who are meritorious by the Law."[64] Grace is therefore not as potent a theologoumenon for Luther as it is for Augustine. For Luther grace is primarily a weapon against those who rely on works. The scholia section of his commentary confirms my suspicion: there is no scholium for Romans 4:16.

Still, we must credit Luther with translating *hilastērion* as "mercy seat" (*Gnadenstuhl*), correctly drawing attention to the way in which this word typologically connects the mercy seat of the tabernacle with Christ. He was followed in this translation by Tyndale, "seate of mercy."[65]

If Romans is not primarily about grace for Luther, the letter definitely centers on righteousness. This can be illustrated by the very beginning of the published version of his Romans lectures, where he states that Paul attempts to break down our own righteousness and show us that we need Christ and his righteousness.[66] The righteousness is of course Luther's "passive righteousness," forensically credited to believers totally apart from works. Those today who still defend Luther's choice to read Paul in this way collapse the works of the law into good works or else think that Paul's insistence that one cannot fully keep the Mosaic law means that Luther got it right.[67] But Paul's insistence that the law cannot be perfectly kept does not eliminate his teaching that faith is accompanied by good works. Living before the Augustinian-Pelagian blinders came over us, Origen correctly saw that "faith" for Paul includes good works.

The Protestant Approach to Romans

Luther credits his experience of Christ in Romans with a wholly new approach to reading the Bible.

> When I was a monk I was a master in the use of allegories. I used to allegorize everything. Afterward through the Epistle to the Romans I came to some

knowledge of Christ. I recognized then that allegories are nothing, that it's not what Christ signifies but what Christ is that counts. Before I allegorized everything, even a chamber pot, but afterward I reflected on the histories and thought how difficult it must have been for Gideon to fight with his enemies in the manner reported. If I had been there, I would have befouled my breeches for fear. It was not allegory, but it was the Spirit and faith that inflicted such havoc on the enemy with only three hundred men. Jerome and Origen contributed to the practice of searching only for allegories. God forgive them. In all of Origen there is not one word about Christ.[68]

Central in Luther's discovery of "Christ" (often his term for his understanding of the gospel) in Romans is this locus, Romans 3:21–28. If 1:16–17 became the locus most associated with Luther's individual discovery of righteousness by faith, 3:21–28 became the locus that contained the hermeneutical key for making sense of the whole Bible and all of human and divine life on this planet. The vista that opens here on the "sins previously committed" from the mists of past millennia allows Luther to find a salvation-historical narrative that explains the whole Bible for him. No longer would he need allegory to find meaning in the biblical text. Descriptions of Scripture that held sway for centuries that emphasized its depth and multivalence (an ocean, a deep forest, a labyrinth, a table of wisdom loaded with food, an abyss) would start to lose ground.[69] Luther begins to relate everything in the Bible to the perspective of humanity in generations past wallowing in sin that God overlooked in anticipation of Christ's death that would bring righteousness to those who believed. Luther's master story for the Bible takes a perspective very different from previous interpreters; the Protestant makeover of Scripture had now begun through Luther's encounter with Romans.

The following features appear in family resemblance among Protestant approaches to Romans: (1) justification by faith in Christ is viewed as the central theme of the letter; (2) this justification is imputed and (3) comes independently of any human works; (4) the baptism language of Romans 6 is viewed as referring to identification with Christ in faith, not with the rite of baptism. In contrast to this Protestant approach, the Catholic approach would involve a broader definition of justification with a full recognition of Paul's descriptions of how humans cooperate in salvation, as well as a sacramental appreciation of the baptism language of Romans 6. One might generalize that some Protestant commentators claim to be Augustinian in their reading of Romans while claiming that Catholic commentators are semi-Pelagian. Catholic commentaries of note today may be counted on two hands: Lagrange, Leenhardt, Kuss, Schlier, Byrne, Johnson, Penna and Fitzmyer, though the last hopes his Catholic "background will not show up too boldly."[70] Alain Gignac's forthcoming commentary will also be worth consulting as a Catholic reading of the letter.[71]

John Henry Newman wrote, "To be deep into church history is to cease to be Protestant."[72] While it is not my goal here to move Protestant readers into the Roman Catholic or Orthodox Churches, it is my goal to bring highlights of the two millennia of conversations on Romans to today's students of the letter. Not all of these conversations occur within the structure of Reformation categories. Those categories must be introduced as we follow the conversation into the sixteenth century, but we must begin listening prior to the Reformation. We should not assume as an a priori truth that the Protestant reading of Romans is at all points the most accurate reading of the letter, as William Sanday and A. C. Headlam seem to do when reviewing other commentaries.[73] Nor can we assume that only we Protestants cherish and understand the righteousness that God grants to believers. From outside the Western Church, Father Zossima's description of his people rings as a rebuke to this assumption: "Our people still believe in righteousness, have faith in God and weep tears of devotion."[74]

Alien Righteousness

The medieval notion of righteousness was the standard by which God would judge all humans on judgment day. God's righteousness would be given to humanity when the rewards and punishments were distributed to humanity at this judgment. Luther's revolutionary break with this notion, which he grounds in Paul's letter to the Romans, is that God's righteousness is organically connected with the righteousness of Christ. So that when one identifies by faith with Christ, then one is clothed with God's righteousness.[75] This righteousness from without is what Luther would call "alien righteousness," and it forms the starting point for any human attempts to do good works.[76] The process of being righteous that became known as "justification" is thus the combination of Christ's righteousness and God's justice that Luther found in the letter to the Romans, for example, 3:22–26: "The characteristic of Luther's doctrine of justification can therefore be designated as the reunification of the righteousness of Christ and the justice of God by which the sinner is justified 'coram deo,' which forms the stable *basis* and not the uncertain *goal* of the life of sanctification, of the true Christian life."[77] This new idea of justification had life-changing consequences for how people lived their lives. No longer would Western civilization be driven by ascetic scruples that looked ahead to a judgment day. The righteousness of God could already be appropriated. The anxiety level regarding human attainment of righteousness would go down, as would pilgrimages and other forms of ascetic behavior. After centuries of Romans interpretation to the contrary, righteousness now included marriage, eating, and drinking.

This righteousness came by faith alone, according to Luther. In the winter of 1515–1516, the Catholic Luther glossed the phrase as "without the help and necessity of the works of the Law."[78] In the translation work that began just seven years later, this gloss was captured with the phrase "faith alone." Luther adds his *allein* to the translation of verse 28, and here the Protestant celebration of *sola fide* begins. Here the unacknowledged ancestor remains influential even when disowned. We have already noted how Origen uses *sola fide* at 3:28, though writing in a different context than Luther's dichotomy between faith and all works. While Luther is famous for inserting *allein* at 3:28, it must be recognized that over ten exegetes between Origen and Luther also used the phrase.[79] It is therefore not a new development in the sixteenth century, but a phrase already accepted with qualifications by Augustine, fought against by Pelagius, and endorsed by Aquinas in the sense that one enters the condition of righteousness without works, since works only follow justification.[80]

Luther's famous tower experience consisted in his reading of 1:16–17 alone in a tower, accompanied by the discovery that justification comes instantaneously on the basis of faith and does not require any antecedent love of God or other works on the part of the human recipient. Charles Carlson reads closely Luther's attacks both on the scholastic understanding of the process of justification and on the nominalists' insistence that a first step could be made from the human side in the movement toward justification. He suggests that Luther's revolutionary insistence on justification by faith as an instantaneous transaction that brings passive righteousness to the believer arises out of Luther's inability ever to feel love for God in the penance aspect of the medieval process of justification in which he was trained. This tension was increased in Luther because he had also been exposed to the nominalists, who taught that one should take responsibility for approaching God as best as one could.[81] The innovation that Luther brings in the interpretation of justification is that he considers it an instantaneous transaction that brings passive righteousness, not actual righteousness, to the believer.[82] This breaks from the pattern of over a millennium, dating at least back to Origen, of viewing justification as a discipleship process that calls one to cultivate and practice righteous living.

BARTH

Barth's explanation of the revelation of God's righteousness in Christ surfaces throughout his commentary on Romans 1–8. It is primarily in what happens on the cross. Barth writes on 8:4 that "the condemnation of sin in Christ is the revelation of the righteousness of God."[83] Also, in Christ's cry of abandonment on the cross—"My God, my God, why have you forsaken me?"—there is revealed to humanity the absence of the true God, the no that God speaks to human existence as we normally know it. This is what Bruce McCormack calls Barth's analogy of the cross.[84] We cannot know Christ and the significance of his death on the cross apart from God revealing it to us.[85] "Men do not stand upright before God in virtue of their religion, any more than they stand upright before Him in virtue of any other human property. They stand upright before Him in virtue of that divine nature by which also Christ stood when His 'religious consciousness' was the recognition that He was abandoned by God."[86] Once one accepts this revelation, that one lives abandoned by the true God as Christ on the cross was abandoned by God, then the way is open for one to know God through God's power that is activated in the resurrection of Christ. By Christ's faithful surrender of himself to God and the resurrection that follows, the questionable nature of human existence becomes evident: "The sinner in will and act, the man whom alone we can see, know, and conceive of, is thrust against the wall and becomes wholly questionable. How shall we, who have been thus placed in question, live any longer in sin?"[87] The final question of this quotation illustrates an irony in *Romans II*. Though both Romans commentaries have been criticized as offering little contribution to ethics, it is in his doctrine of the cross that Barth offers the most pointed ethical challenge. "Because the death of Christ is the end of that life which can and must die, and the final victory of sinlessness over the possibility of sin, it proclaims: Thy sins have been forgiven thee; and because, since the order death-resurrection, sin-grace, cannot be reversed, Christ dieth no more,—therefore I, living to God in Christ, am as such dead to sin. I stand only within the sphere of conversion from sin to grace, a conversion which cannot be reversed."[88]

Barth's picture of the individual human is very negative. Here there is no significant change between the first and second editions. In the first edition, Barth claims that "speech of the human, relative righteousness of this or that person is excluded, superfluous, irrelevant."[89] The human can effect nothing that will stand before God's judgment as righteous or inherently significant. Human existence is at best a parable of a completely different humanity, a humanity transformed by God. Since Barth has chosen to begin with God in these two commentaries, his anthropology is sharply negative. Since humanity is separated from God and utterly impotent to reach God, everything that humanity does in this life ("under the sun" as the Preacher would say) is empty.

What sort of faith brings justification to the human person? Again Barth starts with God: it is God's faithfulness. All that humans can hope for is the time when, bowed and naked under God's judgment, God will clothe them with his righteousness.[90]

On the *pisteōs Iēsou Christou* phrase in 3:22 that Barth translates "through his [God's] faithfulness in Jesus Christ," he writes, "The faithfulness of God is the divine patience according to which He provides, at sundry times and at many divers points in human history, occasions and possibilities and witnesses of the knowledge of His righteousness. Jesus of Nazareth is the point at which it can be seen that all the other points form one line of supreme significance. . . . The life of Jesus is perfected obedience to the will of the faithful God."[91] With this move, Barth clearly anticipates later debate on this *crux interpretum*. The faithfulness of God (as opposed to the faith placed in God) and the faithfulness of Christ (as opposed to faith placed in Christ) make it possible to envision a world in which God saves people irrespective of their own decision to trust God. We could say that the universalism to which Barth seems open is therefore due to his insistence on God's complete faithfulness, independent of human decision or performance. It is not a universalism of enlightened tolerance; it is rather a universalism of radical God-centeredness.

With this negative view of humanity, Barth is reacting against the liberal Protestantism of his educational milieu. His anthropology is in continuity with

Luther; he is more negative toward the human will and capacity for good than is Origen. In his insistence on the subjective genitive for righteousness of God, *pistis Christou*, and the knowledge of God, Barth illustrates his debt and reaction to modernity.

POST-BARTHIAN APPROACHES

E. P. Sanders is attracted to the possibility that Paul's account of righteousness as coming through Christ's expiation in Romans 3 is a traditional formulation that Paul repeats, while his real explanation of the transfer of humanity into the realm of God's righteousness comes with the participation in Christ's death to sin and death in Romans 6 and the power of the Spirit as described in Romans 8.[92] Indeed, Sanders's position that participation in Christ (6:3–11) is the center of Paul's gospel means that he does not invest energy in exegeting the expiation or redemption language of 3:24.[93] Sanders notes how 3:1–29 functions as an argument against the necessity of law keeping for salvation. Romans 3 is thus out to show that the Mosaic law is unnecessary for salvation, not to give a ruling on the question of what part works play within a Christian's salvation or ongoing identity as a Christian.

Sanders is especially concerned to pinpoint why it is that Paul says that God's righteousness comes apart from the law (3:21). He infers from 9:31–10:13 that Paul's real problem with the Mosaic law is simply that it is not faith in Christ. Since for Paul everyone can be saved by faith in Christ, this "soteriological fact" is what eliminates performance of the Mosaic law as a viable path for salvation, not the inability of people to keep the law or their attempts to keep the law in the wrong way.[94] The arguments that Paul uses against requiring Gentiles to keep the law are taken by others as the motivating reasons for Paul's position.[95] People who oppose the new perspective are often not ready to follow Sanders here; they take Paul's negative statements about life under the law as a foundational position in Paul's understanding of God's righteousness, rather than the secondary steps for which Sanders takes them.[96]

The main contribution of the new perspective to this locus has been its insistence that Paul's doctrine of justification by faith arose in the context of the dispute over whether to require Gentiles to keep Mosaic law and not in debates similar to those of the fifth and sixteenth centuries about the relationship between good works and divine grace.[97] Those influenced by the new perspective take pains to point out that this locus is saying that righteousness comes by faith rather than *the works of the Mosaic law* (Rom. 3:28). This approach then emphasizes that 3:21–28 is not discrediting the significance of good works in a believer's life. For example, Douglas Harink, indebted as he is to the new perspective, shows from 1 Thessalonians how Paul's early preaching to pagan Gentiles definitely included the idea of righteousness by works.[98] Simon Gathercole is also honest enough to admit that early Judaism and the New Testament consider works very important when describing a final judgment, and Kari Kuula can even affirm that "Paul's own soteriology is quite legalistic and it lays much weight on human works. It is best described by the terms 'synergism' or 'co-operation.'"[99]

Katherine Grieb's narrative-based reading of Romans also take pains to allow the story of Israel to be evoked with full integrity in this section of Romans. The framework of the exodus story and other instances of redemption pictured in Mosaic law are invoked as foundational narratives behind this locus, which describes God as righteous and the one who makes righteous.[100] The most popular translation of *hilastērion* as "mercy seat," which I explain in a following section, also fits well with this emphasis on the narratives of Israel's Scriptures as the necessary framework for understanding this locus. Thus Grieb summarizes Romans 3:25 in the context of this locus as follows: "God put Jesus Christ forward as a way of dealing with the sins of Israel committed in breach of the covenant and with the sins of the world that resulted from the disobedience of Adam and Eve."[101] Jesus represents Israel as its Messiah, and since narrative-based approaches sometimes emphasize how Israel is marked by God as God's messenger for the world, Jesus comes by extension to represent the world. It is thus no surprise that the subjective genitive reading of *pistis Christou* fits very well with this approach to 3:21–28.[102]

N. T. Wright brings his understanding of the narrative behind the text to land firmly on the side of the subjective genitive reading of *pistis Christou*. Because Israel has been unfaithful (3:2–3), *pistis Christou* within 3:21–22 must mean that "this righteousness, this world-righting covenant faithfulness, has been revealed 'through the faithfulness of Jesus the Messiah.'"[103] The redemption Paul mentions in 3:24 evokes for Wright the narrative of Israel's exodus from Egypt, which is for Wright a central metaphor in understanding what happens in Jesus' death. Wright does recognize that *hilastērion* means mercy-seat. Still, he hears narrative echoes of both the "Day of Atonement" and the "atoning sacrifice" of Israel's martyrs in this term.[104] Wright reads 3:27–31 as a very works-affirming sort of faith. Paul's terminology means that God will declare believers to be righteous before the judgment day, but such redemption still means that believers must live holy lives in worship of the one God of Israel.[105] We turn now to the three key questions of this locus.

Pistis Christou

While Sanders treats *pistis Christou* as an objective genitive, his emphasis on participation in Christ as the essence of Paul's theology supports those who treat the phrase as a subjective genitive and claim that Paul is asking people to participate in Christ's faithful dependence on God. Such writers as Paul Achtemeier and Arland Hultgren are making sure that the subjective genitive does not gain universal acceptance. On the one hand, the objective genitive reading leaves us wondering why Paul did not use the preposition "in" at places like Romans 3:22 and Galatians 2:16. This is a criticism that can be fairly leveled at the objective genitive reading, but seems ably answered by R. Barry Matlock's observation that *pistis Christou* is used to balance "works of the law" and thus points definitely toward the sense of the objective genitive.[106] The common criticism that the objective genitive reading runs the risk of making the believer's faith in Christ a work in itself is really not fair to Luther and has been soundly corrected by Anders Nygren. It is not that faith is a human requirement but that the reconciliation effected by Christ for humanity is a power that evokes faith in Christ by the reconciled.[107] In the end, the best arguments for the subjective genitive seem to be its theological utility, not the lexical or syntactical difficulties of the objective genitive.

On the other hand, the subjective genitive reading can run the risk of making human participation in Christ's faithfulness a work that eclipses the mystery of the redemption accomplished by Christ's death. For Paul, Christ remains a paschal lamb (1 Cor. 5:7) and not simply the supreme example of faithfulness. In the lens of syntax, the subjective genitive reading is the weaker position.[108] Matlock, following the lead of James Barr, has also helpfully called attention to the lexical difficulties with the claim that the subjective genitive is the more obvious reading.[109] C. E. B. Cranfield has also provided a thorough presentation of the problems with the subjective genitive position.[110]

One way out of this disagreement is to return to Origen's view of faith in Christ as putting on the virtues. This would allow one to believe in Christ (objective genitive) and then while doing this to follow the way in which Christ lived out his faith (subjective genitive) and grow in the virtues. The false dichotomy between subjective and objective genitives can even be seen in Hultgren's argument against the subjective genitive. He affirms that it should not simply be read as an objective genitive, but also as a "genitive of quality," which is "adjectival," helping us understand that "Paul's accent is upon faith, but this is the faith which is 'of Christ,' i.e., faith which responds to Christ proclaimed in the gospel."[111] Since Paul drops the *mou* from the Septuagint of Habakkuk 2:4 and the third person ending found in the Masoretic tradition at Habakkuk 2:4, choosing instead to say that the righteousness comes *ek pisteōs eis pistin* in Romans 1:17, it seems best to follow Morna Hooker and Sam Williams in seeing Christ's faithfulness that calls for a human response of faithfulness within the *pistis Christou* phrase.[112] Besides the ancillary texts that Hooker cites in explanation of the logic behind seeing both subjective and objective senses in the phrase, we may also note the *metron pisteōs* in 12:3–5a and the imitation of Christ enjoined on the strong in faith in 15:1–3. The surprising quotation of Schlatter with which this chapter opened also shows that a reading that includes both subjective and objective senses of the genitival phrase *pistis Christou* has a long precedent even within the Lutheran tradition.

Why does it matter whether we read *pistis Christou* as objective (faith in Jesus) or subjective (Jesus' faith)? First, the degree to which we emphasize faith in the human affects how we present the gospel. Proponents of the subjective genitive, who hold that Christ's faith is what saves, will not call for a distinct, conversion-constituting act of placing one's faith in Jesus. They will rather call people to join the church that lives out in a concentric pattern the faith that Jesus displayed. Second, we will begin to read Paul's gospel not as primarily based around the dichotomy of works and faith, which both have a human subject, but rather as a dichotomy between law and Christ. Third, this view of *pistis Christou* moves students of Paul's letters to see that justification by faith is part of a bigger theme in Paul, participation in Christ. And this participation means that justification and sanctification refer to the same process in the life of the church.[113] Finally, our stance on the meaning of *pistis Christou* can also affect how we draw the circle around those we call saved. Proponents of the objective genitive tend to understand faith in Christ as a requirement for salvation that logically precludes those who do not have such faith from salvation. Proponents of the subjective genitive might minimize a christocentric text like Romans 10:9 and include people who have faithfully followed God (the righteous *ethnē* of 2:14–15?) within those who are justified by the faith of Christ.

Those who hold to the subjective genitive of *pistis Christou* must take care to note how the faithfulness of those who imitate Jesus' faithfulness differs from Jesus' own faithfulness: "Jesus' faithfulness is also his righteousness by which he will live forever (Hab. 2:4). Those who trust in him trust also in God's covenant faithfulness because he is God's eschatological deliverer of Israel and of the world."[114]

Hilastērion

Renewed sensitivity to Paul's use of his Scriptures and careful lexicography have brought interpreters in the late-twentieth and early-twenty-first centuries to read "mercy seat" for Paul's term *hilastērion* in 3:25. Lexically, Paul's word never refers to the actual victim on an altar. Thus "expiation" as a cultic act or legal resolution is difficult as a translation. "Propitiation" as legal satisfaction is also not strongly attested in the use of *hilastērion* in Paul's Scriptures. (Those reading German commentators must know that the German language does not distinguish between "propitiation" and "expiation"; *Versohnung* can be translated with either word.) The background in Paul's Scriptures and in previous uses of *hilastērion* thus points strongly in the direction of "mercy seat," the place where the forgiveness of sins was effected. If this rare word in Paul's usage signals Paul's use of this material in a Day of Atonement sermon, we gain an explanation of why there are so many rare words used in this locus.[115]

Faith and Works

Closely related to the question of how faith and works are related is the question of whether justification by faith is the central theme of this letter. The new perspective's emphasis on this doctrine as Paul's way of getting past an improper emphasis on law observance as an identity badge of Jews certainly attempts to reduce the significance of justification by faith within Pauline theology. Also, increased attention to the differences among New Testament authors makes us question whether such a doctrine should be considered central to our understanding of the Christian gospel. Philipp Vielhauer notes that justification by faith as understood in the Lutheran tradition is definitely not the center of "Paul" in Acts.[116]

CONCLUSION

This locus assumes the significance of a key place within the New Testament that describes how Jesus' death brings God's saving righteousness. Though plenty of students remain split over whether to read *pistis Christou* as objective or subjective, Origen's openness to both the objective and subjective senses of *pistis Christou* is repeated now by Hooker and Williams, and seems to be the preferable way to read this text. It is not clear that a native Greek speaker would feel compelled to decide between objective and subjective genitives when using the phrase.

Origen's allegorical reading of "Christ" behind the purely golden *hilastērion* of the Old Testament has not returned. But an analogous tendency to read Christ the *hilastērion* of Romans 3:25 as a literal reference to the tabernacle's mercy seat is returning to Origen's sensitivity to the Jewish Scriptures of Paul and away from the Gentile tendency to abstract from this word a precise, theological doctrine of the atonement.

Luther's explicit departure from the allegorical reading of Scripture that he credits in the quotation above to his encounter with Romans led to a triumph of the Antiochene school in Protestant dress. But such a literal reading, oriented exclusively around the Christian master story in which everything points to Christ, is now being nuanced by the narrative theological approach to Romans. It would be claiming too much to say that the Alexandrian school has now gained the upper hand, but our eyes should be open to the surprising development that narrative layers of meaning, that is, the stories of Paul's Scriptures, are seen beneath this text that once prompted Luther to denounce all appeals to allegorical layers behind the text. This locus, which Origen saw as pointing back to the tabernacle furniture in order to highlight Christ's identity, is once again a connection point for the story of God's dealings with his first love, the Jews.

Locus 4

All Sinned (5:12)

Nothing is so easy to denounce, nothing is so difficult to understand.
Augustine on "the ancient sin"[1]

We move from Romans 3 to Romans 5. Romans 4, the Scripture proof that Abraham exemplifies a faith-based righteousness, is not as controversial a locus in the history of interpretation as loci 3 and 4. The main controversy in Romans 4 is the precise way in which Paul's thought moves from locus 3 to the example of Abraham. For this, I recommend Hays's suggestion.[2] Readers should note that the debate over how the connection between the end of Romans 3 and the beginning of Romans 4 hinges on the relationship between believing *ethnē* and the Jews, precisely the question that Origen locates as the central theme of this letter.

For those engaged in the challenge of trying to outline Romans, the significant question for Romans 5 is whether the chapter belongs with preceding chapters as the conclusion of a section (1:18–5:11/21) describing how Christ's atonement covers sin, which is then followed by a separate description of salvation from sin as dying and rising with Christ (chaps. 6–8; Schweitzer); or whether chapter 5 goes with chapters 6–8 as a description of the life of the believer (later Augustine, Luther, Melanchthon, Bultmann).[3] I think Dunn is right to regard chapter 5 as a bridge, concluding one section and opening another.[4]

ORIGEN

Most significant at this locus of "original sin" is Origen's reading of a hard fall. All humans are affected by Adam's sin. Death spreads to the whole human race as a consequence of Adam's sin, according to Origen's reading of Romans 5:12. He has a lengthy section discussing such heroes as Enoch and Noah. Even these must have been tainted by sin, for Enoch fathered Methuselah, who died! Even though Noah was found to be righteous in his generation (Gen. 6:9), he sinned in the vineyard, after the flood, when he became drunk and naked in his vineyard (Gen. 9:20–21). Especially strong is Origen's favorable quotation of Job 14:4—"No clean person comes from an unclean one, even if his life were only one day."[5] When Rufinus produced this commentary, then, he was no doubt aware that this section of his commentary would counter the Pelagian currents in Rome, which read Romans 5:12 much differently: "By example or by pattern. Just as through Adam sin came at a time when it did not yet exist, so in the same way through Christ righteousness was recovered at a time when it survived in almost no one."[6] Still, Origen does not emphasize from this locus that guilt is reckoned or passed from parent to child because of Adam's sin.[7] He offers two explanations of the fall: either all humans were in Adam's loins and expelled from Eden when Adam and Eve were expelled, or every human unexplainably experiences an individual expulsion from Eden and subsequent condemnation.[8]

As unacknowledged ancestor, Origen's emphasis on the hard fall emerges still as a dominant genetic trait in most Protestant and Catholic commentaries. Orthodox commentators do not see a hard fall here.[9]

As an exegete, Origen significantly notices how the "Therefore as" with which 5:12 begins is awkward. He explains this verse by connecting it with the end of the comparison to which the "as" points in 5:18. Origen says that though this "as" in 5:12 is pointing to a time when righteousness will come to all, Paul constructs this paragraph to hide this connection so that people will not assume all will become righteous in this life or with no moral effort.[10] Origen is also significant because his text of 5:14 omits the word "not," making the verse say that people from Adam to Moses sinned as Adam did, violating a specific command.[11] Origen first explains this reading by saying that death had infected everyone in the world, but death held dominion only over those who sinned as Adam did. He goes on to offer another explanation, that every descendant of Adam could be thought to have sinned in the likeness of Adam, thus extending the dominion of death to every human. Finally, Origen wonders whether "in the likeness of Adam's sin" is a mystery, perhaps referring to the death out of which Hosea prophesies deliverance or referring mysteriously only to certain people who have sinned as Adam sinned.[12] His different approaches will allow later commentators to use his exegesis of this locus in different ways, as can be illustrated by comparing Augustine and Erasmus below.

But Origen is aware of the manuscript tradition that our New Testaments have followed—"even over those not sinning in the likeness of Adam's transgression"—and he exegetes that possibility as well. For Origen this means that there were people who were dying because they were affected by the "law of death," though not affected by any other law related to punishment for specific transgressions.[13] Unlike commentators today, Origen proceeds under no constraint to establish his lemma. He simply exegetes whatever Christians are reading as their text of Romans.

In his section on 5:12–14, where Paul describes sin and death as present in the world before law, Origen notes how the Gnostic scholar Basilides does not understand the law of which Paul writes as natural law. Origen thinks it must refer to a natural law. He disparages Basilides by noting in the same context that Basilides takes Paul's claim in 7:9–10a, "when the commandment entered, sin came to life and I died," to mean that people's souls move from animals into human forms. Origen argues that Paul's sentence has to refer to a single being and that Basilides is wrong. People (and not animals) actually died because they did not fulfill natural law. Basilides is thus incorrect to associate the law that brings death only with Mosaic law.[14] Origen demonstrates here his polemical edge in the commentary, as well as his tendency to distinguish between senses of the word "law," in this case by his sensitivity to Judaism that resulted in a defense of Mosaic law from what he considers an unhelpful association between this law and death.

ROMANS 5, 7, AND 9 AS KEY BATTLE SITES FOR AUGUSTINE

John Buford viewed the hills and open spaces of a town in southern Pennsylvania and realized it would be a very good place to fight a battle, especially if one could locate one's forces on its hills and ridges on the southeast part of the town, a town hardly known to Western civilization before Buford came upon it on June 30, 1863. So Augustine happens upon Romans, and finds it a useful site from which to address some of his own quandaries and a well-situated battlefield from which to fight what he perceived as rebel forces against his Catholic orthodoxy, especially Manichee and Pelagian ideas. More than the theological positions that Augustine derived from Romans, such as his diagnosis of original sin in the human being as child of Adam (locus 4), his emphasis on the inexorable pull of God's grace (loci 7–9), his later insistence on the impotence of the human will, and the inescapable decree of divine predestination (loci 7–9), Augustine's most significant legacy in the history of Romans interpretation is the continuation of the project begun by Irenaeus and advanced by Origen: the reclamation of Paul for the church and the identification and mastery of the text of Romans as a theological battlefield.

On those Pennsylvania hills and open spaces mentioned above, key battles were fought on July 1–3 that affected the outcome of the opposing armies' encounter and invested the topography of the area with an enduring significance.

It is impossible now to see "Little Round Top" or the "Peach Orchard" without thinking of the soldiers on both sides who fought bravely in the battles at these sites. So it is with the battles Augustine fought on Romans. Though we may disagree with Augustine's maneuvers and the outcome of his battles, the topography of Romans is forever charged with theological significance at the sites of key battles Augustine fought here. It is difficult to read Romans 5, 7, and 9 without reliving Augustine's battles. As we approach Augustine on 5:12, we must understand that we are entering a section of Romans that has been thoroughly traversed and utilized by Augustine. Even if you have never studied how Augustine interpreted Romans, if your life has been touched in any way by Western Christianity, the way you have been reading chapters 5, 7, and 9 of Romans has been formatted by Augustine. Origen remains in our plot as the unacknowledged ancestor to whose general (Romans is all about Paul's negotiating between the Jews and the *ethnē*) and specific (Christ is mercy seat; God may save all; the divided *egō* in Romans 7 is not fully regenerated; humans responsibly exercise their wills in ways that have real consequences; Israel still matters to God; "submit to the authorities" does not mean Christians need to obey the government) interpretations Romans readers are returning. But it is because of the way that Augustine surveyed and used Romans 5, 7, and 9 that all subsequent participants in conversations on these chapters find it necessary to identify themselves using Augustine's coordinates.

AUGUSTINE

In a very real sense, all three books of Augustine's *On the Merits and Forgiveness of Sins and on Infant Baptism* are an argument that 5:12 shows that original sin is propagated from Adam. Augustine nuances his interpretation to consider every aspect of the issue: 5:12 shows that the death that entered the human race through Adam is not simply the death of the soul (a Pelagian position), but the death of the body. The original sin that brings this death is passed to all humans not by the Pelagian explanation of imitation; in Augustine's words it is *propagatio*, not *imitatio*.[15] Romans 5:12 is also the key verse from Romans that Augustine uses in the third book of this work, a book added after Augustine had seen Pelagius's commentary on the Pauline letters.[16] The first point on which Augustine attacks this commentary is on Pelagius's argument against original sin that is based on 5:12. Pelagius says that if one holds to original sin, one must also hold to the idea that Christ's death brings grace even to unbelievers. The argument assumes that no one could believe that Christ's death is effective for unbelievers, so in an analogous way, no one could hold that Adam's sin is passed on to infants. Augustine argues with a counterexample that baptized infants do receive grace, or some benefit that even the Pelagians must admit, so the Pelagian argument's parallelism breaks down, for these infants are in one sense unbelievers who do receive divine grace.

Augustine uses the whole of the fifth chapter of Romans, especially its latter half, in this piece. Paul's argument is entirely obvious, Augustine says; the only thing that is not clear is what Paul meant by "Adam, the type of the one who was to come" in 5:14.[17] In his use of the rest of this chapter in Romans, this composition confirms and sharpens an earlier emphasis of Augustine: the law was introduced to multiply sins.[18] While Augustine had already made this point in his *Statements* almost two decades previously, the Pelagian threat sharpened this idea into a weapon that a later Augustinian would use against the very church Augustine sought to defend. For the Pelagians had a very positive view of natural law and Mosaic law. Both were means of bridging the gap between God and humanity that should be used, once the guilt of past sins had been covered by the grace of Christ.[19] Augustine therefore opposes this positive view of the law, coming as it did with an optimistic estimate of a believer's ability to keep it, with an insistence that the law's real purpose is to multiply sins, not to ameliorate them.[20] Thus the famous "second use" of the law can be seen in the forge of an anti-Pelagian battle. The link between sin and death is also covered in this piece, for Augustine uses 8:10–11 to prove that physical death comes from sin, something the Pelagians denied.[21]

The emphasis on the fifth chapter of Romans would continue in Augustine's anti-Pelagian correspondence. Letter 157, written in 414 or early 415, marshals 5:11–12 to contest those Pelagians who say that unbaptized infants will not be condemned.[22] Here as elsewhere Augustine is not employing a pristine argument from Scripture; it is rather that the practice of the church shapes his arguments. Since the church baptized infants, Scripture must be interpreted to show that this baptism is necessary. But the dominant text from Romans in this letter is not the text that Augustine, with the help of some shady biblical translation, was able to forge as the text that proves "original sin," 5:12. It was rather 5:20—"But law entered by stealth, so that the transgression might be multiplied. But where sin multiplied, grace abounded all the more." Augustine repeatedly refers to this text in Letter 157 to argue that the law is not a direct means of salvation, as the Pelagians would argue, but rather that the law leads to more sin.[23] It is only in an indirect way that the law, after leading to more sin, then leads us to desire what we ought to do.[24] By the increase of sin brought on by human nature's attempt to keep the law, the description of 7:23 becomes apt for all humans: a human is born with the law of sin in his or her members.[25]

ABELARD

Abelard follows Origen in noting how the "Therefore as" at the beginning of 5:12 seems incomplete. He offers ways out of this awkward expression by either connecting it to the "reconciliation" in 5:11 or by connecting 5:12 to 5:18, as Origen and most commentators today do.[26]

The complexity or difficulty with the doctrine of original sin as imputed guilt is seen in the series of excurses that Abelard offers while trying to explain it. He begins with "Questions or Objections regarding Original Sin," followed by "Investigation of Solutions, and How Sin Is Described."[27] The excursus that follows is "Brief Consideration of What Is Original Sin." In this excursus Abelard follows Augustine's early assertion that all of God's judgment on people is just and that every human sin or righteous deed is performed by the exercise of a person's own will.[28] This then leads him to the excursuses "Concerning Free Will" and "What Is Free Will?"

In these excursuses he uses both Augustine and Boethius to set out the philosophical problem of free will.[29] The philosophical complexity is heightened by the challenge of the primary sources Abelard knows. Toward the end of the "First Solution" excursus that follows these excursuses on free will, Abelard quotes a letter of Pelagius for the second time in his exegesis of this section of Romans, a quotation he considers as coming from Jerome. The point of this quotation is that while Adam sinned with no prior example and brought on his own death, we who have the witnesses of the Law, Prophets, Gospels, and apostolic letters have no reason to wish to sin.[30] Such a quotation that treats humans as perfectly free to choose not to sin is antithetical to the generally Augustinian direction Abelard is taking on this locus. It illustrates how some medievals still sought to retain a place for the exercise of human responsibility and freedom, though this was generally constricted by the Augustinian framework in which they worked.

Abelard finally offers his excursus on the full definition of original sin. He defines "original sin" in the tradition of Augustine as the guilt with which humans are born that makes them deserving of damnation or eternal punishment. While humans can be faulted for punishing undeserving children, God cannot be so faulted, Abelard argues. He mentions children who died at the time of the flood or in the destruction of Sodom and states that God cannot be faulted, for in the end God's grace can be seen, despite the destruction with which God judged the world. Paul calls people "children of wrath" (Eph. 2:3) as if they are born under God's just anger. Ezekiel 18:1–2, which looks ahead to a time when children will not be considered guilty of their parents' sins, is simply predicting the grace of the new covenant that is mediated through the sacrament of baptism. Without baptism therefore, Abelard considers God to be fully within a description of righteousness to condemn children simply for their inherited guilt. The damnation of infants leads within the whole picture to a magnification of divine grace, Abelard insists. Actual sins that people commit distort human nature and bind these sinners to the guilt already inherited from their parents.[31]

LUTHER

Luther follows Augustine in reading this locus as indicating that Adam's actual sin brought original sin into the world, so that all those born after Adam are sinners irrespective of any actions they have made. Luther's gloss on this verse includes the idea that all humanity sinned with Adam in Adam's sin. Luther also emphasizes the extent of the sin, for he claims that Paul defines "world" in this verse with the following phrase "all men."[32]

Luther has a lengthy scholium on this locus, including a section under the heading "What, therefore is original sin?" and a lengthy "Corollary" that follows. In his definition of original sin, Luther waxes on eloquently against the scholastics, who had defined original sin as a lack of righteousness in the will. By contrast Luther defines it as a complete lack of righteousness in all the parts of a person, and a predisposition to commit evil, a loathing of what is good, a delight in what is evil. He said that the scholastic tendency to limit original sin to the human will leads to pride and hinders genuine penitence.[33] This is a noteworthy statement, given Carlson's suggestion (described in the preceding chapter) that Luther may have come to his position on justification as passive righteousness because he could never seem to experience God's forgiveness in his participation in the sacrament of penance.[34]

At the end of the scholium on this locus Luther describes the Greek (though he had not yet received Erasmus's Greek New Testament at this point in his lectures) phrase at the end of the verse "in which all have sinned" as ambiguous, asserting that the pronoun "which" can be either masculine or neuter. He is implying that if masculine, the pronoun refers to Adam and gives us Augustine's picture of all humanity inside Adam, sinning along with Adam in the garden of Eden. Luther considers the other possibility, that "which" is neuter, to lead to the translation "in that all sinned," meaning that original sin is proven in that all humans are the children of Adam and commit sin. Luther follows Augustine in affirming both interpretations, though he emphasizes the former one.[35]

I cannot leave Luther without making clear how this locus is related to other loci in Romans. We can try to read through 5:12 as if it simply describes that all humans die because of sin. But since Origen we have been given glasses to read this locus as describing a hard fall, a catastrophe for the human race, in which the death-carrying virus of sin infects all humanity. Augustine and Luther radicalize this picture further by finding the Western church's doctrine of original sin here, the guilt that is passed on to each subsequent generation of humans, regardless of the length of their lives or their conduct. As we approach the loci that deal with the human will and divine predestination, we shall see that interpreters who emphasize the guilt of original sin and the inability of the human to do anything untainted by sin (locus 4) are especially prone to emphasize the effective power of divine predestination (loci 7–9) in the order of salvation. The positions just described for these loci are termed "Augustinian" in Romans commentaries.

ERASMUS

Erasmus begins his annotations on this locus by explicitly citing Origen's observation that the "Therefore just as" phrase that begins the verse is not completed and then summarizes Origen's explanations. Erasmus offers a new and noteworthy solution to the puzzle. He correctly includes "so" (the adverb *houtōs*) among the possible connotations of the Greek conjunction "and" in the verse. This results in his translation and explanation: "'Therefore just as through one man sin entered into the world, so also through one man death entered'—so that you understand that both of these have come to us from Adam. Adam sinned, and because of his sin fell into death. So likewise we, since (following him) we sin, are hastening to death."[36] The glaring omission in this explanation is the causal or biological link that the Augustinian approach sees between Adam's sin and later generations' sin.

On the difficult last phrase of this locus, Erasmus labels Augustine's explanation that all humanity somehow sinned when Adam sinned as untenable. Erasmus states directly that infants who do nothing do not sin. Erasmus also blatantly denies, with an allusion to the opinion of Jean Gerson, that children experience spiritual death if they die before being baptized. A third reason why he rejects Augustine's reading of "in Adam" for the prepositional phrase at the end of the verse is that the Greek preposition *epi* in this phrase is not the standard preposition used for someone or something to be inside another person.[37]

Erasmus cites favorably the commentator unknown to him (Pelagius) included in an edition of Jerome's works he knows whose gloss "by example or by pattern" denies the biological transmission of a sin nature (Origen) or sin nature and guilt (Augustine). Erasmus's main argument is that Romans 5:12 does not teach the doctrine of original sin. He is convinced that Paul is referring both before and after the verse to actual sins individuals commit, not to the inherited guilt of original sin. While Erasmus insists he believes in original sin, he alludes to his support elsewhere for this doctrine from Job 14:4; 25:4; and Psalm 51:5, and not this locus in Romans. He also cites Chrysostom on this verse, who observes that all Romans 5:12 is saying is that "when [Adam] fell, even those who had not eaten from the tree became mortal from him."[38] Erasmus tries to use Origen's "slippery" (Erasmus's word) exploration of different exegetical approaches on this locus to argue against this locus as the basis for the hard fall, but in the sixteenth century Augustine's reading of original sin here in continuity with Origen's interpretation that humanity was in the loins of Adam when he sinned and was expelled from Eden continued as the established exegesis of this text.

BARTH

In *Romans I* Barth describes the sin that entered the world as the human desire to be independent in relation to God.[39] All the impulses that seek to present the human being as interesting in herself, and all the possibilities for such activities as "introspection, human knowledge, experience, psychology, historical thought," arise outside God through sin.[40] Barth steers clear of affirming a strong doctrine of original sin. Uninterested in the question of an historical Adam, Barth simply affirms that all humanity is sinful, and that this sin found its entrance into the world through a human. Barth does not treat Adam's sin as the index case of a viral epidemic, as Augustine does in his construction of the doctrine of original sin. Rather, Barth treats Adam's sin as the great precedent, a breach in a dam that held back human perversity.[41] If one had to measure Barth on the scales of past controversies, he would be more Augustinian than Pelagian, more Lutheran than Erasmian, for he affirms that all humans are implicated in sin. But he does not use this text to teach a sort of qualitative original sin with which humans are born.

In *Romans II* there remains the definition of sin as an assertion of human independence from God.[42] In the history of Romans interpretation Barth is unique in defining sin in epistemological and ontological categories, rather than in moral categories. Indeed, he is completely disinterested in cataloging various types of sins: "Sin is the sovereign power in the world as we know it; and it is wholly irrelevant what particular form it takes in the life of each individual."[43] There also remains the caricature of the world as a place where various forces are arrayed against God.[44] In both *Romans I* and *II* he pays extensive attention to death. If sin is the power that dominates the world, death is the law that dominates the world.[45] This is surely appropriate, for Romans spends more space on death as a theologoumenon than any other book in the New Testament.[46]

But in *Romans II* Barth more explicitly rejects any connection between this locus in Romans and the doctrine of original sin. He writes that Paul would regard the doctrine of original sin as "one of the many historical and psychological falsifications of his meaning."[47] Barth's opposition to an interpretation that finds original sin in this locus arises from the way in which he begins with what God has done in Christ. Only because God's righteousness becomes evident in Christ does Adam's sin become visible for what it is: "Adam has no separate, positive existence. He does not revolve round his own pole; he is not a second factor. He exists only when he is dissolved, and he is affirmed only when in Christ he is brought to nought."[48] To support the doctrine of original sin is to reify Adam and sin into entities that exist and can be known apart from Christ. For Barth, for whom everything begins with God's righteous activity in Christ, this would be sacrilege.

This reminds us of a crucial point in which Barth is revolutionary for New Testament scholars' view of the law. Unlike Luther's simplistic second use of the law, in which the law drives a person to the gospel of faith in Christ, Barth held that the law would only be a threat that convicted a person of sin when God had already shown his grace to a person through Christ.[49] Barth divests the law of any independent value, even the negative value of Luther's second use, apart from what God has done in Christ.

POST-BARTHIAN APPROACHES

Approaches to Romans since Barth tend to minimize the Augustinian reading of original sin here and look more at how this text fits in Paul's reconfiguration of Israel's story.

New Perspective

Sanders's treatment of this locus is framed by his general understanding that "for Paul, the conviction of a universal solution preceded the conviction of a universal plight."[50] This approach is somewhat similar to Barth's assertion that the law only convicts after a person has experienced grace. Sanders developed a similar idea in his *Paul and Palestinian Judaism* from an inductive study of the rabbinic sources themselves, where law is not a threat that drives a person to God, but a wonderful gift. Sanders thus coined the phrase "from solution to plight" to describe the formulation Paul offers in his letters for the place of the law in God's revelation to people. Sanders differs from Barth in that he views grace as prompting the possibility for the human to initiate a move from condemnation to salvation. He is thus not as God-centered as Barth. While Sanders has not convinced everyone, there is now a significant current in New Testament scholarship that views the law in this way.[51] This current refuses to absolutize the traditional reading of Romans 1–3 in which one must begin with sin before describing salvation.

The description of humanity under sin in 1:18–3:20 differs from 5:12, according to Sanders. They only cohere in that both end up with humanity under the power of sin and thus in need of the salvation provided by Christ.[52] Sanders considers Paul's admission in 5:13–14 that sin is not counted when there is no law and that people died who did not sin as Adam did to disprove Paul's own assertions in 5:12 and 5:19 that all humanity is rendered sinful in Adam. The reasons that Paul repeats this assertion are, first, that Paul had the definite idea that Christ brought salvation for the world, and so he needed to find ways (such as in 1:18–3:20 and 5:12–14), which, while not as coherent as the solution, at least point toward it; and second, that Paul was influenced by an ontological dualism that pitted the forces of good against the forces of evil (2 Cor. 4:4; 11:14; Gal. 4:8).[53]

Dunn, like Sanders, cannot accept the Augustinian connection between Adam and the moral status of all humanity based on this locus. Dunn comments on the end of 5:12: "The relationship between the one man's initial failure and all men's sin is not an issue to which Paul addresses himself, and the imprecision of the syntax forbids us to press for a clear-cut decision on the point. All that Paul seems to want to say is that this epoch of human history is characterized and determined by the fatal interplay of sin and death."[54] He also emphasizes how "law," understood as Mosaic law, comes up in 5:14 as Paul seeks to show those Jews in his audience that possessing the law magnifies the need Israel has for the redemption Christ offers.[55] This fits with a straightforward reading of 5:20a. It is therefore not simply a chronicle of how humans need Christ's salvation because they are all sinful in Adam. This need is present, but there is also a focus in 5:14 that Israel's possession of the law does not exempt it from the need for salvation; indeed, the law seems to exacerbate this need, according to this new perspective reading of Paul.

Narrative-Based Approaches

Grieb fills in the story only alluded to by Paul's pointed references to Adam, Moses, and Christ. The story as she tells it is that Israel was called to follow God and serve as God's representative for the world, since Adam had failed in that calling. The Mosaic law is part of the means by which Israel is to mediate for God with the *ethnē*. But Israel was disobedient to that law and did not adequately serve as the intermediary between God and the *ethnē*. So God sends Christ, the "second Adam," or, if we follow Barth's reading that we shall encounter in the next chapter, "the first human," to succeed in obeying God and mediating between God and the world where Israel did not. Romans 5:12 functions in this narrative approach as a heading that describes the plight to which both the nation of Israel and then Christ were called to respond as obedient intermediaries between God and the world. Only Christ's obedience has met this need, bringing righteousness both to the sinful *ethnē* and to Israel, whose Torah in the end served only to highlight their need of salvation all the more.[56] The main difference that is evident between the approaches of the new perspective and Grieb's narrative-based approach is that the latter does not emphasize the "solution to plight" movement in Paul's thought. This central tenet of the new perspective is eclipsed by the narrative that moves from Adam's sin to Christ's redemption. Also, while the new perspective highlights the role of the law within Paul's explanation of this locus, a narrative-based approach such as that in Wright's commentary under the heading "From Adam to the Messiah" must necessarily use a narrative that moves from sin to redemption.[57]

Henri Blocher

Henri Blocher seeks to find a middle way between the difficult reading of Origen and Augustine (that humanity was inside Adam and is condemned for his very sin) and a looser reading of the locus. Blocher's solution is to say that Adam's sin makes the imputation of sin to the *ethnē*, who do not possess a law, easier. Since Adam broke the creation covenant of Genesis 2, according to Blocher, humans die because they are viewed through the legal identity of Adam. Blocher retranslates the locus as follows: "Just as through one man, Adam, sin entered the world and the sin-death connection was established, and so death could be inflicted on all as the penalty of their sins. . . ."[58] He goes on to say that this makes the "how much more" comparisons in 5:9, 10, 15, 17 more understandable: "If Adam's role was so dramatically efficacious in securing the condemnation of all people in him, and therefore the reign of death, how much more is Christ's work efficacious for those in him, leading to life eternal!"[59] He later argues for a nuanced view of original sin by dismantling the opposition so easily assumed between one's own actions and one's heredity. This opposition is also seen in the standard pairing we assume we must choose between: Augustine's original sin by

generation and Pelagius's almost universal sin by imitation. In effect he is trying
to show that the generation versus imitation dichotomy is false, and in so doing
Blocher has marvelously steered through the issues surrounding 5:12.[60]

CONCLUSION

Romans 5:12 describes the spread of death to all humanity. On this all agree.
Beginning with Origen, who read this text as possibly describing how all humanity was in the loins of the sinning Adam, and reinforced by Augustine, who con-
cluded from this text and the church's practice of baptism that moral guilt is
passed down from parents to children, the Western church's doctrine of original
sin has been associated with this locus. While Erasmus gave voice to the textual
difficulties already recognized by Origen in reading the text as a proof for original sin, and Barth voiced the theological difficulties with the doctrine, it is only
with the new perspective and narrative theology that we again see Israel and its
law as crucial to this locus. In their readings, 5:12 presents the negative framework in which the Mosaic law, the people who possessed this law, and the Messiah were called to function.

Locus 5

The All and the Many
(5:18–21)

Lord, I believe, were sinners more
Than sands upon the ocean shore,
Thou hast for all a ransom paid,
For all a full atonement made.

Count Nicolas von Zinzendorf[1]

In this chapter we will examine how 5:18–21 has been interpreted through two millennia of conversations on Romans. The parallel in 5:18 between one transgression leading to condemnation for all with the one act of justification leading to the justification of life coming to all humanity is the primary locus of attention. Other texts in Romans that have been aligned with this window of universalism are 11:32, 36.[2] As we examine how people have responded to the universalism question here, I also ask you to consider: (1) whether there are features of this letter as a whole that prompt readers to consider universalism; and (2) if there are exegetical or theological approaches that lead some commentators to a vision of universal restoration with God.

ORIGEN

Origen's Romans commentary notes Paul's use of "all" in 5:18 and "many" in 5:19 and is mostly concerned with how Paul says only that "many" were made sinners when in 5:12 Paul says that "all have sinned." His response draws a distinction between being a sinner, which involves habitual sinning, and having sinned. While everyone has sinned, not everyone is a sinner. Similarly, many will be considered righteous, but not all people, even though all people may perform a righteous act.[3]

In this context Origen does not seem to be entertaining the idea that all will be saved, for he quotes Jesus' words from Matthew 8:11 that "many" and not "all" will join the patriarchs in the kingdom of God.[4] This is unexpected for Origen, who is usually stereotyped as fully in the universalist camp.

In his exegesis of the end of Romans 11, Origen emphasizes the goodness of God, since God ultimately wills to bring salvation to all people. The position of Israel as an enemy of the Gentile church is qualified by Origen using Paul's phrase "on your behalf" (Rom. 11:28) to emphasize that the temporary disbelief that Israel has shown toward the Christ was only to open up God's salvation to the Gentiles.[5] For Origen, the salvation that Paul sees for Israel at the end of Romans 11 is very significant. It illustrates what Origen wants to affirm against the Gnostics: that individuals are not predestined into saved and condemned categories, but that a single, benevolent God continues to work in concert with free humans for the ultimate salvation of all.[6] This ultimate salvation of all, including the devil and demons, is sometimes called the *apokatastasis*, or consummation. Origen devotes a section of *On First Principles* to this idea and its scriptural support, an idea he describes as a matter for discussion rather than definition.[7]

In other places in Origen's commentary he seems to open a window toward universalism. In his exegesis of Romans 3:26, Origen describes how the sacrifices of Leviticus point ahead to the *hilastērion* that Jesus would accomplish not only for believers' sins, but for the sins of the world.[8] This is evidence that this letter contains more windows that can be opened to the horizon of universalism than some of Paul's other letters. The account of how God's righteousness comes to humanity through the faith of Jesus Christ in 3:21–28, the Adam/Christ comparison in 5:12–21, and the description of salvation for "all Israel" after a "full number" of *ethnē* have entered this salvation, followed by the language of disobedience and mercy for all in 11:25–26, 32, can prompt some interpreters to consider universalism.

The interpretive approaches that seem most prone to recognize and follow these prompts are those that emphasize the Jew-*ethnē* pairing as a theme throughout the letter, or those that consider this letter to include more than simply a road to salvation for individuals but a description of God's knowledge and relation to humanity as a corporate whole. Besides the Jew-*ethnē* pairing that Origen sees as central to the letter, in his case there is also a tendency to consider universalism, because he views hell as a restorative rather than punitive experience for sinners. For Origen, hell is a place where sinners are purified for a finite period rather than punished eternally.[9] This doctrine of hell comes through in his other writings. Origen's Romans commentary is not a strong statement for his doctrine of *apokatastasis*, but it is consistent with the trajectory toward universalism found in his writings.

Some Christians consider any teaching that God will ultimately save all humanity as necessarily and fatally weakening one's theology. For these, the moral weight of people eternally burning in hell functions as the necessary ballast in their theological ships. If this ballast is lost or lightened, the ship begins to list and will eventually capsize, in their estimation. Thus G. W. Butterworth notes that what sparked most opposition in Origen's teaching was his idea that demons and reprobate people would have opportunity to acquire virtue and be saved.[10] Thomas Merton's poem at the beginning of this book similarly emphasizes the reputed universalism of Origen as his most controversial idea. For those who cannot accept the salvation of the reprobate in a final *apokatastasis*, their understanding of Christ as the only way seems totally separate from the possibility that God through Christ will save all people.

But an emphasis on the efficacy and particularity of Christ as savior is logically quite close to the affirmation that God through Christ will ultimately save all. If all need to repent and believe in Christ to participate in a salvation they cannot earn, then won't the God who wishes all to be saved and who did not spare the only begotten Son reach out and save all?

AUGUSTINE

Augustine quotes 5:18–19 near the end of number 29 of his *Commentary on Statements in the Letter to the Romans*, but he does so only to show how Paul finishes making distinctions and returns to his flow of thought that was interrupted after 5:12. He does not raise the universalism question in this context.[11] In *City of God*, Augustine begins a paragraph emphasizing how God will judge each individual person according to what he or she has done, and then quotes 9:14 and 11:33 to argue that even though no human can act rightly without God's help, God is still completely just in judging every individual.[12] Later he quotes 8:13 when entertaining the possibility, against his exegetical preference, that eternal hellfire is really for the soul and that Scripture's language about fleshly torment in hell simply means that such torment comes against those who have lived for the flesh.[13] Interpretations that conceive of judgment as annihilation or a restorative, temporary period in hell à la Origen appear on Augustine's radar screen only as wrongheaded readings that must be shot down.[14]

ABELARD

Abelard understands the "justification for all people" at the end of 5:18 as explaining how Christ's act of justification covers all types of people, including those before the law who are mentioned in 5:12 and those who sinned in a way different from Adam's sin (5:14). While Abelard makes no effort to guard against a universally affirmative reading of the end of 5:18, he does not emphasize the "all" as a universal affirmative that extends to every human being. For Abelard, Paul is concerned to show that the justification effected by the one Jesus Christ extends to all types of sinners previously mentioned in the paragraph.[15]

In a standard exegetical move that will appear also in Luther, Abelard begins his comments on 5:19 by stating that Paul cannot be speaking of every last individual at the end of 5:18 because he now uses "many," not "all." Abelard also uses Paul's adjective "many" to refer to people who are forgiven of original sin through the church's sacraments, but then fall into their own sin and are liable for punishment. He compares such people to the unforgiving servant described in Matthew 18:23–34 and concludes that no one who is delivered from the original sin of Adam by the church's sacraments can be said to be predetermined to the condemnation of eternal death. Such predetermination he reserves only for those who have not received the church's sacraments.[16]

AQUINAS

Aquinas efficiently considers and rejects the possibility that the "all" referring to those who fall under Adam's sin is the same "all" in extent as those who receive the justification of life through Christ. It is false because he takes it as axiomatic that not all people are justified through Christ. With wording that might appear to some as sleight of hand, Aquinas uses birth and rebirth to find the extent of the "all" in each case: "It must be understood that as all people who are carnally born from Adam incur condemnation through his sin, so all who are spiritually reborn through Christ obtain justification of life." He goes on to cite John 3:5 to support his idea that all who are reborn reach life through Christ.

While he admits that the justification through Christ is sufficient to cover all humanity in its extent, it is allowed to reach only the faithful with effective justification. Here he quotes 1 Timothy 4:10, which describes Jesus as the savior of all people, especially of the faithful.

He builds from his parallelism regarding birth to a parallelism regarding death: "Just as no one dies unless through the sin of Adam, so no one is justified unless through the righteousness of Christ," and then he quotes Romans 3:22, as if to say that the "all who believe in him" at the end of this verse matches the second "all" in Romans 5:18. Aquinas does enlarge the extent of this "all" by allowing that it includes not only believers living after Christ's incarnation, but also believers before the incarnation, who believed that Christ would be born on the earth and suffer. Aquinas concludes this section with the finality of a logic teacher and a transition to another idea here at the end of Romans 5 : "So therefore it is proven that the grace of Christ proceeds to the justification of the many from what follows, as is evident from the reign of life."[17]

LUTHER

In his gloss on the second "all" of 5:18 Luther cites Augustine to support an exclusivist reading of the locus. The first "all" is used because all who are born physically are born through Adam. The second "all" in the verse is used because all who are spiritually born are born through Christ.[18]

Luther's gloss explains that the "many" appears in 5:19 to make clear that Paul did not mean that all people receive God's grace through Christ, but rather to show how strong both sin and grace are. Luther says on this verse that grace is stronger than sin, since if one sin could affect many—actually all—people, grace is stronger, since it can save many—and even all—people, if they are willing.[19] With this observation Luther's exegetical instincts are surely correct, for it matches the repeated "much more" earlier in the paragraph (5:15, 17). Of course, Luther did not consider that this stronger grace would actually save all people, though he certainly recognized its power to do so.

J. W. COLENSO

One name worth mentioning before we reach Barth is John William Colenso. A missionary to the Zulu people in present-day South Africa, Colenso's universalism came into full blossom while writing a Romans commentary on the mission field. On our locus he writes, "For 'the many' who died in Adam were, of course, the whole race; and therefore also, blessed be [sic] God! 'The many,' to whom 'the grace of God abounded, the free gift by grace of the one man Jesus Christ,' the gift of righteousness, must be the whole race, the whole family of man."[20] Colenso functions in the history of Romans interpretation as the supreme counterexample for those who object that a universalistic reading of 5:18–19 will destroy any missions impulse. John and Harriette Colenso did tremendous work for the Zulu people while continuing to believe that in the end God will save all. There are compelling reasons for mission that those with an exclusively extraterrestrial view of salvation refuse to recognize.

BARTH

In *Romans I* Barth entitles 5:12–21 "The Triumph of Life," and begins with a strong call to consider the divine designs for humanity as a whole. "Walking as in the day (Rom. 13:13) is not our 'personal experience,' but rather a very small part of a world event. The link of a chain by itself, loosed from its context, has no value. A pair of individual 'salvations' of particular little humans is not the goal of God's way."[21] In this opening salvo we see Barth's position on a central question all students of Romans must face, that is, whether this letter only communicates a plan for individuals to reach salvation or whether it is a statement about God's dealings with humanity as a whole. Barth's early answer to this question fits with his main polemic in *Romans I* against liberal theology, a theology that was individualistic in nature. The answer to this question affects how we will understand God's righteousness in this letter. Is it only a vertical relationship between God and the individual who is walking on the Romans road to salvation? Or is God's righteousness concerned with humanity as a whole and therefore to be both vertically and horizontally understood?

If we read this righteousness as coming on "all humanity" or "humanity as a whole" not simply in extent but also in dimensions of existence, the door is opened for the social dimensions of salvation. For centuries, based on Luther's alleged reading of Augustine, we have been led to believe that the righteousness of God as described in Romans does not include social justice. If, as Barth suggests here, God is out to bring righteousness to humanity as a whole, then this points toward a climax in which all dimensions of human existence are penetrated by God's salvation. This is not explicitly found in either *Romans I* or *Romans II*, but an ethical concern is discernible even in other works from this time period of Barth's career, as John Webster has ably shown.[22]

In Barth's exegesis of 5:18–19 in *Romans I* we can read Barth describing in comprehensive terms how Adam's disobedience and the judgment of "Sin!" and the punishment of "Death!" come on all humanity. Then Barth describes just as comprehensively how Christ's obedience brings the judgment of "Righteousness!" and the possibility of "Life!" for all humans. At the end of this section he describes these two lines that extend through history and simply remarks that the distinguishing problem for humanity is the line in which we locate ourselves. That final remark seems to render the early Barth not as a universalist, but only as someone who recognizes the universal possibility of life for all humanity, which the human will must actualize. This position resonates with some strands of pietism and illustrates that at this stage Barth seems to be tracking with Luther's comparison of the strength of divine grace over human sin.[23]

On 3:21–22a in *Romans II* Barth describes the universal call for faith in Jesus, the one who veils God's incomprehensibility. He insists that with Paul we cannot call others to our faith as if the body of faith is potent for salvation. Rather all humanity must be called to faith in Jesus, a movement of faith that Barth describes as possible for all since it is simultaneously impossible.[24]

In Romans 5 Barth emphasizes the fallenness of all humanity in Adam. This then is answered by the justification that comes in Christ. Barth certainly sees this as scripted for a cosmic stage. He clarifies Paul's point in 5:18–19 by rejecting a possible interpretation that affirms that only certain individuals have been made righteous through Christ's obedience. It is rather that the human individual as part of a corporate entity is illumined and shown to be righteous. Christ's obedience (5:19c) incorporates all humanity, just as Adam's disobedience had incorporated all humanity: "In the light of this act of obedience there is no man who is not—in Christ. All are renewed and clothed with righteousness, all are become a new subject, and are therefore set at liberty and placed under the affirmation of God." Barth immediately qualifies this universal incorporation in Christ by locating humanity as standing on a threshold, looking forward in hope to a new world.[25] Neither here nor later in his career does Barth unequivocally claim that an *apokatastasis* will necessarily occur in this new world, or eschaton. It remains simply a hope.

Barth's exegesis of the law entering in 5:20 points to the relationship that this question of universalism has to Judaism as a theologoumenon within Christian theology: "Is there not between Adam and Christ a third figure—Moses! . . . by whose side Aaron stands?"[26] One of the reasons that the universalism question arises in Romans is that this letter considers and grants Christ-less Judaism a place in the divine economy.

When Barth comes to the overflow of grace at the end of 5:20, we must not miss his famous question, asking if Paul is not right to utter 5:20 even, "indeed primarily and specifically," in regard to Judas. Since Judas was so necessary to the enactment of the New Testament, according to Barth, and since Paul's very point here in Romans is that God's grace overflows right where sin is greatest, Barth considers it perfectly appropriate to consider how God's grace overflows even to Judas Iscariot.[27]

Before moving to later works in Barth's life, we need to address the question of early influences on Barth's openness to universalism. Christian Collins Winn has suggested that certain issues in Barth's theology are clarified when it is recognized that he was influenced by Württemburg Pietism, including the hope of an *apokatastasis*. Even the Zinzendorf lines at the beginning of this chapter seem echoed in some of Barth's works.[28]

In a later work on Romans 5, Barth introduces the new idea that really the "first man" in this chapter is Christ. Since Adam is a "type" of the Christ who appears to come later in time (5:14b), the first and original human is really Christ. Our connection to Adam depends on our relationship to the first and original human, Christ. With this emphasis on the stronger link between Christ and humanity rather than between Adam and humanity, Barth is close to affirming that the benefits of Christ's death and resurrection extend to all.[29] He can thus go on to affirm that in the last half of Romans 5 "'religious' presuppositions are not once hinted at. The fact of Christ is here presented as something that dominates and includes all men. The nature of Christ objectively conditions human nature, and the work of Christ makes an objective difference to the life and destiny of all men. Through Christ grace overflows upon them, bringing them pardon and justification and opening before them a prospect of life with God. In short, 'grace rules.'"[30]

Barth arrives at his universalistic horizon by what some might understand to be a supersessionistic reading of Christ's relationship to Israel. Christ is the only true Jew, and with Christ's death and resurrection the covenant that was with Israel is now revealed to be a covenant with the world.[31] But this seems to contradict Paul's insistence that Israel's ancestry and covenants mark them as elect in a way different from the rest of humanity (Rom. 9:4–5; 11:1–2, 28–29; 15:8). While Israel has always been the world's representative in Judaism, Judaism never collapsed the covenant they enjoyed with their God to exactly the same covenant as God has with the world.

Barth's reflections on this passage are also significant for the question that looms behind much of this book: Do we read Romans as a letter describing God dealing with humanity in a corporate, collective sense, or is Romans a description of how individuals come to faith? In the last pages of *Christ and Adam*, Barth explains how the two figures of Christ and Adam relate to humanity. Christ is the head of the human race, while Adam is not. Adam happens to precede other humans in time, but he is not theologically prior to other humans, for every human person besides Christ "is at once an individual and only an individual, and, at the same time, without in any way losing his individuality, he is the responsible representative of all men." Barth thus refuses to say that Romans views humanity only as a corporate personality in which individuals are only parts of a whole, and he also rejects a crass individualism that reads the letter as if each human is theologically sui generis.[32] In other words, Barth concludes that the answer to the question, "Does Romans deal with humanity as a corporate whole or as individuals?" is a resounding "Yes!" This is the same connection we see in the Zinzendorf lines quoted at the beginning of this chapter, lines from his hymn "Jesus Thy Blood and Righteousness," whose every verse is an extended meditation on loci in Romans.

In his 1956 lecture "The Humanity of God," Barth describes a new focus on the implications of Jesus' full humanity as a "turn" in his theology from the emphasis on the absolute transcendence of God that so dominated *Romans II*. What Christ means for humanity prompts him to ask tersely, "Therefore 'universalism' (apokatastasis)?" He first cautions not to raise an alarm at the word before understanding whether the word is meaningful. He then recommends that believers take seriously Paul's word in Colossians 1:19 that through the firstborn of all creation God is reconciling all things back to God. And he intimates that there are far more dangerous theological positions than universalism coming from the critics of the doctrine. He concludes that "there is no theological justification for setting any limits on our side to the friendliness of God towards humanity which appeared in Jesus Christ."[33]

Barth preached his sermon "All!" to the inmates of the Basel Prison in 1957 with Romans 11:32 as his text: "For God has made prisoners of all, that he may show mercy to all." In this sermon Barth correctly sees that Paul could not have dictated the first phrase without knowing that he would conclude with God's mercy. He therefore starts with the second half of the verse, describing how God's mercy is really for all people. This half of the verse Barth describes as "a mountain which we cannot climb, in our thoughts or in a sermon—a mountain from which we can only climb down."[34] It is for those we might consider undeserving, including our enemies. The prison in which all humanity is held is the prison of disobedience to God. What remains for the hearer of this message is simply to admit that one is fully in this prison, and not to attempt to assert one's own superiority to others or argue that one needs the divine mercy less than others. Barth views the mercy to all as fully based on God's work in Christ, for to explain how this mercy comes he quotes 1 Corinthians 5:21a.[35] While this leaves the question open, stopping short of a full affirmation of Origen's *apokatastasis*, there is surely an emphasis not found in Barth's early Romans commentaries. If Barth reads this locus in *Romans II* through the lens of the complete otherness of God and futility of all religion to reach God, he reads it at the end of his life with an emphasis on not restricting any outsiders from God's mercy: "The one great sin from which we shall try to escape this morning is to exclude anyone from the 'yes' of God's mercy."[36]

Barth's early Romans commentaries open the possibility for a universal vision of God's salvation of humanity. The possibility is caressed and warmly encouraged through biblical and theological reflection in his later writings, so that the hope of universal salvation is voiced, though a climax of universal salvation is never affirmed as doctrine.

POST-BARTHIAN APPROACHES

In a way that anticipates other twentieth-century interpreters, G. B. Caird claims that Paul holds three ideas simultaneously: God predestines people to salvation, people are responsible for what they freely decide about God, and all will be saved.[37] This represents one approach to Paul's horizon of universalism; it is increasingly common to read that Paul does hold to God's restoration of all sentient beings in final salvation while also preaching the necessity of faith in Jesus Christ. Proponents of this approach maintain that Paul was not a systematic theologian who constantly checked his teachings against Aristotle's law of the excluded middle.

Sanders also claims in an early work that both God's predestination and the human responsibility freely to place faith in Christ are held in Paul, without explicit attempts at harmonization.[38] Later he also argues that Paul maintains that people must believe in Christ if they are to die to their sins and enjoy God's life while simultaneously holding that in the end God will save all his creation.[39]

After Barth there has also been a weaker move toward universalism by interpreting the Bible as teaching that those not saved will be annihilated rather than condemned to eternal torment. George Hunsinger includes this view of annihilationism in his catalog of four views on "hellfire and damnation." In his catalog, "reverent agnosticism" is the category for those who refuse to say that God will damn the unrepentant to eternal hell.[40] Various degrees of hopefulness for universal salvation may be found in this category. I have added some examples to Hunsinger's categories and summarized the four views in table 2.

A noteworthy addition to Hunsinger's examples is Richard John Neuhaus, whose meditation on the passion of Christ clearly articulates the hope of universal salvation. After quoting Romans 5:15 on how the grace available through Jesus overflowed for "many," Neuhaus quotes 11:32, which describes how God has confined all to disobedience so that he might have mercy on all.[41] This hope of universal salvation comes from more than Neuhaus's Romans exegesis, of

Table 2. Four Views of Eternal Salvation and Punishment

Universal Salvation	Reverent Agnosticism	Annihilation of Unrepentant	Eternal Punishment of Unrepentant
Origen	Clement of Alexandria	Arnobius	Augustine
J. W. Colenso	Maximus the Confessor	John Stott	Martin Luther
F. D. Schleiermacher	Karl Barth		John Calvin
J. A. T. Robinson	Hans Urs von Balthasar		
	Richard John Neuhaus		

course. It is primarily driven by his understanding of the cosmic effects of Jesus' death and resurrection.

Brendan Byrne's 1996 Romans commentary is sensitive to the whole letter's universal horizon. On 5:12–21 he writes, "By setting Christ over against Adam in this passage Paul ensures that the argument for hope contained in the gospel proceeds along truly universalist lines." But on 11:30–32 he summarizes how Romans as a letter is universal in its perspective and limits "universal" to categories, not all individuals: "All is then summed up in a concluding explanatory sentence (v 32) giving perfect expression to Paul's 'inclusive' vision of the gospel. . . . The 'all' (tous pantas) that appears twice in this sentence resumes the universalistic note that has run throughout the letter (1:16, 18; 2:9–11; 3:9, 19–20, 22–23; 4:11, 16; 5:12–21; 9:24–26; 10:11–12). As in the case of these other references, Paul does not have primarily in view all human beings in an individual sense; the sense is communal: 'all—that is, Jews as well as Gentiles.'"[42] By contrast, Richard Bell does not limit the "all" of 5:18–21 to a categorical "all" that simply emphasizes how both Jews and the ethnē are included. The parallelism in 5:18–19 would break down if such a limitation were the point of Paul's "as . . . so also" statements. And the "much more" in 5:15b—and I would also include the "abundantly overflowed" of 5:20b—would not make sense if the grace that comes through Christ's obedience has fewer people as its object than the sin that comes about through Adam's disobedience.[43]

A related question is what the "all" of 11:32 means. Bell asserts that it means all Jews will be saved, but not necessarily all people in the ethnē category, since Paul has only said that a full number of them will precede the salvation of "all Israel" (11:25–26).[44] Perhaps Bell should consider 11:30–31 here, for these verses seem to sum up Paul's vision of God's salvation by juxtaposing the Jews and the ethnē in parallel fashion. If in 11:32 Paul finally concludes that God has shut up all to disobedience in that he might have mercy on all, the immediately preceding context makes difficult Bell's distinction between the scope of salvation for Jews and ethnē.

There is of course resistance to an inclusive reading of this locus such as Bell exemplifies. Many commentators read 5:18–21 and 11:32 and decisively eliminate the possibility of universal salvation.[45] A colleague at another school described to me how he suggested to his students that God might be more inclusive and save more people than we think. After the class a student argued with him, finally admitting that his teacher's suggestion was troubling because it implied that people would be in heaven who did not deserve to be there. My friend then began to open a window on the philosophical problem of rigid particularism: "That would be a novel idea, wouldn't it, that some people who don't deserve it will receive grace to enter heaven?"

Even among those who discuss universalism, there are caveats. We have already seen how Byrne treats Paul's universal language as simply emphasizing that both Jews and *ethnē* will be saved. Bell is certainly correct to qualify his description of the unrestricted universalism of 5:18–19 with the admission that Paul elsewhere holds faith in Christ as necessary for salvation.[46] Wright dismisses a universal reading here by saying, "Our minds instantly raise the question of numerically universal salvation, but this is not in Paul's mind. His universalism is of the sort that holds to Christ as the way for all."[47] The question then becomes how we relate the universal and the particular in Paul's portraits of salvation.

Since I am seeking in this book to take seriously Origen's repeated contention that Paul in Romans is an arbiter between Jews and *ethnē* and since I wish to compensate for commentators' neglect of the universalism in this locus, I leave the last word in this chapter to a paradigmatic example of the *ethnē,* the atheist philosopher Alain Badiou. While his use of the term "universalism" primarily concerns how Paul has transformed the philosophical category of "subject" to a universal, there is at least one place in his *Saint Paul: The Foundation of Universalism* where this philosophical universalism overlaps with the universal salvation we are considering in this locus.[48] Badiou quotes 5:18 as "A single act of righteousness leads to acquittal and life for all," notes how this "all" is also found in 1 Corinthians 15:22, and writes: "As soon as it is a question of contingency and grace, all fixing of divisions or distributions is forbidden. . . . There is no place here for vengeance and resentment. Hell, the roasting spit of enemies, holds no interest for Paul." From here Badiou moves into an assertion that we all have to consider, whether we hold simply to the universal claims of Paul's gospel or more expansively to the claim of universal salvation. He states that our own claim to be included among the saved to whom this gospel speaks inherently seeks legitimacy by making the claim applicable for everyone. "For Paul, it is of utmost importance to declare that I am justified only insofar as everyone is. Of course, hope concerns me. But this means that I identify myself in my singularity as subject of the economy of salvation only insofar as this economy is universal."[49] On the one hand, Badiou's comment should make us consider carefully why and how we impose our constructs of salvation on the human race. The possibility of universalism is worth considering at least because it helps us identify why we want or why we know God has designed a heaven that does not hold everyone. On the other hand, this comment helps us understand Paul's teaching of grace. There is no confident and trusting faith, the faith that gives peace beyond understanding, without including hope for all. The minute I limit the "all" I begin to question or doubt if God's grace is sufficient for me. Badiou might not trust God's promise in Christ, but he understands the content and stakes of that promise.

CONCLUSION

Romans, with its account of how the one God of Jews and *ethnē* remains faithful to past promises and brings righteousness in Christ to both groups, definitely opens windows that force its readers to think of all peoples without temporal or geographical limits. Origen's hope in a final *apokatastasis* might have been condemned in Constantinople, but it has kept reappearing even among some strands of pietism.[50] If someday we mortals find ourselves trembling in ecstasy as God's full salvation penetrates into all humanity, remember that aspects of the interchange were lovingly and slowly nurtured in conversations over Romans. Those approaches like Origen's that see the letter as primarily about how God works with both Jews and *ethnē* and read the "all" in 5:18–21 and 11:32 in light of its contexts and those approaches influenced by pietism that emphasize the sufficiency of divine grace to transform all sinners are especially prone to find the hope of an ultimate salvation for all humanity in this letter.

Locus 6

Warring Laws (7:7–8:4)

In the first place, this entire passage clearly indicates a complaint and a hatred of the flesh and a love for the good and for the Law.

Martin Luther on Romans 7:7–25[1]

ROMANS 6

Some scholars will eloquently and justifiably chastise me for not identifying any locus within Romans 6. It is a significant chapter for how Paul works out the development of Christ's obedience that extends over death and sin. E. P. Sanders, who treats "participation in Christ" as a separate and more central theme in Paul's letters than "justification by faith," rightly points to the first half of Romans 6 as a place where Paul emphasizes participation in Christ.[2] As Catholic interpreters would emphasize, the invitation to participate through baptism in Christ's death to sin and subsequent victory over sin and death has clear implications for Romans readers.[3] Still, Christians differ as to the extent of Christ's victory and the ways in which humanity enacts this victory. Is it only for those who consciously place their faith in Christ and confess with their mouth that God raised Jesus from the dead, or does the victory include even those unaware of it?

Barth's story within his Easter sermon in 1959 on 6:23 presents a helpful starting point for a consideration of all of Romans 6: "Did you read in the paper recently that two Japanese soldiers were found in the Philippines, who had not yet heard, or did not believe, that the war had ended fourteen years ago? They continue to hide in some jungle and shoot at everybody who dares approach them. Strange people, aren't they? Well, we are such people when we refuse to perceive and to hold true what the Easter message declares to be the meaning of the Easter story. Sin and death are conquered; God's free gift prevails, his gift of eternal life for us all."[4] From this section in which Paul answers the question, "Shall we remain in sin so that grace may abound?" (6:1), Paul then has to answer the inevitable question that any law-observing Jew would ask after reading Paul's fleeting references to the law in 5:13 and 6:14–15: How is the law related to humanity's sinful condition that leads to death? This is the primary question driving this locus. In the history of interpretation a second question has often commanded readers' attention: Who is the *egō* who cannot do the intended good? The third major question in this locus is a hermeneutical one, seldom articulated and answered differently by exegetes here: To what extent should human experience be used as a guide to understand 7:7–8:4?

ORIGEN

Earlier in his commentary on Romans 7, Origen waxed long and eloquently (so long that his translator omitted it) on how the New Testament uses the term "law" to refer to different parts of the Bible: "historical" matters in the Torah like Genesis 16 (Gal. 4:21–23), Psalm 35:19 (John 15:25), and Isaiah's prophecy in Isaiah 28:11–12 (1 Cor. 14:21 in Aquila's translation).[5] This prepares for the focus on law that continues through the beginning of Romans 8. It is not that Origen is disinterested in identifying the *egō* here in chapter 7, but he is equally focused on identifying the various types of law that are in view. This concern to balance attention on the laws described and on the *egō* illustrates one response to the first question in the exegesis of this locus that is listed above.

On Romans 7:7–13 Origen surprisingly identifies the "law" in view as natural law. He cites Adam, Cain, and Pharaoh as people who recognize their sin, according to the Scriptures, but since these all lived before the legislation of Moses, Paul must be referring to natural law here. For Origen, natural law also best fits Paul's description that he was alive once before the law, since it is only after reaching an age of accountability that people become aware of this law. Origen for the second time in his commentary offers the example of a child who hits a parent, saying that this is done because the natural law is "dead" within the child who has not yet reached the age of accountability; it cannot refer to Mosaic law that teaches that children who hit parents have sinned, and Paul cannot mean that he was alive before the Mosaic law came, for he was circumcised on the eighth day (almost the very beginning) of his life.[6] Even when he exegetes Paul's reference to the tenth commandment (Rom. 7:7–8), he mentions the Mosaic law as the specific context for this law, but still claims that Paul's point about desiring what is forbidden is valid within natural law.[7]

Here I cannot resist breaking into the conversation. With Hermann Lichten-berger, whose exegesis of 7:7b–13 includes the observation that "here the turning points of the historical thought are Adam and Moses," I cannot follow Origen's identification of "law" as primarily designating natural law.[8] Indeed, as will become clear in my summary of the work of H. D. Betz below, I think Origen's basic framework for this letter needs to be applied to these consecutive paragraphs in Romans 7 as well. Romans 7:7–13 explains the relationship of humanity to law in the Jewish context, while 7:14–24 explains the relationship in the context of the *ethnē*. Paul is arbiter for Jews and Gentiles in this letter, according to Origen. In the locus of 7:7–8:4, Paul is out to show that whether for Jews (7:7–13) or Gentiles (7:14–24) law is a good thing but problematic in its outworking apart from Christ and the Holy Spirit whom Christ brings.

Origen calls attention to the warring laws that are described in the passage. The "spiritual law of God" (7:14, 22) is most likely the Mosaic law, and the "law of the mind" (7:23) is most likely a natural law that agrees with the Mosaic law.[9] The "law of the members" (7:23) is the expression used for fleshly desires.[10] Just as Origen emphasizes how Paul uses *nomos* in different ways, so also he writes that Paul, since he becomes all things to all people (1 Cor. 9:22), uses *egō* in different ways here. When the implied author claims to know that the law is spiritual (Rom. 7:14a), *egō* identifies the speaker as Paul the apostle. But in the next half of the sentence, when the *egō* is of the flesh and sold under sin, Origen explains that Paul has assumed the persona of the weak. Even this weak person whom Origen identifies as the *egō* in 7:14b–24 is outside modern commentators' options here. This weak *egō* is a persona Paul assumes of someone beginning to be converted. This explains why the person is aware of sin and yet struggles with evil habits. These habits are still plaguing the new convert, because there has not been time to develop the virtues of a changed life.[11] It is worth noting that Origen is not simply describing two laws warring against each other—he actually sees at least four laws at work: the law of the mind is pulling the *egō* toward the law of God, while the law of the members is pulling the *egō* toward the laws (plural!) of sin.[12] The apostolic *egō* only returns at 7:25, which Origen translates as "the grace of God through Jesus Christ our Lord."[13] With different referents for *egō* and at least four laws involved, Origen is panoramically staging this locus. According to Origen, Paul is describing much more than a contest between flesh and spirit within an individual believer. Paul is rather using different voices to describe how people at various levels of spiritual maturity are affected by a plurality of laws.

On 8:1–4 Origen urges his readers toward practice and diligent training in truth, chastity, piety, and wisdom, since the voice in 8:1 is now of a person who is fully in Christ, not the one who was only beginning in his conversion who was speaking in 7:19–25.[14] Here is a commentator who has not been exposed to the Reformation virus that divides the letter's chapters into doctrine (1–11) and practice (12–15).

Origen, with an analogy back to the tree of the knowledge of good and evil, understands the "law of the Spirit of life in Christ Jesus" (8:2) to be the law of God, which in its letter can kill, but which the Spirit or Christ can use to bring life.[15] He does not extend this dual reading of the one law back into Romans 7, however. The "law that is weak through the flesh" (8:3) Origen understands to be the Mosaic law interpreted literally. He says that this law is not only weak but even dead, since its requirements regarding Sabbath, sacrifice, and leprosy cannot be kept.[16] Origen's description of "flesh" and "spirit" as aspects of Mosaic law is an early precedent for the exegetical tendency to bifurcate the Mosaic law into literal and spiritual uses in order to explain Paul's negative and positive statements regarding this same law. Christ's death cleanses us from sin and now the law is kept according to the spirit, since in its fleshly aspects it is weak, that is, it cannot be fulfilled.[17] Origen finds ways to read Paul as emphatically against law in ways not always visible to commentators today. Besides what we shall see at locus 10 (Rom. 10:4), here at 8:3–4 where Paul says that God condemned sin, Origen says that God condemned the law that was weak, an explanation too radical even for Rufinus to follow.[18] For Origen, then, this locus is not a snapshot of a particular condition in an individual's spiritual journey. It is rather a chronicle of the warring laws' effects on people at different points in their spiritual journeys.

AUGUSTINE

Augustine shifts the focus off the warring laws and exclusively onto the religious subject who is speaking in this locus. His own change of mind on this locus, based on his experience of the Pelagian threat, introduces a binary approach still very influential to Romans readers whose only question while reading Romans 7 is: Is the *egō* pre-Christian or Christian?

The noteworthy development in *On the Merits* is the transition evident in Augustine's interpretation of Romans 7. In his early works he consistently holds to the interpretation that 7:7–24 chronicles an unregenerate Jew's existence prior to law and under law.[19] But in *On the Merits*, he is clearly on the way to viewing the persona of 7:14–25 as a believing Christian. At first he simply quotes 7:14–25 to show that people really are born into a body of death, that is, they are afflicted with the problem and consequences of original sin.[20] But then he uses 7:18 in parallel with the request for divine forgiveness in the Lord's Prayer to show that believers struggle with sin. Later in the same book he will say that the positive descriptions applied to Job in Job 1:8 could also be applied to the divided self of Romans 7.[21] By the time Augustine writes letter 6*, the shift on Romans 7 is complete. He is clear that the persona of 7:18–20 is a Christian, who cannot accomplish goodness in this life because of the original sin inherited by being born a human.[22] It must be emphasized that Augustine's change from interpreting Romans 7 as a pre-Christian experience to a Christian experience was not occasioned by academic, "objective" exegesis, however chimerical such an activity is. Rather, as Augustine himself tells us, it was the Pelagians who overturned his previous position.[23] By the time he formulates what we know as his final exegesis of Romans 7 for Julian of Eclanum, Augustine walks a precarious line: he argues that this text refers to Paul's own experience under grace without detracting from Paul's deserved sainthood.[24] It was Augustine's view of the church as a body that encompasses all believers, even the mediocre and struggling ones, that forced him to change his position on Romans 7, when his view of the church was threatened by the elitism of Pelagius's view of the church.[25]

Augustine was also troubled by Pelagius's insistence that the human was capable of making real progress toward righteousness: "But we must fiercely and strongly oppose those who think that the power of the human will can by itself, without the help of God, either attain righteousness or make progress in tending toward it. . . . We, on the other hand, say that the human will is helped to achieve righteousness in this way: Besides the fact that human beings are created with free choice of the will and besides the teaching by which they are commanded how they ought to live, they receive the Holy Spirit so that there arises in their minds a delight in and a love for that highest and immutable good that is God."[26]

Origen's young child who hits a parent returns in Augustine's *On the Merits*. Augustine has recast the child into an infant, perhaps to make absolutely clear that this child does not have the rational capacity to understand natural or written law. He therefore is dependent upon and agrees with Origen's point that knowledge is essential to hold people culpable under law.[27] What we call "the age of accountability" becomes firmly rooted in the exegetical tradition, therefore, because of Augustine's use of Origen's example here.

A second composition from this period in Augustine's battle against the Pelagians, *On the Spirit and the Letter*, appeals to Romans for a variety of points. If *On the Merits* was focused on 5:12, *On the Spirit and the Letter* seeks to use more of the battlefield, that is, more of the text of Romans, for a broader assault against the Pelagians. Here Augustine states that Romans interprets Paul's words in 2 Corinthians 3:6—"The letter kills, but the Spirit gives life." Augustine marshals texts from chapters 2–8 of Romans to prove this in what follows. To fight the Pelagian idea that God can justify people through God's law, Augustine sets his artillery on the Pelagian idea of righteousness, and the conversation on Romans is forever altered.[28]

The hints that we have already seen of the second use of the law receive a hermeneutical amplification in this composition to include a stereotypical presentation of the Old Testament as law, in which grace is hidden, and the New Testament as a text that openly declares the grace of God, which is received in faith leading to righteousness.[29] The law-gospel hermeneutic of a later Romans commentator receives its birth here.

While Augustine does not go to Romans 9 in this text to address the conundrum of the human will, he does admit that God cannot be the author of all human volition, since this would implicate God in evil.[30] Augustine seeks explicitly to preserve free will here in the year 412, still relatively early in his battle against the Pelagians. Indeed, he, like the apostle on another point, protests too much, for Augustine asks, "Does grace cancel free will? God forbid! Instead we establish free will."[31]

Romans was very useful for Augustine in countering the Pelagians. In sermon 348A, "Against Pelagius," there are fourteen distinct quotations from the Epistle to the Romans, coming mostly from chapters 5 and 7.[32] Augustine begins his sermon by emphasizing that Christ's incarnation was on behalf of sinners. He quotes the creedal formula of 1 Timothy 1:15, including Paul's self-description, "chief of sinners." Augustine emphasizes that the only reason for so great an event as the incarnation is to bring life to humanity, who has no life in itself. He then quotes the sermon's central text, Romans 5:8–9.[33] Augustine returns to exegete this central text: Christ died for us, not for himself, since he in whom there was no sin did not have the cause of death. Augustine emphasizes that it is not possible for us the guilty ones to free what is bound or to free what is damned. Christ did this in his incarnation: "Christ died for us."[34] Augustine argues from an orthodox soteriology in order to show that Pelagian anthropology would effectively hamstring this soteriology. "And he himself, because he wished to die for us, became our remedy. Great is that mercy, brothers; our physicians wanted it to cure us, but it was not in their medicine chest, it was rather from his blood. 'Much more,' he says, 'now justified.' From whom? 'By his blood,' not by our strength, not by our merits, but 'by his blood, we shall be saved from wrath through him,' not through us, but 'through him.' He has bound us to the cross. If we really want to live, let us cling to death."[35] Augustine goes on in this sermon to update his parish on the news that Pelagius had recently got himself cleared of any charges of heresy by a synod of bishops in the east.[36] Augustine implores his audience to be on their guard against this hidden heresy.[37]

In September of the same year, Augustine preaches in Carthage a sermon on Philippians 3:3–16. Though "Pelagius" or "Pelagians" are not mentioned by name, it is clear that Augustine associates the righteousness of the law that Paul held before following Christ with the Pelagian efforts toward perfection. In this sermon Augustine appeals to Romans 4:25 to make the same point we saw in the previously examined sermon. Our justification is not our own doing.[38] He also quotes Romans 9:30 to establish that the righteousness advocated by Paul is one that comes by faith.[39]

It is in Augustine's rejoinder to the Pelagian counterattack that he is forced to work out his view of free will. A key text that he relies on is Romans 6:20–22. Here Paul makes no attempt to write of absolute freedom, but rather of freedom relative to sin or to righteousness. Augustine thus argues that Adam and Eve were created originally free to choose righteousness. Because of the sin of Adam, however, all subsequent humans are free to choose sin, but lack the freedom to choose righteousness. Here, as in his dealing with the hardening of Pharaoh's heart in *To Simplicianus* over twenty years previously, we may discern Augustine working with his paradigm of evil as the privation of good. The will that is found in an unredeemed person, tainted by original sin, is deficient. It is free to sin, but not free to act righteously or even to believe. This defective will is then restored to a freedom for faith and righteous action only by God's grace.[40] This view of the will becomes entrenched in Western civilization's view of humanity: it will be repeated by Luther at the end of the Middle Ages and again by a hobbit at the end of his epic journey in Middle Earth.

The transition observed above in *On the Merits* to a view that the divided persona of Romans 7:14–25 is really someone under grace is complete by 420, when Augustine writes *Against Two Letters of the Pelagians*.[41] Now Augustine characteristically argues that the only possible interpretation of this text is that it represents someone under grace: how else could Paul in the near context say there is therefore now no condemnation for those in Christ Jesus (8:1), and how else could the persona of 7:22 delight in God's law, unless he were under grace?[42] For Augustine, this final position on Romans 7 was perhaps a more satisfactory answer to the Manichean use of this chapter that had plagued him decades previously. From our perspective, this interpretation on Romans 7 also sets the stage for Luther's *simul iustus et peccator* portrait of the believer.[43] Luther would follow Augustine's focus on what this locus says about the individual believer's entrance into salvation. Their stage for the letter is much narrower than Origen's description of four laws pulling people in opposite directions.

Augustine and Luther were also concerned to identify this individual believer as someone who continued to be plagued by sin. They resisted any intimation of perfectionism. Canon 9 of the Council of Carthage reads, "If any claim that the words of the Lord's Prayer where we say, 'Forgive us our debts' (Mt 6:12), are said by holy persons in the sense that they say them humbly and not truthfully, let them be anathema. After all, who would tolerate persons who lie while praying, not to human beings, but to the Lord himself, saying with their lips that they want to be forgiven, but saying in their heart that they do not have any debts to be forgiven."[44]

ABELARD

Abelard is most influenced by Augustine on this locus, for he does not even consider whether the struggle narrated here may refer to someone not fully converted. Abelard also follows in Origen's pattern of using this locus as a platform for viewing the deficiencies in Mosaic law. Unconcerned with dividing Mosaic law into "spirit" and "flesh," Abelard simply explains this law as a teaching tool for the Israelites, but not a revelation that could make them fully acceptable before God.[45] Christ's command to practice God's love goes beyond what Mosaic law required. Loving as Christ commanded brings God's reward, even as God rewards those who make themselves eunuchs for the kingdom of heaven.[46]

Abelard glosses Paul's "evil that lives in me" (7:21) with "the yoke of bad habits that block the good will," betraying the residual effects of Pelagius's equation of the sinful nature with habit.[47] Abelard does not spend as much energy as Origen in analyzing the different laws mentioned in this locus. Abelard says that 7:21

describes how reason recognizes that God's law (undefined here) is good. In the context following his identification of the "other law" of 7:23, Abelard simply identifies the law of 7:21 as reason. The "other law in [his] members" that Paul describes in 7:23 is glossed by Abelard as *luxuriam in genitalibus* and summarized as the law of concupiscence, which he calls an abhorrence.[48] The law of sin and death in 8:2 Abelard describes as the precepts or suggestions of carnal concupiscence. The "Spirit of life" is the Holy Spirit, the personification of love.[49]

Abelard's word for "righteous requirement" at the beginning of 8:4 is *iustificatio*, and he quickly defines this "righteous requirement of the law" as what the law teaches regarding the things that matter for justification rather than the works of the law themselves. The things that matter are love of God and neighbor, which can never be fully practiced by us, but are perfected in us through Christ. God's condemnation of sin in us is really God's love destroying every accusation and fault so that his highest favor might spread to us.

Here Abelard has an explicit quotation of Origen in which he says that the Greeks got it right that God condemned sin for sin, which he explains as meaning that Jesus himself became a sacrificial victim for sin. (This reminds me of Origen's description of the *hilasterion* of the tabernacle as Christ himself.)[50] According to Abelard, through Christ's offering of himself as sacrificial victim, he condemned, that is, exterminated, sin. This is because he effected remission of our sins by his blood and reconciliation. (Here Abelard seems closer to a model of expiation than to his own earlier explanation of Christ's atonement as supreme example.) Or, though the spiritual and human forces that crucified Jesus incurred sin in so doing, God condemned sin in us and rescued us from it, that is, God employed what was evil for the best goal, converting it to good.[51] (This sounds more consonant with his exemplary model of the atonement.)

We therefore find evidence of a sedimentary exegesis of this locus. From Origen, Abelard inherits some attention to the various laws described, and he even quotes Origen by name in describing how the atonement condemns and eliminates sin. From Pelagius he inherits the idea that "habit" is to account for the law of sin within the human. From Augustine he seems to have accepted the exegetical attitude that this whole locus is all about the struggle of a Christian, and might give evidence of relying on experience in his explanation of the law of sin in his members.

AQUINAS

Aquinas follows Augustine and the *Glossa Ordinaria* in labeling the sin that Paul identifies in 7:9 as concupiscence, since this is a sin that leads to all other sins.[52] Aquinas notes that Augustine has interpreted the *egō* both as someone under sin and as someone under grace.[53] In his exegesis of 7:14–20 Aquinas is focused on identifying which is the better identification. He decides in favor of the later Augustine's exegesis of the *egō* as a speaker under grace.

Aquinas builds on Augustine's definition of evil as privation of good to con-clude that the resident sin (7:17) is not an actual thing but simply a deficiency, a privation of good within humanity.[54] Paul's phrase, "that is, in my flesh," in 7:18 is diagnosed by the angelic doctor to imply that the speaker is under grace, for it would be superfluous to write that of someone not converted and under sin.[55] Also, Aquinas takes the "willing that is near me" to point to someone under the influence of grace.[56]

The polemical potential of Romans is utilized by Aquinas for jabs at both the Manichees and the Pelagians in this context. Against the Manichees, Aquinas glosses "good" in 7:18 as the grace by which we are freed from sin. The Manichees are thus wrong to take this verse as evidence that human bodies were created by an evil god. Aquinas quotes Philippians 2:13 against the Pelagians, who read "the will that lies near me" in Romans 7:18 as evidence that humanity takes the first step in willing and performing good.[57]

Aquinas translates 7:25 as: "The grace of God frees me from the body of this death," understanding it to be spoken by the same speaker as the one who asked the question in the preceding verse.[58] He goes on to identify the liberating law of 8:2 as the Holy Spirit: since the Holy Spirit leads people toward the same goal that Aristotle identifies for civil lawmakers, the Holy Spirit can be called a "law."[59] With the introduction of the Spirit as "law" in his commentary on 8:2, Aquinas then lists all the laws in view in this locus: the Mosaic law (7:22), the law of the passions (7:23a), a natural law (7:23b, "law of my mind"), and a new law that Paul calls the law of the Spirit (8:2).[60] Aquinas does not depict the conflict of these laws as vividly as Origen, nor does he emphasize Paul's defense of the Mosaic law in this locus. He does state that even though the Mosaic law could not bring right-eousness, this does not mean that the Mosaic law itself was defective. It is rather that human flesh is defective (8:3).[61] While Aquinas teaches that the speaker in the last half of Romans 7 is under grace, he is nevertheless looking for righteous-ness to be actualized in the speaker's experience as the speaker encounters the "new law" or the Holy Spirit, who is introduced at 8:2. This is seen by his willingness to align Aristotle's ethics with the freedom from the law of sin that the beginning of Romans 8 emphasizes.[62] In his willingness to look to Aristotle's ethics as a tem-plate for understanding this locus, Aquinas is appealing to human experience, albeit experience summarized by the philosopher, not the exegete's own experi-ence, as we shall observe in a revolutionary sixteenth-century reading of this locus.

LUTHER

Following the later Augustine and many of the scholastics against Nicolas of Lyra, Luther treats this locus as though it refers to someone who is justified. For Luther the "I" of 7:7–25 is a whole person, what would be called the "totus-homo," who is simultaneously justified and an unchanged sinner.[63] When compared with his scholastic predecessors, Luther's distinctive difference is that he claims that the believer lives as an *unchanged sinner* who simultaneously receives God's grace.[64] Although one could proof-text individual passages from Augustine to show that the late Augustine regarded the believer in Christ as both a sinner and a justified person, Luther's emphasis on these simultaneous statuses of the believer receives an emphasis unmatched in Augustine's writings. Luther's famous phrase, *simul iustus et peccator*, derives directly from his exegesis of Romans and does indeed bring theological change to a segment of the church. For those who follow Luther in this teaching, the healing and sanctifying power of grace (maintained by Luther's scholastic predecessors) is minimized, while the ongoing sinfulness of the believer is openly accepted. Those who followed Luther in this theological change would no longer feel the compulsion to participate in the sacrament of confession.

In his explication of Romans 7 (scholium on 7:18), the early Luther is clearly dualistic in his anthropology: "Therefore we must note that the words 'I want' and 'I hate' refer to the spiritual man or to the spirit, but 'I do' and 'I work' refer to the carnal man or to the flesh."[65] In the same context (scholium on 7:20), Luther compares the human being described in Romans 7 to a horseman, composed of human (mind or spirit) and horse (flesh).[66] Luther uses the Augustinian idea that mind or spirit is like a man and the flesh is like a woman: "Therefore we are the woman because of the flesh, that is, we are carnal, and we are the man because of the spirit which yields to the flesh, we are at the same time both dead and set free."[67]

The *simul iustus et peccator* idea seems already present in Luther's early remarks on Romans 7—in his scholia on what he considers the twelfth statement in Romans 7 (Rom. 7:25) he states: "Note that one and the same man at the same time serves the law of God and the law of sin, at the same time is righteous and sins! For he does not say: 'My mind serves the law of God,' nor does he say: 'My flesh serves the law of sin,' but: 'I, the whole man, the same person, I serve a twofold servitude."[68] In his later writings Luther continued to read his idea of *simul iustus et peccator* back into the whole letter of Romans, especially Romans 7.

Luther's emphasis on the resident sinfulness of the human being that results in moral impotence is an underrated factor in attempts to understand his revolutionary exegesis. This emphasis has a clear resonance with Augustine's teachings, and is sounded against scholastic dependence on Aristotle and the nominalist teaching that one could prepare for grace by doing the good that is already inside oneself. Even while the early Luther admitted that one could prepare for grace by doing good works, he always maintained that these good works could only be done through God's grace, and that these good works would never obligate God to grant saving grace and justify the sinner.[69]

ERASMUS

Erasmus agrees with Origen that Paul assumes the persona of an unregenerate person in most of chapter 7, and then in the "Thanks be to God" of 7:25 he assumes the persona of one who has received grace. Erasmus criticizes Augustine's treatment of Romans 7 as found in *Against Two Letters of the Pelagians*, saying that Augustine has forced a reading that does not fit with the way Paul has taken over the personae of humanity as a pagan, a carnal Jew under the Mosaic law, and finally as a spiritual believer whom grace has freed.[70] Though there is no mention of Luther by name in Erasmus's *Annotations on Romans*, this reading of Romans 7 is probably reacting against Luther's idea of passive righteousness that is part of his *simul iustus et peccator* emphasis. Erasmus thus seeks to retain a place for active righteousness at an earlier point in the order of salvation than Luther's schema. He is certainly following Origen in viewing this part of Romans as clearly about Christian practice and progress in righteousness. And while Luther has followed the later Augustine in staging this locus as a monologue for the individual believer, Erasmus preserves Origen's stage notes for this locus. A wider range of humanity is brought onstage in this production in which two or more speakers express different encounters with laws that wage war within and among humanity.[71] Unlike the experientially driven hermeneutic of Augustine, Abelard, Aquinas, and Luther, Erasmus follows Origen's rhetorically driven hermeneutic.

JOHN WESLEY

John Wesley's sermon "The Origin, Nature, Property, and Use of the Law" explains the law in 7:7–25 in ways indebted to Augustine, Luther, and Calvin. He says that the law is the moral law, which has three uses: to slay the sinner, to bring the sinner to Christ, and to keep the sinner depending on Christ's grace.[72] This is similar to the way in which Augustine found at least three stages of human existence in 7:7–8:4, and is indebted to Luther's second use of the law and Calvin's third use.

BARTH

In *Romans I* the section covering 7:14–25 is entitled "The Law and Pietism." Barth sees the struggle between good and evil within a soul as reflecting a pietistic posture before God that is sinful. This pietism is bold enough to claim that the relation between God and any individual should be "I in you; you in me," and the struggle within the soul does not bring salvation, but only moves in a hopeless circle.[73] In his exegesis earlier in Romans 7, Barth's christocentric starting point is precisely the staging ground for an attack on pietism. Salvation is not found in the individual's struggle with sin, as exemplified in such characters as Luther, Arndt, and Spener. Salvation is rather found only in Christ.[74] Barth divides our locus into two parts. He considers 7:21–22 as one side of the human dilemma. Barth glosses the impulse to do good and the inward pleasure in the law of God with the pietistic impulse. It is perfectly expected and understandable, but ultimately hopeless.[75] The other side of the human dilemma comes in

7:23. This verse describes "the law of my members" or "the law of sin," which Barth glosses as "the particular legality of matter, the outer material life, the natural and historical world . . . the arrangement of the world as apostasized from God." Barth goes on to describe the soul as completely helpless, unable to speak or do anything that would lead toward rescue from the law of sin.[76] Here we see Barth with the late Augustine and Luther in his insistence on the impotence of the human soul against Origen, Pelagius, and Erasmus, who all maintained that the human could take steps toward God.

It is tempting to use biographical criticism here and note that a pietistic evangelist, Jakob Vetter, had conducted meetings in Barth's church for about six months during the time that Barth was working on *Romans I*. Despite his horror at the pietistic certainty with which Vetter described the stages of salvation and complete detachment from pietism that Barth felt, he undertook to learn of pietism by reading biographies of such pietists as Ludwig Hofacker, David Spleiß, and August Tholuck.[77] This section of *Romans I*, then, shows how Barth read the angst over sin in Romans 7 as a sign of a pietism. Barth's concern with pietism is evident as well in *Romans II*, although he does not attack it as explicitly as he does in *Romans I*. For Barth, this pietism was unhelpful because it still started with human experience. This becomes transparent in a comment he makes in *Romans II* after quoting 7:15: "If the law of my religious being and having, were itself Spirit; if sensitive 'apprehension of the absolute'—'feeling and taste for eternity' (Schleiermacher)—could seriously be regarded as lying within the realm of human competence; if God and such a man as I am could be treated as co-partners; I should be in a proper position to contemplate and comprehend my words and acts and deeds from the point of view of eternity, or, at least, to think of them as the first stages of a movement in conformity with the movement of the Spirit of God. Then I should be led on to describe and comprehend myself quite properly as the answer to the problem of life."[78]

The change in Barth's treatment of Romans 7 in the second edition partially arises from the more complete separation between God and the world that Barth makes, compared to the first edition. Now in the second edition it is religion itself, including but not limited to pietism, that is a threat to humanity. This seems to account for many of the specific differences between the two editions. For example, while Barth entitled the section on Romans 7 in both editions "Freedom," he changed the subheadings of this chapter to make clear the inadequacy of religion, which he equates with law in the second edition.[79] Romans 7 then becomes more clearly in the second edition a statement of the ineffectiveness of religion to reach God. The first edition by contrast was not as negative in its portrait of religion, for the first edition was modeled on the organic growth of the kingdom of God on the earth, without the dialectical tension between God and the world that dominates the second edition.

Barth does not lose sight of the dangers of pietism in *Romans II*. He quotes the pietist Johann Arndt as saying that as long as one is conscious of the struggle between good and evil, between Spirit and flesh, one can still consider oneself to be faithful. Barth blasts such a pietistic position as "perilous," "the middle way of compromise and resignation."[80] But for the most part Barth's polemic against pietism is replaced in *Romans II* by a focus on the threat of religion for a human being. The "law" (*nomos*), which recurs throughout Romans 7, is read by Barth in *Romans II* as a cipher for "religion."[81] Religion is essentially a threat, in Barth's mind, because it is the one human channel for the questions that expose the human's finitude; in religion the human is confronted with the question of death.

Religion also seems to divide people into two halves, according to Barth. Religion evokes the will to do good, but at the same time it exposes the impotence for actually performing the good. According to Barth, this tendency in religion operates before and after a religious conversion, so that in Romans 7 "Paul describes his past, present, and future existence."[82] Still, the dualistic tension that religion places on someone does not finally break the person. Barth lays great stress on the phrase "Wretched man that I am!" in 7:24. This implies for him that there is still a unified person even after the person has been exposed to religion's balkanizing force. For Barth, Paul "is writing about a man, broken in two by the law, but who, according to the law, cannot be thus broken. Paul is thrust into a dualism which contradicts itself. He is shattered on God, without the possibility of forgetting Him. Do we now understand the meaning of the Grace of God and of His Freedom?"[83]

These sentences conclude Barth's chapter on Romans 7. They illustrate well that here, where most commentators start with the human person and let their exegesis be governed by the question of whether Paul is referring to a human before or after conversion, Barth is still beginning with God and centering his exegesis around what it tells us of God. For Barth, Romans 7 is about how God can meet a person in spite of the devastating encounter the human may have with religion. Barth is thus saying that though religion is a human activity, God may actually meet a person there.[84] The person will be exposed to God's law, which sounds a conclusive "No" over the person's existence. But then by graciously reconstituting the human person who has been devastated by religion, God shows his freedom.

It is common for Romans commentators today to recognize aspects in which this locus is an apology for Mosaic law.[85] Statements in 7:7, 12, and 14 serve to make clear that Paul is saying that the law is good; it is an alien power of sin that is awakened when the law comes that is to blame for the sin Paul experiences, not the law itself (7:9–10). One does not find Barth defending religion throughout Romans 7, but some defense is there. In *Romans II*, commenting on 7:7a—"Is the law sin? May it never be!"—Barth finds a parallel between law and religion and asks why we cannot abandon religion for something that seems better. In the process of asking and answering this question, Barth asks, "Why should we not return to the main theme of the first edition of this commentary, and, joining hands with Beck and with the naturalism of the leaders of the old school of Württemberg, set over against an empty idealism the picture of humanity as a growing divine organism?"[86] Barth goes on in this section to argue that there is no way that the law or religion can be sin, so that although it tragically functions as the highest human possibility and so can be a tempting substitute for an encounter with God, yet it also serves as the primary place from which humanity realizes its own finiteness and impotence to venture into the realm of the Divine.[87]

A cursory reading of Barth on this locus might lead one at times to give credit to Kierkegaard's existentialism for Barth's description of religion as a force that breaks humans into two halves. For example, on 7:7b Barth writes, "If God encounters and confronts men in religion, He encounters and confronts them everywhere. Remembering their direct relation with Him, its loss becomes an event, and there breaks out a sickness unto death."[88] But this is different from the existentialism of Kierkegaard, who labored to preserve the time-bound, individual human being from being swallowed up by the Hegelian Absolute.[89] Barth is primarily concerned with God and the threat and promise God poses for humanity. Barth does not view human existence in itself as contradictory or alienating; it is only when God encounters humanity that the questionable status of human existence is fully realized. Thus Barth is not an existentialist like Kierkegaard or Bultmann, who wrote on Romans 7 that "Man himself is the split."[90] For Barth the record of dualistic pressure on the human being to which Romans 7 points is evidence of what happens when God encounters a human being through religion.

In comparison to the other interpreters of Romans covered in this volume, Barth brings the locus back to the interpretation of Origen. It was Augustine who framed the locus as if it had to refer to someone either in a pre-Christian or a Christian state. Augustine himself entertained each of these positions as though it were exclusively true in separate battles he fought: against the Manichees, Augustine thought Romans 7 described a pre-Christian experience; the Pelagians overturned this interpretation, he says, so that he came to realize that it dealt with normal Christian experience. Barth's treatment of Paul describing "past, present, and future existence" in Romans 7 is exegetically closer to Origen and Erasmus than to any of the intervening commentators. For Origen finds Paul assuming different personae in this section: at times assuming the discourse of the weak who are sinful, a habit that has precedent in Scriptures composed by David and Daniel. Origen is surprisingly nuanced in his interpretation, for he writes that when Paul affirms his sin, he is simply assuming the position of sinner in order to communicate to sinners and to those believers who have been converted but still find sinful temptations inside themselves.[91] When Paul concludes in 7:25b, "So then I myself serve the law of God in my mind, but the law of sin in my flesh," Origen thinks Paul is not speaking for himself, even though he says, "I myself," but actually assuming the persona of someone who has been converted but is still on the path toward training his body to resist vice and follow the virtues that his mind accepts.[92] Barth is distinct for his insistence that the human being is simultaneously broken and reconstituted in an encounter with the question of God within religion. But he is like Origen in refusing to be constrained to say that the implied author of Romans 7 is writing as someone either before conversion or after. Contemporary commentators, who still impale themselves by climbing toward only one or the other side of Augustine's fence, might do well to enter the open pastures first cleared by Origen on this locus.

NEW PERSPECTIVE AND NARRATIVE APPROACHES

The new perspective has taken a step past the anthropological lens with which Augustine read Romans 7 and emphatically views this section as an apology for the Torah.

On Paul's flow of thought in Romans 7, Sanders writes: "Paul's logic seems to run like this: in Christ God has acted to save the world; therefore the world is in need of salvation; but God also gave the law; if Christ is given for salvation, it must follow that the law could not have been; is the law then against the purpose of God which has been revealed in Christ? No, it has the function of consigning everyone to sin so that everyone could be saved by God's grace in Christ."[93]

Dunn's exegesis of this locus as an apology for the Mosaic law at least focuses more on the warring laws and less on the identity of the speaker, which at times has been the exclusive focus of exegesis in this locus, due to Augustine's influence. Dunn especially likes the possibility that the warring laws in this section actually refer to the same Mosaic law that is experienced differently depending on what power, sin or the Holy Spirit, animates a person's encounter with it. Dunn's position on the Augustinian question of whether the latter half of Romans 7 refers to a pre-Christian or Christian experience is heavily influenced by his eschatology and by his understanding of the believer's experience. He repeatedly describes the *egō* here as a believer who "is stretched between the old epoch of sin and death (and law) and the new epoch of grace and life (and Spirit)."[94] One wonders why "law" occurs only with the old epoch in this quotation, since Dunn definitely holds a place for Torah in the new epoch as well. The conflict between the laws that is evident in 8:2 is also explained as the tension between the epochs: "The law of the Spirit is the eschatological law (cf. Jer 31:31–34; Ezek 36:26–27); 8:1–2 speaks from within the perspective of the new epoch introduced by Christ, whereas 7:23 speaks from within the old epoch of Adam."[95]

The new perspective has made it possible for narrative-based approaches here to highlight the experience of Israel as indicative of human experience under law. On 7:21–25 Wright summarizes, "Israel, it seems, has been called to hold on to the enormous tension between being called to be the light of the world and discovering itself to be, like everyone else, soaked in sin." Wright sees Messiah Jesus as the answer because Jesus "sums up in himself *both* Israel according to the flesh *and* the God who comes to the rescue."[96]

It is inevitable that a reader's experience will affect exegesis. Still, we can respect this whole letter best if we do not appeal to human experience, whether our own or what is scientifically described in psychology textbooks, and instead exegete this locus in light of the literary and rhetorical conventions it reflects. My bias no

doubt goes back to a moment in graduate school when I was kept from writing
on this text due to a lack of acquaintance with psychology, the science of human
experience.

Professor Betz would often tell our Romans class what still needed to be done
to understand various questions within Paul's letter to the Romans. His example
of identifying unsolved problems and offering possible steps toward their resolution is one of the best gifts I received from him. When we got to Romans 7 he
spent some time describing what still needed to be done to identify the *egō* of this
locus. After class, back in his office, I asked if I could take on such a study for my
dissertation. Betz discouraged me from such an undertaking: "Oh, to do that one
would need a thorough knowledge of psychology, both ancient and modern.
Have you read Freud?" I had to reply that I had not. "Then you wouldn't know
what the problems are," he responded. So my deficiency in the field of psychology ruled out the exegesis of Romans 7 as a dissertation topic. Weeks later I
recounted this exchange to E. A. Judge, who was visiting Chicago for a guest lecture. "I should think one would *not* want to have read Freud if one were going
to exegete Romans 7" was his reply!

Now we are well served by psychological analyses of Romans 7, Lichtenberger's comprehensive history of interpretation, tradition-historical analysis and
exegesis, and Aletti's rhetorical analysis of the passage.[97] The various appeals to
human experience that have haunted the exegesis of this locus since Augustine
must be resisted as far as is possible. Augustine's experience with the Pelagians,
Aquinas's appeals to Aristotle, and Luther's angst in the cloister must not be
allowed to program the exegete's approach here. Barth's concern not to read this
text from a pietistic perspective thus wisely avoids the interference of a perception of human experience that we cannot prove to be Pauline. Lichtenberger's
exegesis, with eyes open toward past approaches, is preferable to any appeal to
human experience for understanding this locus.

While Lichtenberger's emphasis on the laws as warring over a soul is less than
Origen's, he does emphasize the unity of the "I" of Romans 7 and the "you" of
the beginning of Romans 8, and Paul's emphasis on the incompatibility of these
as simultaneous modes of living. The voice of the wretched man in 7:24 is Paul
speaking from the perspective of the earthly condition of the death-bound
human. The thanksgiving in the next verse is not Origen's different speaker, but
rather Paul's thanksgiving in light of the future redemption of the body
(8:18–23).[98] Lichtenberger cogently argues from the context that the "law of sin
and death" in 8:2 cannot be the new perspective's reading of Torah as perverted
or co-opted by sin and death, for the Torah is always presented as holy (7:12,
14).[99] In this sense we are returning with Lichtenberger's exegesis to seeing more
laws at work here, rather than simply one Torah abused and used by vying powers. The "I" of Romans 7 is not Luther's believer who is statically "*simul iustus et
peccator.*" Lichtenberger's favorable quotation of Barth's statement that here
"Paul preaches the 'beginning of justification in the very midst of man's sin'" is

quite close to Origen's identification of the voice speaking in 7:14–24 as someone who is not yet fully converted.[100]

Jean-Noël Aletti's article on Romans 7 reads the locus with a stereoscopic
vision usually not found among exegetes. He is able to see both the biblical language in 7:7–12 and the influence of Greek philosophy in 7:14–20. His study
independently confirms Lichtenberger's work, that the *egō* is someone, either Jew
or Greek, who is not in Christ. The *egō* feels the conflict of warring laws and is
helpless to rise above the conflict and act fully in accord with the good law.[101]
Both Aletti and Lichtenberger are confirming the earlier study by Kümmel,
which also speaks of the impossibility that the *egō* can refer to a Christian.[102]

Both Aletti and Betz are sensitive to the cultural and intellectual software
available for the production of this locus in the first century. This points to
another difference in how interpreters read Romans. Some think the awareness
of first-century cultural, historical, and intellectual trends should definitely affect
our exegesis, while others see no need to utilize our growing knowledge of such
trends in their exegesis. I speak as a human according to the flesh, but perhaps
this example will be helpful: compare the recordings of Bach's harpsichord works
by pianists Glenn Gould and Vladimir Horowitz.

Since our conversation years ago, Betz has also written on this locus within
the framework of Pauline anthropology. He follows Christoph Markschies in
characterizing Paul as taking over and reconfiguring the Hellenistic concepts of
the inner and outer human.[103] Instead of a mind-body dualism of the sort found
in Platonic thought, Paul preserves the essential integrity of the human person.
The inner human is identified with the "mind" that recognizes law as good. The
outer human is represented by the body's "members" that do evil against the
knowledge and intentions of the inner human. That Paul uses the philosophical
term "inner human" at 7:22 should be a signal that he is situating his remarks in
light of Greek debates about anthropology and responding to questions in
Corinth about his own understanding of the human being.[104] My approach in
this chapter is not as anthropologically oriented as Betz's work, since I have followed Origen's emphasis on the "warring laws" described in this locus. On this
note, Betz helpfully identifies the "law" in 7:21 as a "rule" or principle that sums
up the self-knowledge available to the inner human.[105] To return to an anthropological question from which I cannot escape, Betz cites favorably Kümmel's
judgment that the *egō* of 7:14–25 represents the generally human experience of
a pre-Christian seen through the eyes of a Christian. Still, Betz repeatedly emphasizes that this does not mean that Paul considers Christian life to be free from the
sort of inner turmoil described in this locus.[106]

As Romans moves outward among the *ethnē*, this locus will continue to generate new approaches that are specific to the readers' cultures. For example, after
offering a thorough summary of the Western debate on this locus, Yeo Khiok-
khng observes that "the Pauline discussion of Torah and Spirit in terms of Pharisaic and Christian perspectives for both Jewish and Gentile audiences is a

cross-cultural endeavor." From this he proceeds to exegete the text cross-culturally in his section entitled, "The Pauline 'Torah and Spirit' Compared with Confucian *Li* and *Jen*."[107] As the Western church becomes eclipsed by Asian and African Christianities, such approaches as this will appear more frequently.

The lens of Greek philosophy, especially the origin of the "inner human" as a philosophical concept in Platonic thought, helps us see that Paul is recasting a conflict that would be familiar to educated Greeks. Given the way in which 7:7–13 quotes from the Decalogue and seems to evoke Adam imagery and what we have seen now in regard to how 7:14–25 seems to evoke the discussions of the Greek philosophers, we encounter Origen's general framework for this letter. Paul is an arbiter between Jews and Greeks, and in this locus he wants to show both that law is good, but that when mixed with the human being, law serves to identify sin and highlight the human's need for salvation. Origen himself did not exegete this locus in this way, but he provided the framework in which to do so.

CONCLUSION

Ever since Augustine's controversy with the Pelagians, a dominant reading of this locus has been that it is all about Christian experience. Luther reinforced this reading with his doctrine of *simul iustus et peccator*. But careful exegesis helps us see that this locus is in the first place an apology for law, whether the Mosaic law or law as understood by Greek philosophers. Once the main thrust of the locus is identified, we can go on to respond to the secondary question, Who is the *egō*? Close readings of the text itself and in relation to the culture and contemporary literature available to Paul shift identification of the *egō* back to Origen's persona who was not yet fully converted.

As for the role of human experience in interpreting this locus, a responsible consideration of the rhetorical and intellectual framework in which Paul wrote seems to be a better control on our exegesis than conscious or unconscious appeals to human experience. In Romans 7 a multiplicity of laws wage war over people, whether Jews or pagans, who are not yet in Christ.

Locus 7

Calling, Foreknowledge, Predestination (8:28–30)

There seems to me to be two causes why what was written to the Romans is considered more difficult to understand than the rest of the letters of the apostle Paul: first, that now and then in its utterances, expressions that are confused and lacking explanation are used; second, that it raises many questions by itself, especially those on which people with heretical leanings are accustomed to construct a cause of every individual action, due to be credited not to an intention but to the diversity of nature, and from the few words of this letter they attempt to overturn the meaning of the whole scripture that teaches a freedom of the will given by God to humankind.

Origen[1]

Romans 8:28–30 is the first place in the letter where "foreknow" (*proginōskō*) is used and the only place in the letter where the verb "predestine" (*proorizō*) is used. It represents therefore a bird's-eye view of what happens within the process of salvation and must be faced by any reader who wants to know what Romans says about predestination. For the last two millennia, this locus has been the site, the first of a series of three loci, where humanity's puzzle regarding determinism and freedom is most pointedly addressed by the apostle Paul, who had to explain to the *ethnē* what God's election of a people means. The following three short chapters on these loci, which all deal with predestination (8:28–30; 9:16–19; 9:20–23), show how Gentile Romans readers have moved in full circle on the determinism and free will debate in Romans. The specific aspects of predestination covered in these three loci are as follows: locus 7 concerns providence (8:28) and the place of predestination within the order of salvation (8:29–30); locus 8 concerns the status and function of the human will in salvation (9:16) and the significance of Paul's description of the hardening of Pharaoh's heart (9:17–18); and locus 9 concerns the significance of the potter and clay analogy (9:20–21), the question of double predestination, the idea that God elects some people for salvation and others for damnation (9:22), and the question of whether God elects individually or corporately (9:22–23).

We tap in here to a set of questions centering around determinism and freedom (or predestination and free will) that many readers bring to Romans. After teaching on Romans for three Sunday evenings in a church near my home, a college professor who attended my class confessed that he had disliked Romans for a long time. When we discussed why he held such distaste for Romans, he said that he did not like the way the letter was used to prove that God has determined every individual who will be saved. Some students come to Romans exulting in what they might call the truth of sovereign grace, that God predestines specific individuals for salvation. They cannot wait to get to these three loci, for in them they believe this doctrine that gives them such a secure feeling is most clearly taught. Other students approach Romans ready for a fight; these seek to assert human freedom wherever another reader of Romans thinks the text teaches predestination. Most of my students seem to be between these poles. They come to Romans with a sense that this book addresses the question of predestination and human freedom, and they enter the class hoping to learn what Romans *really* says on this vexed question. We will see godly, learned believers on either side of this question. Prior to increased understanding, our main goal in discussions on questions of this sort should be to be affectionate in Christian love and respect for one another.

The "called" language here in 8:28 and 33 that follows Paul's adoption metaphor (8:15, 23) within his sonship language (8:14–17, 29) represents a bold transfer of Scripture's terminology for ethnic Israel onto those Gentiles and Jews who follow Jesus. We will consider this transfer when we come to the loci on Christ the *telos* of the law at 10:4 and the salvation of Israel at 11:25–27.

ORIGEN

Origen defines the "all things working together for good" of 8:28 in a corporate, eschatological sense. He considers this phrase appropriate in light of the liberation of creation pictured in 8:21 and the Spirit's help in 8:26. His paraphrase—"the divine nature does not disdain to be a guide for the journey toward the good"—is less individualistic and optimistic than the way later readers would understand this verse.[2] It is easier to assert that "the good" simply means that God's children will be redeemed when creation is liberated than to assert that circumstances in each individual believer's life fit into a coherent pattern of good in this life.

A retired professor has repeatedly told me, within the safe walls of the faculty lounge, that he does not believe that "all things work together for good." Tragic events in his own life have disproved his individualistic understanding of this verse.

Though I have not tried to salvage this locus for my colleague, Origen's eschatological and corporate interpretation might help. Origen is reading the paragraph beginning at 8:18 with the eschaton in view, not this first life. Then he reads the promises of eschatological renewal as if they are for God's people as a whole. The body's redemption in 8:23 refers not to an individual human body, but to the whole church, the body of Christ.[3] Origen's reading certainly makes sense in the context of social consciousness in which this letter was written. After all, Paul wrote Romans before Western readers, thanks to Augustine, Luther, and the Enlightenment, came to view the individual human as the primary subject within religious discourse. Origen interprets Romans with corporate personae in view.

The assertions of this locus regarding calling, foreknowledge, and predestination are central in Origen's mind, for even when exegeting the phrase "separated to the gospel of God" in 1:1, Origen quotes 8:28–30 in order to understand Paul's claim to be "separated." Origen's basic approach there at the beginning of his commentary is that God's foreknowledge precedes his predestination (based on the order of the verbs in 8:29) and that God's effective call comes only to those God has predestined (based on the order of verbs in 8:30).[4] He continues at this locus to pay close attention to the order of verbs in verses 29–30.[5]

For Origen "foreknow" means "to receive in affection and to unite with oneself."[6] God does not foreknow or predestine evil people: "Everything that is evil is deemed unworthy both of his knowledge and foreknowledge."[7]

Human effort is included in the process of becoming like Christ: "Whoever would attain to this height of perfection and blessedness should steer towards that one's image and likeness."[8] Human agency in the process of justification is emphasized, for Origen refuses to locate the cause of someone's salvation only in God's foreknowledge or calling, and he asserts that Paul refuses to remove humanity's part in the process of being glorified.[9] He goes on to cite 1 Corinthians 9:27 as evidence that it is the human's purpose and actions that form the cause of salvation, rather than God's foreknowledge.[10]

What then of God's call? Since Matthew 22:14 teaches that not everyone who is called responds to the divine call, Origen takes pains to distinguish different senses of Scripture's use of "call." Here in Romans 8:28–30 those who are "called according to purpose" are in view. It is these people's own purpose that Paul refers to, according to Origen, a view that Chrysostom follows. Where such purpose is lacking, there was a call; otherwise the people could not be held responsible for their apathy toward God.[11] Everyone is called, but not all are "called according to purpose." The example of Origen that resurfaces in Abelard and Barth is Judas Iscariot. According to Origen, Judas was called but not justified. Origen takes pains to assert that people who are not justified have not responded to their calling, for he is concerned that an overemphasis on God's governance in the process will eliminate human responsibility.[12] This concern is a driving force in his exegesis of the next locus as well, where Origen will pioneer the influential approach of viewing 9:16–18 as spoken by Paul's opponent.

AUGUSTINE

In a letter written in 412 or 413, Augustine quotes 8:28 to encourage a Christian woman to allow the cares and evils of the world to work patience in her, preparing her for the life to come. This letter thus illustrates the way in which Augustine interprets Romans as concerned with the individual believer.[13] Like Origen, Augustine's exegesis of providence in 8:28 is focused on the eschaton. But Augustine's exegesis is focused on the individual believer's spiritual journey to salvation and represents a much narrower focus than Origen's corporate framework. Of course, I must concede here that we have lost most of Origen's pastoral letters. Perhaps he too used Romans 8:28 to encourage individuals; in that sense the difference I am highlighting in this paragraph would not be so neatly exemplified. Beyond the question of how to interpret "all things working together for good," we must also examine Augustine's trajectory on predestination.

Augustine did not emphasize predestination in his early writings on Romans. The dominant foil behind his early exegesis was the Manichean interpretation of Paul. Since the Manichees portrayed a deity as the author of evil and denied free will to humanity, Augustine sought to avoid crediting God with the evil of reprobate humanity and described the freedom of the human will more readily than in later writings. Just as there appears to be a progression in Augustine that emphasizes the essential sinfulness of humanity when one reads the *Commentary on Statements in the Letter to the Romans* (written in 394–395), the *On Eighty-three Varied Questions* (388–396), and the letter *To Simplicianus* (396–398),[14] so there appears to be an intensification of the doctrine of predestination. With *To Simplicianus* we see an increasing emphasis on God's election and a decreasing emphasis on the human will, though the new bishop does not refer to this locus there. Still, *To Simplicianus* represents the beginning of Augustine's more predestinarian reading of Romans. When reading Augustine on Romans, therefore, one should at least determine whether any work was written before or after *To Simplicianus*, which functions as a watershed for Augustine on predestination.

In *On Eighty-three Varied Questions* Augustine deals with chance, an issue that surely any reading of 8:28 must consider. Augustine states that since that all that truly exists is good by virtue of its participation in God's providence, there are no chance occurrences in the world. At the same time, he still affirms that the human will can freely choose to sin or to act well.[15] Augustine at least at this point affirms that humans make real choices. This is a contention that some make also for Luther and Calvin. I still think the question must be asked repeatedly when reading these authors: Do Augustine, Luther, and Calvin portray people's choices as making an actual difference in this world or in their entrance into salvation?

In *Commentary on Statements in the Letter to the Romans*, Augustine asks whether all who are called will be justified. His answer is that while many are called, it is only those who are "called according to purpose" who will be justified. So far Augustine is tracking with Origen. Yet Augustine is already moving toward his later position by clarifying here that the purpose originates with God, not with the human subjects. Still, this is the early Augustine, who also affirms that God does not predestine anyone unless God knows that the person will believe and follow God's call. It thus seems to be a position within the model of simple foreknowledge. God knows those who will believe, so these are called according to God's purpose. Besides a discussion on the senses in which Christ is both "only begotten" and "firstborn," Augustine does not address sanctification and glorification in verse 30 in this work.[16]

In a letter written in 409, Augustine states that those from other nations than Israel were worthy of salvation and received it. He claims that this salvation came to everyone who was worthy, and if anyone did not receive his or her salvation, that person must have not been worthy. Since this could be taken to mean that people earn their salvation, Augustine explained in his *Retractions* that in this letter "worthy" meant to have God's calling, and he cites Romans 8:28; 9:11–12; 2 Thessalonians 1:11, and 2 Timothy 1:9. Augustine forms these Scriptures into a tableau that emphasizes God's calling as the determinative factor in an individual's attainment of salvation rather than any sort of human merit.[17]

These more deterministic views on predestination that are evident later in Augustine's life are what the label "Augustinian" often signifies. Such views were carried into the medieval period and sometimes quoted by commentators also influenced by Origen. They will also appear when we examine Augustine on the loci in Romans 9.

ABELARD

Augustine won his battle against Pelagius. In 529 a moderate form of Augustine's views on predestination was adopted by the church. At the Second Council of Orange in this year, bishops in France marked Pelagius and the rigidly deterministic readings of the later Augustine as out of bounds. They thus effectively set the playing field for the Middle Ages, when scholastics theologized at different points along the continuum from Pelagius to the later Augustine. Now a millennium of replaying Augustine's battle against Pelagius in new settings would begin. Medieval commentators explicitly began with Augustine. If this book were only describing the history of Romans interpretation through the end of the sixteenth century, Augustine would be the hero. But we seek to understand how Romans is being read even into our own time, and even in the medieval period Origen was copied by monks and used by Romans interpreters, sometimes alongside Augustine. Abelard certainly made use of Origen and Augustine when commenting on Romans.

On identifying those who are called according to God's purpose, Abelard sounds Augustinian in offering a dichotomy between those who are called according to God's purpose and those who qualify based on preceding merits. He rejects the latter option, saying that those who love God, for whom all things work together for good, are called by an internal, inspiring call that is from God; their call is not based on their own merits.[18]

In his exegesis of the next verse, however, Abelard seems to reintroduce the criterion of human merit. For he explains that God foreknows those whom God approves, who are worthy of God's notice. The texts Psalm 1:6a, Luke 13:25, and 27 are combined to show that God knows the righteous and does not know the wicked. While dependence on Origen cannot be proven, Abelard also notes the order of verbs here, how "predestine" follows "foreknow." This predestation is described as a gift of grace that God prepares, grace that is found only in the elect.[19] "So those are said to be foreknown, whose future election God earlier approved."[20]

Abelard continues to exegete what the goal of predestination is: conformity to the image of the Son. Abelard jumps to ethics from this locus, a move all commentators influenced by the Reformation find nearly impossible to do, citing Colossians 3:9 and 1 John 2:6 to help explain what it would mean in terms of human behavior to be conformed to the image of the Son.[21] So with regard both to the verb "foreknow" and the verb "predestine," Abelard wants to preserve a vibrant place for human responsibility.

In one long sentence on 8:30, Abelard takes Paul's description of the order of salvation and fills in the details: "The elect are predestined, i.e., they are prepared for eternal life through the faith of illumination, which first they take as the foundation of all blessings; afterwards they are called through hope in that one, when now the mercy of God and the known power of the sacraments are added to work effectively, since it is known that they have an eternal reward; thus [the elect], having a sincere love, are justified now by God not so much on their own account as on account of him whom they are holding; in the end they are praised when they are raised into the heavenly homeland."[22] Note here how Abelard like Origen combines divine mercy with human effort, though human effort is never presented as a ground for boasting.

After this, Abelard inserts a "Question," as he did at 3:22. Here he asks how predestination interacts with the human will. Is it necessary that a man be an adulterer if in God's providence this is decreed? His question presents the stakes very well, for he notes how an act decreed by God in the sense that it is inevitable could not then be credited as a sin for the human agent. In addition there is the problem of locating evil in the providence of God. His conclusion is that God's foreknowledge does not mean that the man must by necessity commit adultery, and refers the reader to a book where he has already distinguished between predestination, providence, and fate.[23]

LUTHER

Luther emphasizes the divine activity of predestination by piling up synonyms in his gloss on Romans 8:29—"For those whom He foreknew, whom He foresaw before they were born, He also predestined, predetermined, preestablished, chose ahead of time, proposed, to be conformed. . . ." Against Origen, Luther also glosses

God's foreknowledge of those God will predestine as unconditioned by their merits.[24] Luther has a lengthy scholium on predestination, in which he cites Romans 8:28c; 9:8–13, 15, 17–18 as all teaching predestination. He answers objections by siding with the later Augustine that the human will is bound and not free in regard to things above its power, such as salvation, and explains the divine desire for all to be saved in 1 Timothy 2:4 as actually limited to the elect. To the objection that it is unjust for God to predestine some to damnation, Luther replies that everyone is by necessity in sin and condemnation, but that no one is forced to be in this situation against one's will. Luther admits that the strongest argument against predestination is that God causes some to sin and enter damnation. His response is a surface reading of Romans 9:20–23 that leads him to say that God indeed wills in election those in whom he will show mercy, and his will is that those not chosen will be condemned to show his anger; since this is God's will, Luther claims it cannot be evil. The voice that still questions the justice of this model is labeled "the prudence of the flesh" and considered too selfish; one should rather be God-centered in one's thinking, according to Luther.[25] Love for a God who absolutely wills every human soul is considered sweet and delightful, according to Luther.[26]

For Luther, the main message of Romans was contained in the first eight chapters of the letter. From Luther on, the theory behind how one entered into passive righteousness would be considered "doctrine," and would be limited to Romans 1–8, or perhaps 1–11. The rest of the letter would be relegated to the category of "application." This division of Romans into doctrine and application was a real setback in the interpretation of the letter, for it minimized the so-called ethical portion of this letter, chapters 12–15, which actually have plenty of doctrine in them. Most letters have crucial material in their latter halves and Romans is no exception. Of course, not everyone reading Romans in the sixteenth century was ready to jettison the latter material in the letter. Erasmus was still reading Paul's statements about the moral agency of humans in Romans.

ERASMUS

Erasmus is very alert to pass on anything Origen says about predestination, even preserving Origen's remarks about the topic that he makes on Romans 1:1 and 4 regarding how Paul is a "called" apostle and how Jesus was "predestined" God's son.[27]

On Romans 8:29, the verse that says God "foreknew" and "predestined" those described as "called" in the preceding verse, Erasmus chooses to unpack foreknowledge in a way that leaves human freedom intact. Foreknowledge is God's foresight of something that could be changed. The next step in the process, predestination, is a more certain decree that cannot be changed. Erasmus admits that others might object that he has eliminated foreknowledge, but claims Theophylact as an authority for his interpretation.[28] For the sixteenth century, Erasmus is a crucial tradent who brings Greek commentators' readings of Romans into the

Western church. Erasmus's view that foreknowledge means that God foreknows who is or will be worthy of being saved has the support of most patristic sources, though of course not the later Augustine.[29]

The jousting match between Luther and Erasmus on the question of the human will can be usefully viewed as a contest to determine whether Augustine or Origen should be followed on the efficacy of the human will to make choices with real consequences. In a letter written in 1518 to someone who would later become an enemy of Luther, Erasmus claims to have a high view of Augustine but asks his addressee, John Eck, to study Jerome carefully. One of the reasons Erasmus offers in support of Jerome is his understanding that Jerome used Origen's work more than Augustine did: "I learn more of Christian philosophy from a single page of Origen than from ten of Augustine."[30]

Still, it would be simplistic to say that Erasmus always sides with Origen. Even at the end of his notes on Romans 8:29, Erasmus caricatures Origen, Augustine, Thomas Aquinas, and scholastic theologians as philosophizing too much on this locus and touts his own interpretation as "simpler and more genuine."[31]

BARTH

Like Origen, Barth interprets this locus for humanity as a whole in light of the eschaton.[32] Barth explains "those who are called according to his purpose" as not referring to an identifiable, quantifiable group of people; he says that we are not allowed to count or specify who is within God's love.[33]

In *Romans II* Barth glosses "the image of his son" with Jesus' death, citing Philippians 3:10. To be conformed to Jesus' death means the tribulation that the redeemed value (Rom. 5:3), which cannot be engineered or self-inflicted, but must come from God. Though Barth mentions once in his exegesis of Romans 8:29 the witness to Christ's resurrection as the end of this process, he most emphasizes the predestination to join Christ in his suffering and death.[34] This is the goal of the predestination: witness to Christ's death and resurrection. Barth demythologizes the doctrine of predestination taught by Augustine and the Reformers by removing its cause-and-effect connection in individual believers who live within time. For Barth, predestination means that the love humanity shows for God does not essentially occur in time; it has its origin in God and thus is located outside time. Predestination therefore cannot be predicated of an individual life that is unfolding in time; predestination rather involves the recognition that all human love for God originates outside time in God alone.[35] For us to say that God's election causes certain individuals to believe and join the redeemed is to bring God into our world's time, to reduce God's grounding of all existence to mere causality within temporal existence. Barth's location of predestination outside time is consistent with Aquinas's teaching that both foreknowledge and predestination are from eternity past, but it seems to reject Aquinas's emphasis on the causal force of predestination.[36]

Barth is not a second Origen. Origen had not read Kant, who taught that human will is not bound by time and that pure reason cannot track how free will and nature interact to spawn human actions.[37] Barth's later exegesis of this locus as describing the election of only one individual is a christological move away from Calvin's doctrine of the election of individuals.[38] Though different from Origen, the effects of Barth's interpretation on prayer and preaching bring us back toward Origen. Barth pulls Romans discourse on this locus toward the insistence on the robust exercise of the human will in Origen and away from the meticulous determinism of the late Augustine and Luther.

POST-BARTHIAN APPROACHES

Neither the new perspective nor narrative-based approaches have attempted any strong connections between this locus and Israel's faith or story.

New Perspective

In *Paul and Palestinian Judaism*, Sanders mentions 8:28–30 as representing the way Paul can at times present his message without focusing on humans' response of faith. Note how Sanders returns us to a cosmic stage for the proclamation of Paul's gospel but cannot let go of individuals on this stage in his comment preceding his quotation of 8:28–30 and 33: "What God is doing is of cosmic significance and affects 'all things,' and it is this that Paul preaches about; but individuals will be affected differently, depending on whether or not they believe."[39] In a later work, Sanders glosses the "good" of this locus as "the salvation of the entire cosmos."[40] Sanders also maintains that Paul can speak of predestination while wanting to encourage people with God's action on behalf of humanity, while he speaks of humans' necessity for faith when presenting human responsibility, with no compulsion to harmonize the two.[41]

Dunn notes the Jewish background of the expression "those who love God" as well as the Jewish tendency to associate "saints" (8:27) with "called" (8:28).[42] Dunn clearly interprets 8:28 in a corporate and cosmic stage: "The thrust of the *eis agathon* ['for good'] is eschatological . . . as of the corporate experience of the people of God."[43] The foreknowledge described in 8:29 is "Hebraic," encapsulating a relationship rather than simply knowing something in advance. Without citing Origen, Dunn is quite close to Origen's definition of foreknowledge as God's loving embrace. With regard to predestination itself, Dunn leaves room for the human will without emphasizing its place as Origen had done.[44]

Narrative-Based Approaches

Grieb surprisingly relates this locus only to the Christians in Rome.[45] N. T. Wright lists 8:28 as a place where Paul may be alluding to the Jewish Shema and 8:29 as possibly linked to the "image" language in Genesis 1:26–27.[46]

Yeo Khiok-khng

This Chinese Christian compares this locus with classical Confucianism and finds similarity between the eschatological understanding of "all things work together for good" and the Confucian concept of heaven: "Not all things serve the comfort of the people of God, but all things work together to their salvation. God does not cause everything but God uses every event, good or bad, towards an eventual greater good. . . . Paul gives the faithful assurance that the future belongs to the children of God."[47] Without mentioning Barth, Yeo defines the object of predestination as "primarily not believers or unbelievers but Christ, the purposeful creation of God by means of God's ideal community characterized by faith and grace."[48] With regard to this community, Yeo hears the Jews-*ethnē* challenge behind this text when reading it from his Chinese background: "Confucius' political context is a helpful lens for me to reread the political power of Paul's gospel mission—an ecclesial space that will transform and replace the larger political space. Confucius' ethical insights have led me to observe the communal problems faced in Romans with regards to group behavior and identity."[49]

CONCLUSION

The providence of God described in 8:28 is understood by Origen and interpreters beginning with Barth as an orchestration of events for the people of God—usually defined in this locus as Christians—in light of future existence with God in the eschaton. The actual meaning of predestination is expanded to include the exercise of human purpose by Origen and Chrysostom, limited to God's exclusive volition by the later Augustine and Luther, and once again expanded by Barth, first in a temporal sense and second in a christological sense.

This locus does not fit neatly into the argument of this book concerning the theme of Romans, for neither Origen nor any commentators except Dunn and Yeo connect it meaningfully with the Jews-Gentiles question that Origen and I consider to be the energizing motif of this letter. As the dominant interpretations of Romans begin to come from non-Western interpreters in the next century, we may see more interpretations like that of Yeo, whose reading charts the corporate and social dimensions that have often been untapped in this locus.

Locus 8

Not Willing or Running (9:16–19)

This is very strong wine and the most complete meal, solid food for those who are perfect.

Luther on Romans 9:16[1]

In this locus we step beyond the first eight chapters of Romans and into the section in which Paul deals with Israel, Romans 9–11. In the two millennia of conversations about Romans, Augustine and Luther have played major roles in focusing attention on the first eight chapters of Romans as the most significant. Augustine's battles employed Romans 5 and 7 against the Pelagians. He also wrote on Romans 9, which we begin to enter with this locus. Since Luther took part of Augustine's teachings on Romans and radicalized them into his doctrine of justification by faith alone, Romans became valuable as the letter that describes the approach of the individual soul to God, and this approach was primarily located in chapters 1–8. My friend Richard Pervo recounts how he took three different Romans classes in Lutheran schools and in all three of them the professor never took the class beyond chapter 8.[2] Jürgen Becker's statement on Romans 1–8 is typical of this past preoccupation: "Romans 1–8 does present the last unfolding of the Pauline gospel."[3] Romans 9–11 was then for centuries viewed as simply a "parenthesis" or "tangent" in which Paul talked about Israel. The marginalization of chapters 9–11 occurred over time as commentators mined these chapters of Romans for what they could offer on the question of the predestination of individuals while ignoring what the chapters say about the people of Israel.

95

Luther continued such a focus. Even in *On the Jews and Their Lies* there are very few references to this section of Romans. Barth's *Romans II* reads Israel in these chapters as the symbol of human religion. It would only be later in his career that he would start to see the centrality of Israel in Pauline and Christian theology. It is primarily exegesis of Romans that has occurred after the Holocaust that has observed how the people of Israel are present throughout the letter to the Romans. Now chapters 9–11 are more frequently called the "center" of the letter rather than a "tangent." For people still stuck in the model that views all of Paul's letters as divided into the halves of doctrine and practice, the doctrine section has now expanded from chapters 1–8 to chapters 1–11. At the beginning of locus 12, however, I shall take up again the matter of the halving of this letter.

The main questions in this locus are the identity of the voice(s) in this section and the purpose of Paul's reference to Pharaoh. Is Paul the only speaker in this section or is an imaginary opponent given voice here? Is God's intervention in Pharaoh's life the norm or a special situation that illustrates the power God can wield?

ORIGEN

While this is the first place in Paul's letter where the verb "will" is used in connection with human volition, the question of the human will has already been broached in Origen's commentary. Origen responds to the first Pauline theologians, the Gnostics of the second century who taught that all human natures were fixed (determined) and relied on Romans to present their deterministic model of the world. So the impression that many readers of Romans have, that this book— perhaps of all the books in the Bible—touches on questions of determinism and free will, is something we Western readers have inherited at least from Origen. Never mind that Paul was more interested in Israel's corporate destiny than he was in a philosophical statement about an individual's place along the "free" to "determined" continuum. The challenge has been set before us by the first Pauline theologians, and in the Western church this challenge has been replayed in different generations—Origen against the Gnostics, Augustine against the Pelagians, Luther against Erasmus—with claims for orthodoxy switching between sides. This reputation of Romans is arguably confirmed by the very beginning of Origin's commentary. In his exegesis of what the phrases "called apostle" and "separated to the gospel of God" mean, Origen immediately jumps to the question of God's predestination of individuals. His basic strategy is to say that Paul can speak of God predestining or calling Paul because God foresaw Paul's meritorious life. This interpretation does not begin with Origen; it began at least a century before, where we find it in the *Shepherd of Hermas*. But Origen will turbocharge this interpretation so that it becomes persuasive and useful for Pelagius, and it will live on then through the popular commentary of Pelagius for over a millennium.[4]

We may begin our survey of Origen on this locus by noting that he takes the question in the middle of 9:14 ("Is there injustice with God?") to be spoken by an opponent of Paul, an imaginary sparring partner sometimes referred to as Paul's interlocutor. Origen reads Paul as responding with the "Not at all!" at the end of the verse. But then Origen takes 9:15–18 as all spoken by this opponent of Paul, supporting the questions of 9:19 ("Why does he still find fault? For who resists his will?") that Paul introduces as coming from someone else: "You will say to me then. . . ." Thus Origen teaches that the clause "It is not of the one who wills nor of the one who runs but of God who has mercy" and the two Scripture quotations that bracket this statement are all spoken by the opponent.[5]

After setting up 9:14–19 as mostly spoken by Paul's opponent, Origen explains how Paul would nuance the opponent's assertions. Origen aligns our locus, "So therefore it is not of the one who wills nor of the one who runs, but rather of God who shows mercy," with Psalm 127:1–2 and 1 Corinthians 3:6–7. These two texts do not imply that humans are not to invest any effort in working for God, he writes. Rather, humans work and God works. God gives the blessing without which any human effort is in vain (Ps. 127:1–2), but Origen points out that still the text does not imply that human builders do nothing. In 1 Corinthians 3:6–7 as well, Paul does not deny real actions that he and Apollos have done in establishing the Corinthian church. But it is ultimately God who "gave the increase" according to Paul. So here too Origen says that Paul is not saying that humans do not exercise their will or cooperate in their salvation, but that in comparison with God's saving activity, such human agency may be regarded as nothing. Those who are convinced that humans do not have a free will and that Paul is saying that God predestines all people as God sees fit may not find this controversial, since they too would agree that God is the more potent agent of salvation when compared to merely human agents. But note that Origen does retain a place for human activity in salvation: "It is assuredly pious and religious, while God and man do what is in themselves, to attribute the chief part of the work to God rather than to man."[6] Origen concludes this section by agreeing that no one resists God's will, but that the question of 9:19 ("Why does [God] still find fault?") is unnecessary ("*superfluum ergo . . .*"), since people make choices as independent moral agents: "That we may be good or evil depends on our will; but that the evil man should be appointed for punishments of some sort and the good man for glory of some sort depends on the will of God."[7]

AUGUSTINE

Already in *On Eighty-three Varied Questions*, Augustine affirms that 9:16 is true. The early Augustine here affirms that God does show mercy and harden those God wants, but this is done justly, in response to the merits hidden inside people.[8] In discussing 9:15–21 in proposition 62, Augustine says that Pharaoh deserved or merited the hardness of heart inflicted on him because of earlier infidelity.[9] He is therefore at pains to say that God did not arbitrarily harden Pharaoh, but that the ultimate responsibility for the hardening of Pharaoh belongs to Pharaoh himself. This same idea is voiced in *On Eighty-three Varied Questions*, the basis for God's predestination, whether for salvation or judgment, is located in people's previous behavior.[10] But Augustine goes on to say that God's call of a person precedes anything that person can do.[11] By the time we get to *To Simplicianus*, while only two years after he began writing the *Commentary on Statements in the Letter to the Romans*, the emphasis has shifted. After a lengthy discussion, Augustine concludes that Romans 9:16 ("So then, it is not of the one who wills, nor of the one who runs, but of God who has mercy") means that in the order of salvation, God's call precedes any act of the human will.[12]

Augustine also agonizes over the question of how God could "hate" Esau before he was even born. His solution is analogous to the explanation for evil that finally satisfies him in the *Confessions*.[13] Augustine uncritically accepts Paul's example of Pharaoh.[14] When God hardened Pharaoh, he simply chose not to have mercy on Pharaoh. God did not actively do something that made Esau or Pharaoh into evil people; he simply chose not to have compassion on them. Though it is not an active evil that God renders on Esau or Pharaoh, but simply the privation of compassion, it is still God who is ultimately responsible.[15] This is a definite change from what he had written two years before.[16]

Henry Chadwick claims that the essentials of Augustine's doctrine of predestination were already in place when he wrote the *Confessions*, though he would work it out, with a distinction between God's foreknowledge and predestination, when embroiled in the Pelagian controversy.[17] Augustine's doctrine of predestination thus develops in the thrust and parry of theological battle, but it also has roots in his own metaphysical assumptions. Augustine's idea of predestination seems to derive its energy from his understanding of the gravity of original sin and from his insistence on the vibrant strength of divine grace.[18] At the same time, in ways that prefigure Barth, Augustine has a clear idea of Christ as the predestined one in whom believers find their own identity.[19] The difference between our spiritual identity and that of Christ is keyed to our sinful nature: Augustine reminds Julian of Eclanum that Christ inhabited only the likeness of sinful flesh (Rom. 8:3), while the rest of humanity inhabits sinful flesh itself.[20] This reminder that the old Augustine gives Julian has roots in an earlier battle Augustine fought.

Augustine drew early impetus for his emphasis on predestination from his controversy with the Donatists. Their idea that the church was an isolated, pure group seemed to Augustine to deny the predestination of the church to expand and take over the world.[21] The emphasis on a church that is built on those elite who can keep themselves pure ran against Augustine's dynamic vision of a church that contained a continuum of members, from sinners to saints. It is this vision of a church that prompts Augustine to read Romans 9 in a more predestinarian way in *To Simplicianus*. His exegesis of Romans 9 in *To Simplicianus* is not the result of an academic or pristine reassessment of the text. His exegesis is rather the result of a desire to preserve the church for everyone. In this sense Augustine's

exegesis of Romans follows his responses to ecclesiastical and theological challenges; it does not serve as the primary catalyst for Augustine's responses.[22]

The insistent claim that humans have freedom in exercising their wills, both
before and after baptism, limits the role of the Divine in such texts as Romans
9:16—"So then, it does not depend on the one who wills nor on the one who
runs, but on God who has mercy." Augustine had written Simplicianus on this
text that "the power to will he has willed should be both his and ours, his because
he calls us, ours because we follow when called. But what we actually will he alone
gives, i.e., the power to do right and to live happily for ever."[23] Pelagius follows
Origen by insisting that Paul is taking the voice of someone who questions. Paul
himself cannot say this and thus take away human freedom and responsibility,
according to Pelagius, because in 2:4 Paul mentions divine kindness that leads to
repentance, in 2 Timothy 2:20–21 (a text Origen uses to explain locus 9 on Rom.
9:20–23) Paul says that one can cleanse oneself from being a vessel for common
use and become one for noble use, in 2 Timothy 4:7 Paul describes his life as a
race he has run, and in 1 Corinthians 9:24 Paul instructs his audience to run.

Origen's explicit commentary on this locus is now available only in Rufinus's
translation.[24] As he worked on it in early-fifth-century Rome, one can imagine
the relevance he thought it would have. There was tremendous interest in Western readers regarding Paul's example of Pharaoh in this text. The anonymously
written *On the Hardening of Pharaoh's Heart* is evidence of this. Note how its
author caricatures a God who predestines people by his power alone, without
regard for the freedom of the human will, in order to discredit a form of predestination that does not take seriously the exercise of the human will.

> But because the will of God is in every way good, "he turns it" [the king's
> heart; Prov. 21:1] here and there as reason and justice dictate, not by power
> alone. If therefore he creates such a kind who would be forsaken by God,
> there comes a spirit who with the devil is called "a forge" and it is necessar-
> ily like clay hardened by fire. Of course the Lord was foreseeing the heart of
> Pharaoh sagging toward evil and inflamed from below by the devil to burn
> for the destruction of the blameless; he let himself harden his heart for this,
> as it is said, that he would abandon the rather dull unfeeling heart that was
> keeping them [the Jews]; so that after being beaten for a long time its func-
> tion was displayed rather late, the choice of free will, which is naturally
> maintained. Because he exercises it with reason, not with power, the free-
> dom of the will is not subject to an earlier decision, through which in the
> ruin of all things an alien creator God is made known, who therefore threat-
> ens torments, not recognizing whom he kills or damns in eternal fire.[25]

The rhetorically charged language of this text illustrates the intensity with which
the predestination–free will debate raged in Western Christianity around the turn
of the fifth century. Pharaoh is not regarded as an exceptional case, but rather as
someone whom God let harden himself, along with some help from below.

Pelagius completed his commentary on the Pauline epistles; Augustine never
finished his. But still, due to Alaric's invasion of Rome in 410 and Augustine's

more secure ecclesiastical position, Augustine had the last word.[26] North Africa had become a temporary refuge for Pelagius and his disciple Caelestius, and it was Augustine the North African, newly victorious over the elitist Donatists, who would now recognize another form of elitism in the Pelagian revolution.[27] Augustine served as an officer in military intelligence for the church. It was indeed Augustine who by 411 had put the pieces of the puzzle together, linking Caelestius with Pelagius and framing their teachings into a system that attacked divine grace and the true identity of the church.[28] Augustine's self-appointment to guard duty for the church would continue for years. In 417 he would write a letter that included a summary of what really happened at the synod in Palestine that declared Pelagius free of heresy.[29]

The late Augustine is known for a rigid predestinarian reading of these texts of Romans. While some of his advocates continue to claim that Augustine always taught that people made real choices, Augustine himself writes of his transition on the exegesis of Romans as an experience in which divine grace triumphs over the human will: "I have tried hard to maintain the free choice of the human will, but the grace of God prevailed."[30]

ABELARD

Without mentioning Origen, Abelard follows the unacknowledged ancestor by describing verses 16–18 as written from the perspective of Paul's opponents.[31] Abelard explains the Scripture quotation (v. 17) regarding the good job God does in raising up Pharaoh as Paul's attempt to show this position as morally unacceptable. "And in order to increase God's culpability, he adds: 'in order to show in you,' etc.: as if he damned some for the reason that he might glorify himself and seek his glory in the death of some, which seems most iniquitous."[32] This explanation of 9:17 is analogous to what contemporary interpreters of Galatians have argued: Paul at times selects the very Scriptures his opponents have been using for his own quotations in order to subvert his opponents' position.[33]

Abelard claims that Paul or one of the faithful is marked in the conversation in verse 19, with the opening phrase "You will say *to me*" (my emphasis). The word "still" (*eti*) in "Why does he still find fault" functions as grounds for indictment of this God. How could God go on finding fault with people whom God alone has raised, hardened, or pitied? Abelard seems to mean here that Paul sharpens the opponent's question to prepare for Paul's own position, in effect bringing God's faultfinding in this model to a reductio ad absurdum.

Abelard then prepares his readers for the possibility that people do resist God's will, for he offers two definitions of God's will. First, that it is whatever happens, since "God performs all he wills" (Ps. 115:3). But he ends his exegesis of 9:19 with a second definition of God's will as counsel that is not always fulfilled, citing Matthew 23:37 and 1 Timothy 2:4.

We cannot learn exactly how Abelard concludes this section until we hear him describe the potter and clay in the next locus. But it should be clear that he is definitely following in the tradition of Origen in his identification of 9:16–19 as words Paul wrote to describe what an opponent to Paul's position would say.

LUTHER

In his early lectures on Romans, Luther glossed 9:9, on the promise to Abraham regarding Isaac's birth, "He wants the sons of the promise also to be understood as the sons of election and predestination."[34] When commenting on "Jacob I have loved, but Esau I have hated" (9:13), Luther glosses with: "All these statements have been written and adduced in order that the grace of God might be commended and the presumptuousness of human powers be utterly destroyed."[35]

Luther is Augustinian in hearing Paul's own voice in 9:16. He explains that human will and exertion do matter, but that God is the one who graces the human subject so that she can will and perform actions that are the work of God.[36]

Luther notes that Paul's word for "power" in 9:17 is the same word as he uses in 9:22 (though it is a cognate word, not the same). Luther decides that this "power" must refer to God's ability to destroy. He concludes that if someone does will or run, God has had mercy on that person. If God has not had mercy, then one comes under the hardening power of God that destroys.[37] Here Luther seems to be on the same page as Augustine's *To Simplicianus* and bolder to apply perdition directly to God than Augustine. (The only Augustine explicitly cited in this context, regarding 9:21, is his *Handbook on Faith, Hope, and Love*.) For Luther, God thus actively hardens the reprobate; for Luther, the hardening of Pharaoh cannot be attributed to any agent other than God, since Paul is concerned to emphasize God's power over people.[38]

ERASMUS

On the provocative statement of 9:16 ("So it does not depend on the one who wills or runs, but on the merciful God"), Erasmus favorably cites Chrysostom's view that this is actually an antithesis, that is, an opponent's objection, which receives Paul's response in 9:20 ("Who are you, o mortal, who answers back to God?").[39] Erasmus is thus significant for the dialogue he prompted with Luther on the freedom of the will. In the humanist tradition, Erasmus published *On Free Will* in 1524, the same year that Luther stopped wearing his monk's garb. With this work, Erasmus demonstrated that he stood in continuity with a long line of philosophers and theologians who asserted that the human will was free: Plato, Carneades, Plutarch, Alexander of Aphrodisias, Justin Martyr, Origen,

Theodoret of Cyrus, and the early Augustine all considered the human will to be free.[40]

Unlike the *Annotations*, Erasmus's *On Free Will* treats Romans 9:16 as being spoken by Paul: "Just as he turns the efforts of the wicked to the benefit of the godly, so the efforts of the good do not attain the end they seek, unless they are aided by the free favor of God. Without doubt this is what Paul meant by: 'So it depends not upon man's will or exertion, but upon God's mercy' (Rom. 9:16). The mercy of God preveniently moves the will to will, and accompanies it in its effort, gives it a happy issue. And yet meanwhile we will, run, follow after—yet that which is our own let us ascribe to God to whom we wholly belong."[41]

BARTH

In *Romans I* Barth takes 9:15–18 as a lump and strongly affirms that all things come from God's will. God's choice or rejection of humanity is not performed according to human justice; it rather occurs only in accord with divine justice (*Recht*).[42] "So Moses and Pharaoh, the great preacher and deliverer of divinely covenantal grace and his hellish counterpart in history, both equally come out of the same divine workshop as what is and must be: not by virtue of a mechanical destiny, but also not by virtue of their own decision and choice of direction, but rather by virtue of the will of God, who gave form to their being and living."[43] But as his exegesis continues through chapter 9, it becomes clear that Barth does not paint a picture of a deterministic God who stands outside creation while directing its fate. Rather, Barth treats the question of 9:19 as arising from an "unconvincing" and "awkward" picture of God's rule. God's will is not some sort of fate, but is rather "our deepest freedom, question and answer, proving stone on which we test ourselves, what becomes for us either a cornerstone or a rock of offence. . . . O human! When will you have respect before God? When will you quit representing your God to yourself as a blindly working foreign substance? When will you grasp that God's will has no why and acknowledge this, since he is not a mechanism that pushes from the outside, but rather is your own creative life? When will you truly acknowledge God and yourself?"[44] We see here the beginning of what would become the double agency for which Barth argues in his *Church Dogmatics*.[45] Here in *Romans I* there is no impulse to separate God from the creature. The misreading of a mechanistic determinism is resisted simply by asserting that Creator and creature are related intimately in the unfolding of the will of God.

In *Romans II* Barth again wants to affirm the potency of God's election and the impotence of all human willing and running when seeking to give an account for the course of events. But against *Romans I*, Barth emphasizes more strongly the distance between God and humanity. As in *Romans I*, Barth refers to Moses' request to see God in Exodus 33, a natural exegetical move, since Paul quotes Exodus 33:19 in Romans 9:15. But Barth adds something in *Romans II*: Exodus

33:20—"And we must not forget how the passage continues:—*Thou canst not see my face; for no man shall see me and live.*"[46] The emphasis on the simultaneous rejection and election by God is new in *Romans II*. This emphasis is captured by Barth's meditative exegesis of the context of Paul's quotation from Exodus 33. We have just seen how in *Romans II* he emphasizes the fatal nature of a look at God. He goes on to exegete the actual theophany in Exodus 33 in a similar way: "How can we comprehend election, save as the transformation of our rejection? Even Moses could see God only when he took up his position—in the cleft of the rock: and then he only saw Him from behind, as he passed by. . . . To see Him otherwise would involve our death."[47]

The mechanistic stereotype of election and reprobation is resisted in *Romans II* first of all by an emphasis on the universal reprobation under which all humanity stands. This stereotype is resisted in a second way in *Romans II* by an emphasis on the otherness of God as primal source (*Ursprung*), in sharp difference with the emphasis of *Romans I* on the immanence of Creator and creature: "The freedom of God confronts men neither as a mechanism imposed upon them from outside nor as their own active and creative life (see the 1st edition of this book!). The freedom of God is the pure and primal Origin of men: the Light, the presence or absence of which renders their eyes brightness or darkness—the Infinite, by the twofold measurement of which they are great or little—the Decision, by which they stand or fall."[48] Barth therefore resists mechanistic determinism in both *Romans I* and *Romans II*. In the later work the condemnation under which all humanity stands and the distance between God and humanity come to replace the intimate collaboration of creature and creator that we saw in *Romans I*.

POST-BARTHIAN APPROACHES

New Perspective

Sanders does not mention this locus in either *Paul and Palestinian Judaism* or in the shorter *Paul*. Dunn treats 9:16 as uttered by Paul for the limited purpose of showing that God's ultimate purpose for Israel is finally conditioned not on Israel's performance but on God's choice, which is driven by mercy. Dunn like Origen notes that Paul has said plenty about human responsibility to perform good, so that this locus cannot be isolated to imply that God's election means the believer is totally passive.[49]

Israel emerges as central in this locus for the new perspective, a move Origen did not make. Calvinists will be uneasy with the way Dunn uses Paul's focus on Israel to shift the implications of this locus from a textbook explanation of how willing and running interact with God's mercy: "It is important to bear in mind the chief focus and thrust of Paul's argument. It is an in-house Jewish argument. In responding to those who make great play of Israel's covenant responsibility as an integral part of God's electing purpose, Paul naturally puts all the emphasis on the divine initiative. He is not at this point attempting a fuller and more rounded exposition." Dunn goes on to show that the general statements at the beginnings of chapters 6–8 have to be read along with the descriptions of human responsibility that follow later in those chapters. In this context, Dunn marks the introduction of human responsibility as beginning at 9:30.[50]

Calvinist Approaches

Some adult converts to what is called a "Reformation faith," whether locating Luther or Calvin as their apical ancestor, continue to emphasize the divine election of individuals in history and to minimize or eliminate the place of the human will in the order of salvation. When I taught Romans for the first time to undergraduate students I invited my Calvinist friend, the Romans scholar Tom Schreiner, to speak to my class. He noted that the questions in 9:14 and 19 ("There is no unrighteousness with God, is there?" "Why does he still find fault? For who resists his will?") flow naturally from reading 9:11–13 as he reads them, that God elects specific individuals in history.[51] What is most memorable about that guest lecture was the opposition it aroused in one of my students. She stood up and said that this determinism applied to individuals made her very angry. The student's response illustrates how not everyone, as we saw in Origen's and Abelard's positions above, can agree that for God to elect some and damn others, independent of their willing or running, is a clear testimony to God's righteousness.[52] Any claim that this does illustrate God's righteousness would do well to distinguish between this sort of righteousness and capriciousness or arbitrariness, while showing how such righteousness coheres with the idea of righteousness in Paul's Scriptures.

CONCLUSION

As Romans continues to move in a full circle among the nations, many believers will be reading this letter who do not have the luxury to debate the question of free will and predestination as it has been posed in the past two millennia. Origen's insistence on real choices that people make and the pastoral sensitivity for which he is known may provide some inspiration to readers who must first understand that God elects the nobodies and marginalized of the world.[53]

Locus 9

Potter and Clay (9:20–23)

If one regards this comparison as an allegory of the ultimate consequence, then it is God who is on the scene with human nature, before each act to intervene in the physical world according to a moral order. And in that case this naturally suits the system of Calvin and determinism, since the clay is passive under the potter's hands. God by himself determines which person will be good and which person will be evil, to conduct some to glory and others to infamy; he is the cause of evil as well as of good. But the hands of the potter are never blamed for the vessels that are constructed for vulgar use. And consequently the allegory will be deficient without speaking of the moral teaching of Paul, which is absolutely contrary to this fatalism.

M.-J. Lagrange[1]

The main questions in this locus are the identification of which Old Testament potter text is most behind Paul's use of the metaphor and how the "vessels of wrath" statement functions in Paul's argument.

ORIGEN

On the vessels made for honor and dishonor Origen refers to Jeremiah 18:2–6, where God can start over and remake a vessel if at first it crumbles. He also refers to Sirach 27:5, a metaphorical description of temptation as a furnace testing the potter's jars. But his main resource is 2 Timothy 2:20–21, which he identifies as similar because he hears Paul describing humans as vessels there as well. In this text, Origen claims that Paul explicitly portrays the basis on which some vessels are designated for honor and others for dishonor, a matter on which Romans 9 is silent.

The basis is the human agent's own moral condition. When a person cleanses oneself, then one becomes a vessel for honor (2 Tim. 2:21). From here he goes back to the Jacob and Esau portrait in Romans 9:10–13 and says that Jacob cleansed his life and was morally pure. God knew the pure condition of Jacob's soul even before he was born, and in response God said, "Jacob I have loved; Esau I have hated."[2] The potter and clay reference in verses 20–21 therefore means that God's dealings with people can change depending on their disposition toward God.

Origen begins his commentary on the "What if" section of this locus (9:22–23) by noting its syntactical infelicity: "We have often commented on the awkward expressions of the apostle and their defects, which are found in the present place as well. For he has not completed what he says in the beginning of the section, 'What if God, willing?'"[3] Origen cites 11:16b as another example of this sort of anacoluthon. But he says that the actual sense of 9:22–23 is easily discerned. It is that God bears with much patience those unbelievers who deserve punishment in order to give them opportunity to repent and to show his glory to those people who do believe and receive God's mercy.[4] He thus reads the end of the comparison, verse 23, as the whole point of the comparison.

For Origen, then, the point of the potter and clay analogy is that God the potter works in relation to the clay to make appropriate vessels. The clay vessel's disposition or response to the potter affects how the potter shapes and treats these vessels. The vessels fit for destruction in 9:22 are not highlighted by Origen as individuals that God handpicks for hell. They are rather people with whom God is being patient, so that they and others may inherit God's glory.

AUGUSTINE

Number 68 of *On Eighty-three Varied Questions* is a lengthy discussion of 9:20 in its context. Pharaoh is hardened for previously committed sins, which is certainly just and a clear example of how God hands sinners over to an unfit mind.[5] In this early work we still have a respect for the human will that will disappear in Augustine's later works. Because God's peace comes to men of goodwill (Luke 2:14), human willing here is prior to God's mercy. But even this willing arises from God's call and from the way God produces the willing inside us.[6]

By his letter *To Simplicianus*, Augustine chooses to explicate the potter analogy of Romans 9 with the quotation of Sirach 33:10–15.[7] Here we come to what is now considered "Augustinian" when discussing the human will: "Free will is most important. It exists, indeed, but of what value is it in those who are sold under sin?"[8] Humans, whom Augustine describes as created from the mass of sin, cannot be free to choose God. God's mercy must call and stimulate the wills of those created as vessels of mercy. The vessels of wrath, called by Augustine "vessels of perdition"—such as Pharaoh and his army—are indeed created by God to help the vessels of mercy repent, enter God's salvation, and so accent God's glory in comparison to the vessels of wrath.[9]

Slightly after this time, Augustine links Romans 9:20 with the benediction at the end of chapter 11. Since Paul knew God's ways to be unsearchable, what right does anyone else have to question God?[10] This is the straightforward reading of 9:20 that ignores how Paul is answering back to God and wrestling with his Scriptures for all of chapters 9–11.

For Augustine, the potter analogy comes to mean that God is the potter who unilaterally shapes the clay. There is no meaningful give and take between the clay and the potter, such as we see in Jeremiah 18. Augustine is influenced here only by Paul's explicit quotation of Isaiah 29:16 in Romans 9:20. The vessels of wrath are prepared by God for destruction, since God chooses not to show mercy on them. Like Pharaoh, they are real people earmarked for hell.

ABELARD

Abelard identifies the apostle in this verse now speaking for himself in answer to the opponent's objections that were raised in 9:16–19, which seemed to frame God as responsible for human faults. Abelard finds Paul's use of the parable of the potter to refute thoroughly the opponent's objections. Paul's "O human being" identifies a carnal, more bestial than spiritual person whose retort to God is similar to the question Paul allowed him to voice in 9:14—"Is there unrighteousness with God?" Paul's point is that the matter formed out of clay really cannot question the potter.[11]

Abelard argues that verse 21 shows that the potter can make vessels for different uses. If the potter can do this, who does not even make the clay, God has an even greater right, who is not only the potter but also the creator of the clay.

He continues on in this verse to argue that even supposed mishaps can be used by God, supporting his assertion "from even Plato in his *Timaeus*: 'Nothing happens,' he says, 'without legitimate ground or reason preceding its origin.'"[12] From here he cites Origen's example of Judas, used here by Abelard as a bridge to his discussion of vessels of wrath that will follow:

> For who of the faithful does not know, what wonderful use came of that highest impiety of Judas, by whose accursed betrayal the redemption of the whole human race was effected? How most definitely beneficial what was effected by the sin of Judas than by Peter's righteousness, and the evil work of this one has a better and longer advantage than the good work of that one—not, I say, as far as it pertains to Judas, but for the benefit of the common whole, which is the family always prioritized. Indeed, by Peter's preaching and life example some were converted and saved, but by that transaction of Judas all were converted into salvation, which was also effected by Father and Son equally, but with different intention. So however many evils might occur, they are ordained by divine will for the best; and in all things, which he performs or allows to be performed, he himself creates causes, although they are hidden and inscrutable to us, why evidently he thus acts or allows to happen. Otherwise he would do or permit some things irrationally.[13]

Abelard's "Question" section that follows, still on 9:21, is raised to investigate whether there is inequity with God. The answer is that this locus is arguing against such inequity; the fault is with the sick person who does not acccept the medicine.[14]

Abelard's exegesis seems to be more on the side of Origen than Augustine when he exegetes the "vessels of wrath" verse (9:22). Abelard emphasizes that God is not responsible for the condemnation of a Pharaoh or Esau. Rather, Abelard says that 9:22 shows that God shows patience to someone like Pharaoh so that he might come to his senses. When Pharaoh proved himself to be incorrigible, then God used his evil for the best advantage of others.[15]

For Abelard the influence of an approach like Origen's is apparent. As we saw in the last chapter, he follows Origen by identifying Romans 9:16–19 as spoken by Paul's opponent. The potter and clay analogy is here taken as a logical response to Paul's opponent. Though God is free to make any sort of clay and any sort of vessel (à la Augustine), the sunny side of the vessels of wrath are emphasized in Abelard's example of Judas Iscariot, through whose sin God brought great good. And in continuity with Origen's general approach, all vessels of wrath are given judgment because of meaningful choices they have made, after God has waited for them to repent.

LUTHER

Luther glosses the patience of God on the vessels of wrath by explaining that God lets the reprobate rule over the elect and do whatever they want to them, all in order to prepare the elect for life in glory. Paul's word *katērtismena,* which describes how the vessels of wrath are related to destruction (9:22), Luther helpfully translates differently from Paul's different term *proētoimasen* that describes how the vessels of mercy are related to glory (9:23), though he then glosses the former verb with a cognate word, *parata,* to what he used in 9:23, *praeparauit.*[16]

Luther has a scholium on 9:21 in which he quotes Augustine's statement that God is entirely just to condemn every human being and would remain just if not a single person were saved from this condemnation. Luther emphasizes that the main point of Paul here is to destroy all human presumption. In an echo of Augustine, Luther says that God's grace intervenes even before the human will can respond to God.[17]

In his glosses and scholium on the potter who has the right to make fancy and common dishes from the same lump of clay, Luther misses Paul's allusion to Jeremiah 18. This is significant, for in the Jeremiah passage there is a strong case made for repentance from the human side changing God's decree concerning a given people (Jer. 18:7–11). By missing this allusion, Luther situates himself firmly in the tradition of the late Augustine: people are divinely willed either to salvation or damnation, and there is no effective role for the human will in our passage to either destination.

CALVIN

In his *Institutes*, Calvin takes Augustine's call not to question God and follows him in forbidding any inquiry into the reasons behind God's election and reprobation.[18] Rather than granting humans any freedom, Calvin then silences the objection that humans cannot be held responsible by reasserting that God does not simply foreknow the future but determines it.[19]

Calvin's Romans commentary is fascinating for its explicit comment on how Paul is using the Old Testament for his potter analogy: "He represses this arrogance of contending with God by a most appropriate metaphor, in which his allusion seems to have been to Isa. 45.9 rather than Jer. 18.6. The one truth which we learn from Jeremiah is that Israel is in the hand of the Lord, so that, on account of its sins, God may break it in pieces, as a potter does his vessel of clay. But Isaiah goes further. 'Woe unto him,' he says, 'that striveth with his maker.'"[20] Origen finds more than that "one truth" in Jeremiah 18.

Calvin's attention to detail is apparent in his paragraph on the two words that begin 9:22, "What if?" Calvin says that these function to make the "elliptical" sentence in the following two verses into a question whose implication is, "Who then can accuse God of unrighteousness or arraign Him? For nothing but the most perfect rule of righteousness is here to be seen."[21] The elliptical question here is definitely at the center of the varying interpretations of this locus. Calvin's explanation is that the question is simply asking if anything is wrong with God delaying the destruction he has prepared for the vessels of wrath in order to display his power more effectively.[22]

For Calvin the potter and clay analogy functions to show God's righteousness in mysteriously choosing some and damning others. We must be careful not to caricature Calvin's theology as all about predestination. John Hesselink helpfully notes how Calvin simply takes up Augustine's doctrine on this point in order to explain why some responded to the preaching of the gospel while others did not. Also, the doctrine provided a real anchor for faith and motivation for witness among Calvin's flock. Calvin makes no attempt to distinguish between God's action in preparing vessels of wrath or vessels of mercy in his commentary, thus confirming his reputation as someone who teaches double predestination, though Hesselink asserts that Calvin did not hold the decrees of election and reprobation as symmetrical decrees in the divine economy.[23]

BARTH

Barth uses the term *Ursprung* in his exegesis of 9:21 in *Romans I*. But he uses it to emphasize God's complete right to make of creation whatever he wants.[24] In *Romans II* the term is used to show the disjunction between God's election and human conceptions of causality. God's election is not simply an approval of some humans, for all humans stand under his reprobation. God's election is not something that can be traced into the world of time, for God exists in eternity: "God confronts men as their Primal Origin, not as their immediate cause. . . . God must be apprehended as the God of Jacob and of Esau; otherwise we shall not understand that, whilst He is, in every moment of time, the God of Esau, He is in eternity the God of Jacob." He ends the paragraph by observing how the complete disjunction between God and humanity securely protects the idea of human responsibility.[25]

Bakker notes how Barth's teaching on election in *Romans II* is grounded differently than Calvin's teaching. He finds an agreement between *Romans II* and the *Church Dogmatics* on this teaching, for both works picture election as happening outside time, in God's relationship with Jesus Christ. Barth therefore does not place predestination under the theological locus of providence as Aquinas and then Protestant theologians did. The difference between *Romans II* and the *Church Dogmatics* occurs in emphasis. In *Romans II* Barth pictures God's election as an exercise of divine freedom; in the *Church Dogmatics* he pictures election as an exercise of divine love.[26]

Barth is as adamant to fight the interpretation of this locus as teaching the predestination of individuals irrespective of their own choice or behavior as is Origen, the unacknowledged ancestor of later Romans commentators. Still we cannot smooth over real discontinuities. Origen has a much more robust view of the human's effort on the path toward righteousness than Barth, who writes as a true child of the Reformation. Barth's affirmation of the reprobation of all humanity and their simultaneous election is without parallel in the history of exegesis. The parallels between Origen and Barth consist in their refusal to take the easy way out in their exegesis and affirm a unilateral and individual view of predestination such as depicted in Augustine's *To Simplicianus*, later solidified by Luther. Barth differs from Origen, for no one before had said that the vessels of wrath were the same people in time as the vessels of mercy were in eternity.[27] Barth's exegesis here in Romans 9 thus constitutes a revolutionary move, rendering as chimerical the theologoumenon that appeared solid for a millennium and a half, the idea that arose from a reading of Romans 9 of God's directly causal determination of individuals' destinies.[28] Barth's later focus on God's election of Christ has served as a resource for commentators who wish to explain that God's election is not arbitrary or does not include the damnation of humans.[29]

POST-BARTHIAN APPROACHES

New Perspective

While Sanders does not comment explicitly on this locus, his standard approach to the question of predestination is to assert that the Judaisms of Paul's day, perhaps except the Sadducees, all affirmed both human responsibility in the exercise of a free will and some form of predestination.[30]

Dunn notes how *plassein*, the verb for the potter's activity in 9:20, is also used of God's election of Israel, emphasizing that the place of Israel within the divine activities of creating and electing is the unifying theme for chapters 9–11.[31] He argues that the picture of God's authority to make whatever God chooses from a lump of clay does not concern individuals at a final judgment, but rather "Israel's sense of *national* distinctiveness."[32] Paul counters the standard Jewish link between God's patience and vessels of mercy by linking this patience with the vessels of wrath, all for the sake of overthrowing Jewish particularism, not expressly to weigh in on the philosophical question of predestination versus free will.[33]

The new perspective differs from Origen in reading all of chapters 9–11 as more Israel-centered than Origen did. The unacknowledged ancestor is too threatened by Gnostic fatalism to keep the exegesis of these chapters driven by the question of God's election of Israel, rather than the philosophical question of predestination versus free will. Still, in the practical result of the new perspective, plenty of room is reserved for the exercise of the human will. Proponents of the new perspective are thus not scaling the mountain range of Romans 9–11 by finding the individual's place within God's plan of salvation; their approach is rather similar to Origen's sensitivity to ethnic Israel (that we shall see in locus 11) and insistence on a robust role for human will.

Narrative-Based Approach

In a manner distinct from the new perspective, exegetes who read Romans with a narrative substructure of God's relationship with Israel in view find Paul "thinking analogically about the role of Israel in God's plan and the saving work God has done in Jesus Christ."[34] In her exegesis of this passage Grieb writes, "Now [Paul] is forging an imaginative connection between the smashed vessel of Jesus Christ for the sake of sinners with the possible destruction of Israel, a vessel perhaps destined for destruction for the sake of the formation of the messianic people of God. That thought is terrible enough to make anyone break off in mid-sentence. . . ."[35] In explanation of her exegetical insight regarding this analogy or "connection" between Israel's role and Christ's role, Grieb cites Nils Dahl's insight that Paul is indebted to the Akedah here and Barth's *Church Dogmatics* section on Jesus as God's elect one.[36]

CONCLUSION

Paul's discussion of the potter and the clay comes from an ample lump of such texts in Paul's Scriptures. He does quote from Isaiah when using the analogy. One cause of the difference in the exegesis that we have surveyed is the identification of which texts Paul wants us to hear when he uses the analogy.

The precise point of the elliptical question in 9:22–23 is also a gap that is completed differently. For some it is a textbook definition of predestination. For others, it is Paul's first approach at an explanation for why not all Israel believes in the Messiah Paul proclaims.

Locus 10

Christ the *Telos* of the Law (10:4)

This word which is most alien to Christ yet signifies Christ.

Martin Luther on the law[1]

The primary question in this locus is what the word *telos* means. It is usually explained as meaning either "end" in the sense of termination or "goal" in the sense of fulfillment.

ORIGEN

On 10:4 ("Christ is the end of the law for righteousness for those who believe"), Origen says that "the end of the law" means the perfection or completion of the law (*perfectio legis*). He writes that the righteousness of Christ is only for believers, so that unbelievers do not have Christ and therefore do not possess the completion of the law. He also writes that the completion of the law that comes through Christ brings eternal life, since Jesus is both righteousness and the source of eternal life. By contrast, Leviticus 18:5 promises only life for the righteousness from the law, not eternal life.[2]

Besides the exegetical precedent of distinguishing between senses of "law" noted above at Origen's exegesis of the "made righteous by Christ" locus of Romans 3:21–28, there are two other points of significance in Origen's treatment of law. Riemer Roukema correctly observes that the repeated identification of *nomos* as natural law "actualizes" Paul's letter for the Gentile, allowing everything that Paul asserts about the Jews and the law of Moses to be equally valid, mutatis mutandis, for the Gentiles. (This is not dissimilar from Barth's move, a millennium and a half later, to read "religion" when he finds "law" or "Judaism" in Romans.) Thus for Origen the intersection of Mosaic law with Jewish humanity is mirrored by the intersection of natural law with Gentile humanity.[3] A final point of significance is also that Origen is basically pessimistic about "law" in most of its occurrences in Romans. The "natural law" is not the same as the law of faith.[4] While Paul says "you have died to the law," Origen rectifies the inconsistency in Paul's analogy by equating this letter of the law with the man in Paul's analogy of 7:3–4, and thus he says what Paul has chosen not to say: the law is dying.[5] Nor is the Mosaic law in its literal sense a helpful tool for reaching divine salvation. Pelagius reacts against this pessimism by granting "law" an energizing, salvific potential, but it is Origen's pessimistic appraisal of "law" that wins out in the history of Romans exegesis.

Elsewhere in his commentary, in an exegetical move that would remain paradigmatic for Christian exegetes for at least another millennium, Origen notes that the Mosaic law must be understood not according to the letter, but according to the spirit. Origen begins with the phrase "whom I serve in my spirit" in 1:9 and connects it to "the letter kills but the spirit brings to life" (2 Cor. 3:6). From there he draws a connection with "For when the law was weak through the flesh, God sent his own son in the likeness of sinful flesh" (Rom. 8:3). Origen then deconstructs the letter of the Mosaic law by listing commands he considers irrelevant. After quoting Paul's "the law is spiritual" of 7:14, Origen goes on to close his exegetical loop by stating that those who understand the law to be spiritual are the ones who serve God with their spirit (1:9).[6] Origen sought to steer between a Marcionite rejection of the Old Testament that still threatened the church and a judaizing tendency among some Gentile Christians, who wanted to keep the Mosaic law as literally as they could. The spiritual understanding of the law advocated by Origen would allow him to use the law allegorically and so navigate between what he perceived as extreme reactions to the Old Testament.[7]

AUGUSTINE

Augustine's favorite battle sites within Romans are chapters 3, 5, 7, and 9. Since not as much material is available regarding his comments on this specific locus, I shall consider Augustine's treatment of "law" in Romans generally, on the way to hearing what he would say on this locus.

In his early work *Commentary on Statements in the Letter to the Romans*, Augustine describes four stages of the human being: prior to law, under law, under grace, in peace. In his description of the "under law" stage, Augustine gives a classic expression of the "Lutheran" or "second use" of the law. Within this description he quotes 5:20: the law entered by stealth so that sin might abound.[8] Luther's "second use" of the law is very similar to Augustine's description of existence "under law."

Augustine always assumes that the human being passes through a stage described as "under law." We can imagine the exegesis taking a different turn here. Augustine could have said, "The person described in Romans 7, who is under the law and not yet under grace, is a Jew who was given the law. Gentiles were never given the law, and so Paul's description of a law that identifies and magnifies sin does not apply to Gentiles." But this is not what Augustine said. One of the tensions placed on the law by the author of Romans relates to the law's audience. Paul knows that the law is only given to the Jews (Rom. 3:19a; 9:4). Still, Paul in his theologizing cannot escape from the law and attaches a significance of this law to every human being (3:19b, 28–31; 10:4). Augustine concentrates only on the latter side of this tension, an influential move that will prepare the way for both the second and third uses of the law in Christian theology.

Even though Augustine could write in his early writings about an "eternal law," his early writings on Romans give no indication that he has thought about the different ways that Paul uses the concept of *nomos* in Romans.[9] By the time he came to write *To Simplicianus* (396) he began to qualify what he meant by "law." In commenting on 7:14a, "We know that the law is spiritual, but I am fleshly," Augustine says that the law cannot be fulfilled except by spiritual persons, and then he says that the closer one is aligned to "the spiritual law" the more one will fulfill the law.[10]

I have already had occasion to note in this chapter how Augustine seems to emphasize what will later come to be known as the Lutheran, or "second," use of the law. When he attempts to answer the Pelagians' accusation that he teaches that the law was given not to justify people but to make people's sin greater, he simply quotes texts from Romans in order to show that human sin is stimulated by the law, resulting in more sin.[11] Because of his emphasis on law as leading someone to Christ, Augustine represents the "end" or "termination" side in the question of how to read *telos* here.

AQUINAS

Aquinas notes that the philosophers consider the legislators' purpose in making laws is to make people just. In this case, Aquinas notes from Paul's letters (which included Hebrews in his perspective) that the Mosaic law did not reach this purpose. He cites Hebrews 7:14, Galatians 3:24 (the second use of the law text), and Psalm 119:96a to teach that the Mosaic law comes to an end. He also cites Romans 8:3 ("What the law could not do . . .") to illustrate that the Mosaic law was limited in its potency and in Christ is limited now in its lifespan. Aquinas's "*finis*" is surely, in continuity with Augustine, used in the sense of "termination."[12]

LUTHER

The heading for this chapter is Luther's early scholium on Romans 10 that captures well his approach to the Mosaic law. This law is *alienissimum a Christo*; the law is different from Christ's words of the gospel. Still, the law signifies Christ. It leads up to Christ. This approach has significant hermeneutical implications for how one reads the law. In his gloss on 10:4 Luther states that the law without Christ is nothing, since he considers the law to be reaching ahead for Christ as its "fulfillment and the consummation, the fullness, . . . its end."[13] There is no scholium directly on this verse in Luther's Romans lectures, so we will survey Luther's general view of law.

Luther's split between gospel and law continues to drive Lutheran exegesis.[14] We have already seen that Augustine has what could be called a "Lutheran" or "second use" understanding of the Mosaic law as primarily something that highlights human sin. In his scholium on 5:20, Luther's view and its dependence on Augustine are apparent. After saying that the Mosaic law "came for the increasing of sin," Luther quotes from proposition 30 of "blessed Augustine" on this letter: "By this very word he has shown that the Jews did not understand the purpose for which the Law was given. For it was not given that it might give life—for grace alone through faith gives life—but it was given to show by how many tight bonds of sin they are held who presume to fulfill the Law by their own powers."[15]

Luther follows Paul in associating the Mosaic law with sin. In his scholium on 6:14 he states that sin has mastery over everyone who is under the law: "The Law is the power or strength of sin, through which sin remains and holds dominion."[16] Thus like Augustine, Luther applies the law to humanity in general, and not simply to Israel.

Luther's exegesis of Romans 7 leads toward his new understanding of the law and the gospel. The law is not the exact opposite of the gospel. It is rather that the gospel lies beyond what the law can offer, since the gospel offers grace mediated through Christ and the Holy Spirit to the believer.[17]

The continuity that is discernible between Luther's treatment of the Mosaic law and Augustine may at some points have traveled through Staupitz. On the question of law, Staupitz writes in the tradition of Origen by distinguishing the senses of "law," and he also serves as a forerunner of what Luther would do with the law in Romans. Staupitz begins his chapter "On the Lessening of the Law's Burden" within his book *On the Execution of Eternal Predestination* with a description of how difficult natural law, Torah, and the law of Christ are to keep. These laws keep one from depending on oneself.[18] Yet paradoxically Luther can say that faith in Christ is what fulfills the Mosaic law.[19]

Luther's general position on this locus is that Christ is the termination of the law, for the law leads to faith in Christ (second use of the law). Once the law has introduced someone to Christ, it might exert some influence in civil law (first use of the law), but it does not play a role in the personal piety of the believer (third use of the law) as it does for Calvin and John Wesley.

CALVIN

As a Reformed theologian and not a Lutheran, Calvin emphasizes that the Mosaic law in its moral dimension continues to serve as a guide for the Christian. In his commentary he surprisingly begins on this locus by agreeing with Erasmus's glosses of "completion" or "perfection" for *telos*. He then shows real sensitivity to Paul's need to show that the Jews' possession and obedience to the law does not guarantee the righteousness to which the law points. The implications he offers are basically Lutheran in orientation. But in the *Institutes* Calvin invests considerable space to explicate the Decalogue in relation to the Christian, after describing the law as something to which Christ has now offered the proper understanding.[20] So Calvin has a place for the civil (first) and pedagogical (second) uses of the law, but on the question of the Christian's relationship to the law, Calvin is most known for his emphasis to Christians that they live while consciously measuring their lives against the moral claims of the law. In that sense he would read *telos* as "goal," since the Christian is still to use it for a guide. Calvin's influence even spills over to John Wesley, who explains 10:4 in an attack against what could be construed as a Lutheran dismissal of the law.[21] Wesley is adamant that Christ is not in every way the law's termination. Christians still need to look to the law for guidance in their living.

BARTH

On the question of Paul's relationship to the law, Barth treats the term "Law" (his capitalization) as equivalent to the Bible and religion. There is no significant change discernible between Barth's treatment of the law in the two editions of his commentary. In the first edition he states that the law comes to a place of honor because it does just what it is supposed to do, though he admits that "the law outside the power of God, as self-standing mass, as mere object of knowledge, as challenge that itself judges humanity who cannot follow it—this law has henceforth disappeared and shall not rise again."[22]

If anything, Barth becomes more positive toward the law in his second edition. There is no negative qualification of this sort in the second edition, no admission by Barth that there is sense in which the law has passed into oblivion.[23] In the second edition, even where Paul criticizes the Jew for relying on the law (Rom. 2:17), Barth does not criticize the law in his paraphrase: "Thou art stamped with the marks of the living God; and thou art busily engaged in preserving these marks."[24]

For Barth in the second edition, the law is the sign of God's judgment over the historical, temporal realm in which humanity exists and is therefore highly significant. We can see Barth affirming this significance as he proceeds from God as the starting point on this question of the value of the law: "We demand the subjection of all human being and having and doing under the divine judgement, precisely in order that it may always and everywhere await the divine justification, and because, seen from God and for God, nothing can ever be lost."[25] Since Barth starts with God in his exegesis of the texts in Romans that deal with law, he cannot relegate the law into insignificance. The law is a sign from God, and as such it is retained in Barth's theological world. When Barth stands with Paul in establishing the law, then, he is not claiming that Paul the apostle to the Gentiles observed all 613 commandments of the Torah of Moses. But he is saying that Paul's gospel affirms the authoritative command of God, and that faith appears within the affirmation of this command. The faith that the law reveals is first of all God's faithfulness, but of course Barth never separated this subjective genitive from the objective genitive. God's faithfulness includes human faith in God.[26]

On our locus that "Christ is the *telos* of the law for righteousness for those who believe" (Rom. 10:4), Barth says that there is only one righteousness of God, which can come to humanity either through God's faithfulness or through keeping the law. Since the goal of the law is the righteousness of God, he says that the church is "concerned with the law." He goes on to express the wish that the church would know how to use the law as a signpost to God.[27]

In his affirmation of the law in *Romans II*, Barth seems both Reformed and Lutheran. He is Reformed in the sense that he sees no essential separation between the righteousness that comes from performance of the law and the righteousness that comes from faith in Christ. The continuity that he sees between the law and Christ and the ease with which he claims the law for the church makes him appear Reformed. Yet he is Lutheran in that he considers the law to point beyond itself to Christ. In this vein he writes that the law is not an end in itself; one gets the sense that Barth is quite comfortable with Paul's picture of the law as a tutor who leads to Christ (Gal. 3:24), a picture Luther emphasized. I am not simply claiming that Barth had a place for the second use of the law, as Calvin and any Reformed theologian who reads Galatians 3 do. Rather, I am saying that in the way Barth locates the law in the realm of the transient, "as a human possibility," he acknowledges that the law might point to Christ but holds resolutely to its ultimate illegitimacy in a way Calvin and even Luther never do. (The strongest contrast to a previous Romans commentator would be to Tyndale, who thought that the central message of Romans was God's law.) Perhaps the tension between Barth's emphasis on the second and third uses of the law can best be illustrated by a quotation in which Barth leaves the law floating ambiguously between heaven and earth: "The law has its invisible foundation and meaning from God; and we are bound to search it out (iii.31). This is the relative justification of the whole acceptance and confession and defence of religion. But, as a human possibility, it manifestly appears and has its reality in history, it is woven into the texture of men, it belongs mentally and morally to the old world, and stands in the shadow of sin and death. The DIVINE possibility of religion can never be changed into a human possibility."[28] Barth therefore dialectically emphasizes both the second and third uses of the law and so would translate *telos* both as "termination" and as "goal."

BEYOND THE NEW PERSPECTIVE

Dunn explains what has come to an end in 10:4 as "the law misunderstood as a means of establishing and fixing firmly righteousness as Israel's special prerogative."[29] In other words, Paul is not saying that the God-given Torah itself is coming to an end, or that the text of the Mosaic law is a problem. It is rather how it has been used to divide believers in Jesus that must come to termination in Christ. In its properly understood sense, Paul would say that the law is fulfilled in Christ, according to the new perspective.

Philip Alexander has helpfully called attention to the way in which the new perspective has uncritically accepted traditional Protestantism's categories: grace is good and legalism is bad. The new perspective has simply shifted first-century Judaism from the legalism category to the grace category.[30] What Simon Gathercole and others are doing is helping us see that legalism and grace were not mutually exclusive.[31] If this is so, Paul would not have been concerned primarily about the *ethnē* being kept separate from Jewish believers because of the identity badges of the law; he might have even allowed or encouraged Jewish believers to follow their law. In this reading, Paul may have defined *telos* in 10:4 as "end" or "termination" for Gentile God-fearers who had trusted in Jesus, and as "fulfillment" for Jewish believers.

But another critic of the new perspective, Francis Watson, argues from the preceding and following contexts of 10:4 to show that in Paul's usage *telos* has to mean "end." It is not simply a disposition to keep the law that is the problem; it is also the text of the law that is "implicated in the failure of Israel's quest, in its contrast to the Gentiles' unmerited success."[32] The dichotomy between the righteousness that comes by law and the righteousness that comes by faith is just too marked for Watson to find any sense of "fulfillment" in the *telos* of our locus.

CONCLUSION

This locus, coming right after Paul's comparison of Jews and Gentiles, clearly shows Paul in the position Origen finds him frequently in this letter, as a referee between Jews and Gentiles.[33] Since Paul has taken care to say that God's righteousness has come apart from the law while being witnessed to by the law (3:21), that his gospel establishes the law (3:31), and that the coming of the good and holy law triggers death in humans (7:9–12), the interpretation of this locus is highly charged. Its resolution depends on how closely one reads its context (9:30–10:13) and how one pictures Paul's understanding of first-century Jewish law observance.

Locus 11

Israel's Salvation (11:25–27)

God will give them back the free exercise of their will so that, because their unbelief did not spring from malice but from error, they may be put right and afterward be saved. . . . Paul quotes Isaiah in order to prove that God has reserved a gift for them, in order to teach that they can be set free by the same grace by which the believing Jews have already been set free, because he is not empty but always full of grace.

Ambroasiaster on Romans 11:26[1]

The main question in this locus is, Who is the Israel whose salvation Paul predicts? Some who begin their response to this question from 9:6–13 tend to say that Paul has redefined Israel, so that this locus says, "And so all Israel will be saved," in the sense that the growth of the church is already fulfilling Paul's words. Others, who start from the immediately preceding context of chapter 11 or from their assent to Origen's observation that Paul is moving back and forth between Jews and *ethnē* in this letter, read the locus as "And then all Israel will be saved," in the sense that at some future point in history, ethnic Israel as a whole will turn in faith to Jesus Christ.

ORIGEN

While the standard topoi that have driven the church's supersessionism and anti-Semitism can be found in some of Origen's writings, he rises above his generation in his openness to Jews.[2] Origen is fixated on Paul's address to both Gentiles and Israel in Romans.[3] He is sympathetic toward Torah observance practiced by Jews who believe in Jesus and by those who do not. He does not denigrate physical circumcision, for it has an allegorical relationship to inner circumcision.[4] Origen emphasizes Paul's point in Romans 11 that the Jews have not "fallen" and expresses surprise at the number who exposit Romans as if the Jews have already fallen. Origen notes that these commentators have contradicted Paul.[5] Peter Gorday well captures Origen's critical acceptance of Israel and their faith in his description of "the characteristic affirmation/critique of Judaism found throughout Origen's work: that which limited God's saving work to Judaism is overcome, while that which constituted the saving work (giving of the Law through Moses) is upheld in such a way as not to dispossess its original receivers."[6]

Given the church's record with Jews in the first four centuries of its existence, Origen's commentary is remarkably tolerant. Origen's openness toward Jews is not even erased in the translation of Rufinus, who is known for a Christian anti-Semitism typical of the late fourth and early fifth centuries.[7] His translation retains Origen's analogy of Paul in Romans as umpire between Jews and Gentiles, calling both to faith in Christ, without asking Jews to give up Torah observance and without asking Gentiles to observe the letter of this law.[8]

Origen especially emphasizes that the mystery he is sharing is directed to Gentiles who might triumph over (*insultare* in Rufinus) the Jews. To think in this way would be to focus on what is humanly noteworthy rather than on God's wisdom, and would be to neglect God's mystery. Origen even predicts that this mystery (Rom. 11:25) will be hidden from those Gentiles who triumph in their own qualifications, a prediction that came true in the nations' exegesis of this locus for well over the following millennium.[9]

Origen holds out hope for Israel's salvation by describing how Israel will see Christ and then choose to return to her first husband. His quotation of Hosea 2:7 is appropriate here, given Paul's earlier quotations from this prophet.[10] He also quotes Jeremiah 31:37 (LXX Jer. 38:35) regarding how God will never reject Israel.[11] Six million Jews would have to be executed in one generation before any Romans commentator would again think that Jeremiah 31:37 was relevant for understanding this text in Romans.

Origen states that only God, God's Son, and perhaps God's friends know who the "all Israel" are who will be saved, as well as what "the fullness of the Gentiles" means. Not all Gentiles will be saved, but only those who are within "the fullness." He is careful to note that there is a remnant of Israel that believes and is accepted by God; he therefore describes a divided Israel. The prophets' promises refer to the remnant, while their harsh words refer to those who have been blinded (Rom. 11:5).[12] The torment ahead for those who do not believe is one that leads to purification, how long this torment lasts is known only by the one who wants all to be saved and come to know the truth.[13]

Origen's commentary on this locus concludes by commanding the faithful to keep this "mystery" quietly to themselves and never to reveal it to immature ones, with a proof text on how royalty's secret must be hidden.[14] It is unfortunate that for most of the last two millennia Romans commentators have followed Origen's command so closely.

AUGUSTINE

In the *Unfinished Commentary* 2.1–5, Augustine moves from Paul's use of the words "called" and "set apart" in Romans 1:1 to an etymological presentation of the words "church" and "synagogue" to argue that "synagogue" is used more often for animals, which he claims the Bible uses as symbolism of people who are not spiritual. Despite this bias, Augustine attempts impartiality by saying that God chose some of the Jews and some of the Gentiles when he exegetes 9:24—"those whom he called, us, not only from the Jews but also from the Gentiles."[15]

In his digression on the unforgivable sin against the Holy Spirit in his *Unfinished Commentary*, Augustine asks how the Jews could have recognized the Spirit's presence in Jesus since, quoting 11:25, there was a blindness on the part of Israel until the fullness of the Gentiles should come in. He then promises to speak more on that issue if God allows. It is again worth noting that Augustine focuses on Israel's exclusion, and not on their future salvation (11:26).

The repeated refrain in all of Augustine's writing is that Paul in Romans is telling the Jews not to take pride in their works of the law.[16] What is commonly regarded as the Lutheran view of the law has a possible precedent in Augustine. I must make sure to say that Luther's views, whether on the Jews or on predestination as we considered it in loci 7–9, are not the same as Augustine's. Their contexts were very different. Luther often starts his theologizing with something he remembers from Augustine, but his ending position is not exactly the same.[17]

Augustine's repeated explanation that Paul's favorable comments toward Israel or their law are designed to check Gentile pride has the inevitable result of muffling the content of these positive statements.[18] Augustine is nowhere ready to say that Paul writes such positive things as 3:1–2 and 9:4–5 because they are true in the divine economy. Here he appeals to his understanding of the occasion behind the letter to transmute the commendations into warnings against Gentile pride.

Augustine clearly sees the Gentiles as gaining at the Jews' expense: "Though it awaked last, because as it is said, the last shall be first, a people hoping in the blessing of God gleaned from the remnant of Israel and filled its winepress from the riches of the harvest which the whole earth produces."[19]

ABELARD

Abelard writes his commentary while Christian Europe is mobilizing for the Second Crusade. His commentary on this locus displays a negative disposition toward the Jews within an apocalyptic framework.

Abelard's first concern when exegeting 11:26 is to assert that "neither at the end of the world nor at the coming of Christ will all Jews be converted, but only 'the remnant of the Lord.'"[20] He quotes Jerome's use of Isaiah 10:22 again to touch on the remnant theme. He then quotes the texts from Isidore of Seville's book, *Against the Jews*. Here the salvation of Israel is placed in a distant, eschatological future where prophecies like Genesis 49:27 can be imagined to come true.[21] Abelard quotes texts that his sources consider significant for this locus, like Remigius on Psalm 14:7, which Abelard explains as a description of the Jews' punishment in captivity, resolved only by the preaching of Elijah and Enoch, when all those Jews who are in Christ will have believed.[22] He returns to an actual scripture Paul quotes when he names Origen as the source of his ideas regarding why Paul says that a redeemer will come from Zion when Isaiah 59:20 reads differently.[23] Abelard exegetes this locus to say that a remnant of the Jews will be saved in some distant future.

AQUINAS

Aquinas lectures on Romans and then edits his lectures after the apocalyptic furor over the Crusades is spent. Only the Crusades of Louis IX occurred during his adult life, and these did not catch the attention of Europe in the way that the earlier Crusades did. As one might expect, therefore, Aquinas is much more positive toward the idea of the salvation of ethnic Israel than Abelard was over a century before him.

Aquinas notes how Paul is moving "to the case of particular Jews" with his prediction in this locus. Especially eloquent in Aquinas's commentary are his explicit quotations of all the Old Testament texts that Paul quotes. When these are lined up, there is an impressive sense of God's salvation coming on ethnic Israel, as the prophets foretold.[24]

LUTHER

Wittenberg's city church had an inscription, still visible to those who walked by in 1518, that the Jews were expelled from that city in 1304.[25] In his early lectures on Romans, Luther's christocentric reading of Scripture led him to view Jews as disconnected to their own heritage. Unable to see the promises of Isaiah 54, Jeremiah 31, or Ezekiel 36 in their national aspect as directed to the physical nation of Israel simply because God has chosen them, at Romans 9:4 Luther glosses "covenants" with "the old and the new law," and later in the verse he glosses "promises" with "concerning Christ and the life to come."[26] In a marginal gloss at 9:6 Luther writes, "The meaning is the same as that above in chapter 3:3. 'Does their faithlessness nullify the faithfulness of God?' It is as if he were saying that although they had the promise, and it was not imparted to them, because they did not receive it; yet it was nevertheless imparted to others of the same blood, but not because they were of the blood but because they were of the Spirit."[27] With the phrase "not because they were of the blood" Luther shows that he has little sense of the elect nature of physical Israel.

In 1523 Luther had written, citing Romans 9, that the Jews of his day were in the same ethnic group as Christ, and that the Christians were really the heathen and only indirectly related to this chosen group of people.[28] But in 1536, when Luther was sought out by Josel von Rosheim for help in persuading the elector of Saxony to cancel the expulsion of the Jews from his electorate or at least to allow Jewish merchants to pass through the area, Luther refused. This refusal appears as part of a downward spiral in Luther's theological position toward the Jews, though Heiko Oberman has argued that Luther always held out the hope that the Jews would come to faith in Jesus, and that Luther's cruel counsel regarding the treatment of Jews in his electorate, given in 1543, was for Luther a "harsh mercy" that had become so because of his conviction that there was little time left for the Jews before the final judgment.[29] This work of 1543, *On the Jews and Their Lies*, is replete with scriptural references. Citing Romans 9:5, Luther admits that these Jews are the descendants of the biblical heroes and heroines and the people among whom Christ came.[30]

Luther's evaluation of Judaism in this text, beginning with a quotation of Romans 10:2, helps establish the Protestant evaluation of Judaism and Roman Catholicism for the next four centuries. For Luther both Jews and papists attempt to live as God's people based on outward form and works, rather than relying purely on grace, as the prophets and the righteous children of Israel considered necessary.[31]

The most repeated phrase from Romans 9–11 in *On the Jews and Their Lies* is Paul's command in 11:20 to "fear God." Luther combines this with his understanding that Judaism is under divine wrath, and exhorts his Gentile Christian readers to fear lest they find themselves under God's wrath, the position of Jews and Muslims already.[32]

But how, just after offering his version of 11:20 ("Fear, O Gentiles, lest you too fall under God's wrath!"), can Luther begin his enumerated recommendations for eliminating Judaism? The list amounts to a Christian blueprint of a pogrom: synagogues are to be burned and their ruins covered with dirt so as to remain forever out of sight; Talmuds and prayerbooks are to be taken from the Jews, since for Luther they amount to lies and curses; rabbis are to be killed, so as to eliminate Judaism.[33]

Why doesn't Luther mention the "all Israel shall be saved" of 11:26 in this work about the Jews? Paul's promise of Israel's salvation is actually what is perversely driving Luther. Since Luther cannot give up the idea of Israel's salvation, he is driven to recommend the harsh measures to make them convert before the imminent end of the world. The apocalyptic vision—Daniel 9 is explicitly cited more often than Romans 9–11—that drove Luther combined with his preference for conversion at any cost resulted in this scandalous text. Paul's promise of Israel's salvation in 11:26 is not without its problems.

Luther's fixation on the Jews' existence apart from Christ continued with him to the very end of his life. In a sermon preached three days before he died, Luther claimed that in their unconverted state Jews would kill Christians, if they could.[34] In an echo of 11:28a, Luther tells his church audience that the Jews "are our open enemies."[35] The second part of that verse, where Paul says that the Jews are "beloved according to election," finds no resonance in Luther. Aside from the heritage that Paul himself values (9:4–5), the only positive point that Luther can identify about his Jewish contemporaries is the possibility of their conversion.[36]

It is no coincidence that Luther, the theologian whose work turned so directly upon his reading of Romans, would remain troubled by Judaism as an "other" to the end of his life. This troubled Paul as well, and Romans 9–11 has not provided a clear enough signal for Christian interpreters throughout history to value Israel as "beloved according to election" (11:28b).

BARTH

Like all Christian interpreters of Romans except Ambrosiaster and Origen, Barth approached the issues of Mosaic law and Jewish people with the perspectives and tools that Christian history and theology provide, not from a literary or theological appreciation of how Judaism interprets them.[37] When summarizing the catena of Old Testament texts that Paul uses to indict all humanity's sin, Barth writes, "We have just (iii.10–18) heard the voice of the law, of religion and piety. The empty canal speaks of the water which does not flow through it. The sign-post points to a destination which is precisely where the sign-post is not. The impress (*form*, ii.20) speaks of the genuine signet-ring which is not where the impress is, but which has left upon it its—negative. And so it is history as a chronicle of the nobility of men, not history as a chronique scandaleuse, which contains the accusation of history against history."[38] This description indicates how Barth views the law of Moses as the Jews' possession. He describes it as an empty canal.[39] It is empty. Barth does not view it as the life-giving mediator of orthodox Judaism. But as a distinct canal, it is a witness to the water that once filled it and to the divine hand that made the canal. So the Mosaic law, and the existence of the Jewish people, is an indication of God's revelation to the world and a valuable testimony to the inadequacy of religion by itself to reach God. When exegeting Romans 3:1–4, where Paul affirms that the Jews definitely have an advantage, Barth writes in a way that is surprising for someone who holds God and the world apart as rigidly as he does elsewhere in *Romans II*. After quoting Paul's "much in every way" of 3:2, Barth writes, "Strangely great and strangely powerful are the connexion and relation between God and the world, between there and here. For . . . we are able to see in every impress of revelation a sign-post to Revelation; then, too, we are able to recognize that all experience bears within it an understanding by which it is itself condemned, and that all time bears within it that eternity by which it is dissolved." Twice, well after the section in which he exegetes 3:1, Barth affirms that the Jews do indeed have an advantage.[40]

On the phrase "by the law is the knowledge of sin" in 3:20, Barth describes the law as "the impress of revelation" and writes positively of the possibility of Jews who possess the law realizing the divine indictment against them and coming to await with expectancy the kingdom of God.[41] So for Barth it appears that the law of Moses and the distinct identity of the Jewish people function as a pointer to divine revelation and a clear indication of the inadequacy of religion on its own to reach God.

Indeed, this view can frustrate some readers of Barth's Romans commentaries. There are places where Barth treats Mosaic law and the Jewish people simply as examples of religion and religious people; in these contexts there is no sense for the divine promise that the Jews would be God's very own possession. Katherine Sonderegger thinks that Barth is closer to a nuanced description of the law of Moses than simply its translation of "religion." But she thinks that in the Romans commentaries Barth has not yet shown how God takes up history, including the Jewish people, into himself. God touches history as a line touches a circle, but the line does not yet enter the circle.[42]

On 11:25–27 on the salvation of Israel Barth says, "But even this happening is not an end in itself, only a point along the way, a pointer to the still wholly other, much greater possibilities, to a *plērōma*, to a resolved problem, hypotheses made fruitful, providentially filled positions, deposits brought to fullness."[43]

When Barth exposits "All Israel will be saved" in his second edition, he treats Israel as if it were a symbol of the church. He does not seem focused on carnal, physical Israel: "Now, this salvation concerns *all Israel*, the whole Church, every Church. And so, the Church is the figure of the Coming One, the fulfillment of prophecy, the canal through which flows the living water of salvation."[44] Barth does seem to consider physical Israel in this context in his text-critical decision to include the second "now" of 11:31. By including this second "now," Barth makes clear that he considers Paul to be saying that unbelieving Israel remains under God's mercy.[45]

Barth relies on Paul's olive tree metaphor to underscore how Israel remains the elect: "Without any doubt the Jews are to this very day the chosen people of God in the same sense as they have been so from the beginning, according to the Old and New Testaments. They have the promise of God; and if we Christians from among the Gentiles have it too, then it is only as those chosen with them, as guests in their house, as new wood grafted on to their old tree."[46]

Long before he wrote this, Barth preached a sermon and even sent a copy of it to Hitler, in which he insisted that the Christian faith must hold onto the fact that Jesus was Jewish, and he emphasized that Jews and the *ethnē* should be considered children of God. In that same year, 1933, Barth wrote in a letter: "The solution of the Jewish question that is currently being sought in Germany is an impossibility—humanly, politically, christianly. . . . It is necessary that the Evangelical Church make itself heard with a resounding 'no'" and "enter the fray in diligent support of the members of the synagogue."[47]

BEYOND THE NEW PERSPECTIVE

Exegesis and the theology that results from it are never done in a vacuum. The exegesis of this locus is affected by our stance in a post-Holocaust world. Dunn helpfully shows how in light of the use of "all" in Romans 1:5, 16, and 4:16 Paul needs to say and we must understand him to say "all Israel." Dunn mentions a work just published in 1984 that insists that "all" in this locus means "all the remnant."[48]

Both the new perspective and a narrative-based approach provide examples of how powerful a model of first-century Judaism or "Paul's story of Israel" can be when exegeting Romans. N. T. Wright has been influenced by both approaches and continues to help people understand Romans in light of the central problem of Jews and Gentiles in the letter's implied audience. He reads Romans with a model in which he sees Jesus the Messiah (and sometimes also the people of the Messiah) replacing Israel.[49] He therefore contradicts E. P. Sanders's view that in 11:25–27 Paul has reversed Jewish eschatology, which predicted that when Israel was finally restored, the nations would come in their fullness to Zion. For Wright, the restoration of Israel has already happened with the resurrection of Jesus, who is the new Israel. Since Jesus the new Israel has been raised by God from the dead, it is the sign for Paul that the eschaton is beginning and that the nations must learn to worship the God of Israel.[50] A little more attention is paid to Israel in Wright's commentary, but he has not changed his position: "In this passage Paul speaks of the ultimate salvation of all God's people, not only Gentiles but also an increasing number of Jews."[51]

Wright's model has now been challenged by Douglas Harink, who thinks Wright's idea that Israel was called in order to be a light to the nations is wrong and considers Wright's model as leading toward supersessionism.[52] This challenge should serve as a lesson to us all to make sure the story we use as a framework for our exegesis is accurate and true to God's irretractable covenants to Israel.

CONCLUSION

Israel's salvation comes at the climax of Romans 9–11 and arguably at the climax of all of chapters 1–11. Origen's sensitivity to how Paul is an arbiter between Jews and Gentiles allows him to take the references to ethnic Israel very seriously in this locus. As in Origen's day, so also today, we are debating the precise relationship between the *ethnē* and Israel that Paul sketches in 11:25–32.

Locus 12

Let Every *Psychē* Be Subject to the Authorities (13:1–7)

The Bible . . . has a message for the governments and governed of the world. Thus we read in Romans 13 that every person be subject to the governing authorities. There is no authority except from God. Rulers are not a terror to good conduct, but to bad conduct. Do what is good, and you will receive the approval of the ruler. He is God's servant for your good.
P. W. Botha addressing the black denomination,
Zion Christian Church, April 7, 1985[1]

This locus is our only one outside what is now the so-called doctrinal section of Romans, chapters 1–11. It is such because no other paragraph in 12:1–16:23 has commanded the sustained attention of interpreters in the last two millennia of Romans conversations. This is beginning to change, however.

From a variety of vantage points, Romans students are beginning to see that material in chapters 12–16 is integral to the letter, offering significant fruit. In the conclusion of his chapter on Torah and spirit in Romans 7, Yeo Khiok-khng refers to 13:8 in support of a Spirit-controlled life of love as the mark of the righteousness of God in the community.[2] In a summary chapter on Pauline theology, N. T. Wright helpfully says, "Paul is thus driven to ask and answer (what we call) 'situational' and 'theological' questions at the same time, in the same breath, with the same words. I suggest . . . that he would not have understood the difference between those two categories."[3] When I was twelve years old, I used to accompany my father to the growing city of Ageo, where he preached once a month through Paul's letter to the Romans at a newly planted church. Years later he told me that all the while he was preaching what he then thought was the most significant section of Romans—chapters 1–8—the people held his message at arm's length, not fully accepting it. He said that it was only when he got into chapters

129

12–15 that the people fully accepted the message, for their response was, "Oh, if this is what the community that follows this teaching looks like, then we can accept it."

As the church continues to grow among the *ethnē* not constrained by Western individualism, these latter chapters of Romans will rise in prominence. If someone rewrites this book one to three centuries from now, there will be more than just one locus from the last five chapters of Romans. As people's use of a given train line grows, more stops are added to the express train's route.

ORIGEN

While none of the Greek fragments of Romans covers chapter 13, Rufinus's translation of Origen here adequately shows us the direction Origen takes on this locus. By noticing that Paul addresses every "anima" (for Paul's *psychē*) and not every "spiritus," Rufinus's Origen makes the point that this command is really for those believers who still have a foothold in the world. Origen implies that the truly spiritual are above this command. The apostles Peter and John, for example, would not have to obey this paragraph, for they had no money that they could have used to pay the taxes mentioned here (Acts 3:6; Rom. 13:6–7).[4]

Origen raises the question of how Paul can say that the only governments are those that are from God, when some of them persecute believers. His response is that authorities on earth are like the senses that God gives to the human being. Like the senses, "authority" is from God; but also like the senses, authority can be misused. Those governments that violate God's laws will receive God's judgment.[5]

Unlike most commentators, Origen admits that Paul's description of government as "a minister of God" disturbs him. Origen works to find an explanation that would make sense of this description. His response is that in its enforcement of what he takes to be basic moral standards (e.g., prohibitions against murder and theft), the government does serve as a minister of God.[6]

Origen then backs up in Paul's paragraph to contradict the statement that obedient subjects receive praise from government. Since governments do not praise law-abiding citizens, Origen reaches for the final judgment, saying that praise or reward will come from God for those who have been obedient in their lives on earth to government's authority on behalf of moral order.[7]

Martyrdom, such as Origen's father received and Origen himself almost attained, functions as a driving idea even in Origen's exegesis of this passage. He interprets 13:5–6 along the lines of quietism, stating that if Christians disobey the government in such civil matters as tax payment, they might deserve execution by the government, but such execution would not be viewed as a martyrdom. Here Origen's approach is entirely different from Luther's, for Origen almost assumes that believers will have to disobey the government. The question is simply whether the disobedience is for a cause that would bring reward in God's eyes rather than some trivially amoral breach of civil law.[8]

Origen treats martyrdom as a means of destroying Christless government: "The martyrs in Christ disarm the principalities and powers with Him, and they share His triumph as fellows of His sufferings, becoming in this way also fellows of the courageous deeds wrought in His sufferings. These deeds include triumphing over the principalities and powers, which in a short time you will see conquered and put to shame."[9]

It is worth considering martyrdom when studying this locus, for the only other reference to "sword" is in 8:35–36, where it clearly refers to martyrdom. The "sword" in 13:4 is a far cry from Justice Scalia's attempt to use this verse to argue for the righteousness of the death penalty.[10]

Taxes are to be paid not because the Christian owes them to the government, but simply to keep the surrounding society from stumbling. If Christ did not owe Caesar anything, but still paid taxes to keep people from stumbling, we too should pay taxes. The fear and honor that Paul mentions we owe to God more than to any human authority (13:7; Mal. 1:6).[11]

I hypothesized once that the anti-Christian social contexts behind Origen and Barth led to their deconstructive exegetical approaches to this locus, approaches that emphasized when and why Christians do not obey the government.[12] J. Patout Burns responded by characterizing most early Romans commentators' responses to this locus as a balance between the Gnostic approach (which would view government as irrelevant to the spiritual) and the absolutist approach (which no one espoused except Eusebius when supporting Constantine). Origen, who admits to being troubled by Paul's reference to government as a minister of God, serves as a forerunner to later interpreters who would also labor to find exceptions to Paul's "obey the government" theme in this locus.

AUGUSTINE

In his early *Commenary on Statements in the Letter to the Romans*, Augustine devotes three paragraphs to sentences from this locus. His opening paragraph counsels us toward a balanced interpretation. Since we are in bodies and must live in this temporal world, Augustine writes, we should be obedient in terms of temporal things. But with regard to our souls, we must not submit to any temporal authority that would seek to destroy our spiritual identity. Nor should we ever regard a temporal power to be authoritative over our faith. He refers to Matthew 22:21 in support of the balanced approach to this locus, concluding his first paragraph with the call to be most obedient to God, who is the one who commands us to be obedient.[13]

Augustine is drawn to the question of praise from government, just as Origen was. The bishop of Hippo goes on to mention how some might offer martyrs as a counterexample to Paul's logic in Romans 13:3. Why does Paul say that people who do good will receive praise, when in fact sometimes such people have been martyred by the temporal authorities? Augustine's response is that this "praise" can refer either to what one wins in the temporal world by doing good or to the martyr's crown. In a similar way, he explains 13:4 by saying that the authorities are God's ministers for the believer's good (note second-person singular pronoun "you" in both Greek text and in Augustine's Latin text of 13:4), even if they show themselves to be evil in how they treat believers.[14]

Augustine goes on to explain the statement of necessity in 13:5 as a call to give up whatever temporal goods the temporal authorities wish to take from us. Paul mentions conscience in this verse to keep the reader from a hypocritical submission to authorities; Augustine tells us that Paul is asking readers genuinely to submit to the temporal authorities and cites Ephesians 6:6 as an analogous command.[15]

In his sermons beginning in the year 404, Augustine repeatedly emphasizes how Catholic Christianity ought to become the religion for the whole world, absorbing not only the Donatists but also pagans into its fold of repentant and baptized believers.[16] Romans is ably suited as a text for such an agenda, for this of all Paul's letters is driven by an insistent conviction that the Pauline gospel accounts for Jewish and pagan past and present, calling all to a faith that leaves no one ashamed. But in his compositions against Donatism Augustine offers no formative interpretations of Romans. The Romans text most often referred to is 4:5, which he uses to make the distinction that it is God who justifies the ungodly and God who grants righteousness in response to faith, rather than the actual human minister of baptism.[17] In another sermon from the same period, he mentions 13:1 in a call for his congregation to obey the authorities.[18]

ABELARD

Abelard on this locus is rather unremarkable. He advocates obedience to authorities and does not expend as much energy as Origen or more recent commentators in trying find loopholes for obedience to the government. He notes that if a tyrant gains power through violence, then Christians can resist, but in all other cases Abelard calls for obedience.[19] He also quotes Origen on 13:7, "tributes for land; fees for trade."[20]

AQUINAS

Aquinas is also rather unremarkable here. He does mention that apostles and martyrs who resisted authorities did not get punished by God but received a reward instead. This leads him to say that when Paul tells his audience to submit to authorities, he means for them to submit to lesser authorities that are established by God.[21] On the phrase "they are ministers of God for you for good," Aquinas raises the question of how this could be true for evil rulers. He remains conservative here, saying that even evil leaders can minister for good by doling out punishment, like King Nebuchadnezzar.[22] This locus did not receive much attention until the modern nation-state was born, so there is little else to say about the medievals' exegesis of it.

ERASMUS

Erasmus and Luther were caught up in the new theological topos of political theology. It was also in 1516 that Erasmus published his *Education of a Christian Prince*.[23] The work is a product of its time, exemplifying the *novum* that there could be a science for Christian rulers, and that the Bible might actually provide guidelines for such rulers. In the first section, he tells the young Christian prince to whom he is writing that it is best for a leader to serve his people. He argues from the greater to the lesser: if God's gift of free will to humanity glorifies divine creation, a Christian ruler's respect for the freedom of his subjects will glorify that ruler's kingdom. Erasmus paraphrases the emerging locus of Romans 13:1–7, but argues that Paul wrote this in regard to pagan rulers. Paul was asking his readers to honor and be subject to the pagan rulers of their day, but the Christian prince is not to subjugate his realm's citizens as portrayed in the scenario of 13:1–7. Instead, Erasmus says that the Christian prince should go by how Paul instructs believers to live among themselves in the following context: "Owe no one anything, except to love one another."[24] It is an irony of history that this prince to whom Erasmus directed his advice, this early piece of Christian political philosophy, was Charles V, before whom Luther would stand at the Diet of Worms. Erasmus's advice went unheeded, for Charles's response at Worms was, "I have decided to mobilize everything against Luther: my kingdoms and dominions, my friends, my body, my blood and my soul."[25]

LUTHER

But how could that Wittenberg monk stand up to the Holy Roman emperor less than five years after concluding his lectures on Romans? The answer does not consist solely in theological innovation based on Luther's reading of Romans. The theological and political repercussions of Luther's revolution would not have occurred without the influential cooperation of the elector of Saxony, Frederick the Wise. Within Saxony, Frederick was politically prior to the emperor. Frederick had guarded against the church's effective taxation on his province at least since 1502, when he and his brother seized indulgence money collected by the church, after they realized that the pretext for that indulgence campaign, a crusade against the Turkish Empire, would not occur. This may help to explain why Luther, who railed against Rome's collection of indulgences also for theological reasons, was protected by his elector.[26] Frederick the Wise had thus been preparing for Saxony's political break from Rome long before Luther nailed his Ninety-five Theses to the door of the castle church in Wittenberg: "The supreme ecclesiastical authority of the German prince was not a result of the Reformation, as often claimed: it preceded the Reformation and provided the cradle for its early emergence and ultimate survival."[27] Luther's early protests would no doubt have been smothered as heretical if Frederick had not provided an environment in which they could grow in the consciousness of a critical mass of Germans as "the true gospel."

Luther baptized the quest for independence from the church (and by necessary implication from the Holy Roman Empire) of Elector Frederick the Wise and his nephew and successor, John Frederick the Magnanimous, with a theological legitimation of the local, secular magistrate. Indeed, Luther later remarked: "God before the last day has brought back marriage and the magistracy to their proper esteem."[28] This legitimation was effected by Luther by an exegesis of Romans 13:1–7 that shows continuity with the attention paid to this locus in the Middle Ages that we observed in the last section. But Luther raises the stakes for the interpretation of Romans by identifying these seven verses as the ultimate reference point for biblical teaching on the state, a move that had not been transparent to previous exegetes. In *A Sincere Admonition by Martin Luther to All Christians to Guard against Insurrection and Rebellion* (1522) he cites 13:4 and argues for the necessity of submission to government. To rise against the government's divinely approved role of fighting against evil people and protecting the upright would lead to a "horribly unjust" situation.[29]

One milestone in the exegesis of Romans 13 occurred in Luther's doctrine of the two kingdoms. While some might claim that the doctrine of the two kingdoms can be found in Augustine's *City of God*, the teaching gained a name and an edge that it never had in Augustine's day through the exegesis of Romans 13 that Luther employed in the stormy circumstances of a region moving from feudal toward early modern political structures. Luther's exegesis of this chapter was affected by the apocalyptic picture of the end of history that he received from Augustine and from Bernard of Clairvaux. If the antichrist was at work through the Roman Catholic Church, then this church's designs on ruling Germany and other nations in (what we would now call) a political way would need to be resisted. Some other government besides that of the Roman Catholic Church must instead be willed by God.[30]

Years after his Romans lectures, Luther's later exegesis of Romans 13 was also affected by the anarchical tendencies of the Radical Reformers. In order to avoid association with the Schwärmer involved in the Münster uprising, Luther endorsed the heavy hand of the secular state in maintaining the status quo, even at the expense of justifiably aggrieved peasants. Luther's reading of Romans 13 gave rise to the doctrine of two kingdoms. This doctrine granted independence to secular government and church regarding the spheres they rule: the government was allowed free rein in secular matters, while the church was allowed to govern the spiritual sphere of a society's existence. Luther's doctrine of the two kingdoms did not connote two places, but rather two rules or ways of God's ruling the world, which were distinguished but not divided.[31] The first step was

Luther's distinction between what he considered to be incompetent church authorities and competent secular authorities. Then when the peasants threatened his sense of order that Frederick's rule maintained in Saxony, he argued on the basis of Romans 13 that the secular authority must be obeyed.[32] This distinction, impossible to conceive of in premodern, Western states as well as in some non-Western nations today, is now securely lodged, for better or worse, in Western civilization.

This locus that began to appear in medieval discourse would prove very useful for Luther's navigation through the political turmoil of his times. Luther asks Origen's question on 13:1, but responds to it completely differently. He asks why Paul directs "every soul" to be subject, instead of "every person." He suggests that Paul uses this word to indicate that one's submission should be a genuine, heartfelt submission.[33] Though Luther goes on to distinguish between body, soul, and spirit and notes that the Christian's spirit remains free, his exegetical approach is quite different from Origen's, whose exegesis also highlights the difference between soul and spirit here. Origen explicitly calls attention to the fact that Paul does not say that every "spirit" is to be subject to government. He indicates that Christians who own material goods must obey government, while those who are truly spiritual, who own nothing, need not obey the government.[34] Luther by contrast makes the point that Paul does not raise the question of liberty when discussing everyone's duty to obey the government.[35]

Luther's scholium on 13:1–7 turns on a dichotomy between church and state. The church authorities he describes as thoroughly corrupt, while the secular authorities he considers much more competent.[36] In his gloss on this passage he interprets Paul's point to be that believers should not use their status as members of the church to claim exemption from civic obedience. Luther asserts the Jews are portrayed as doing this in John 8:33, and that Christians are instead to submit to all governing authorities. Church order is enjoined in Romans 12; civic order is enjoined in Romans 13:1–7.

Order is a good thing for Luther, who weighs in on the question of civil versus church order. In his composition from the year 1520, *To the Christian Nobility*, Luther takes pains to demolish the Roman Catholic claim (that he calls its first "wall") that the church is above the secular authorities. Luther quotes the opening of Romans 13 ("Let every soul be subject . . .") and tersely glosses "every soul" with the parenthetical remark "I take that [to mean] even the pope's [soul]."[37] In his 1523 publication, *On Governmental Authority*, Luther uses Romans 13 against the Anabaptists to argue that to work in the service of government is allowable and proper for Christians. His emphasis here on the moral calling of government leads him to approve of civil service as a career choice, though he does not make the parallel move to describe the moral responsibility of the state.[38] The moral calling of government is thus viewed from the top of the social hierarchy, not from the bottom, as becomes evident in Luther's fierce reaction to the peasant uprising in 1525: "Even though the powers are evil or unbelieving, yet their order and power are good and of God."[39]

The political repercussions of Luther's teaching did not uniformly strengthen the authority of the secular government, however. The *Twelve Articles*, which the peasants wrote in 1525, demanding fair taxation and access to fish in the rivers and firewood in the forests, attempts to be thoroughly grounded in Scripture. Peasant unrest had been simmering for a century; we cannot ascribe the revolt of 1525 simply to Luther's call to put Scripture above all other authorities.[40] But still the peasants' *Twelve Articles* treat Scripture as the final authority in a way that undoubtedly shows Luther's emphasis. Luther's response, *Admonition to Peace concerning the Twelve Articles of the Peasants in Swabia*, however, is an altogether unnuanced invocation of Romans 13:1–7, demanding that they keep silence. Early in the section of the work addressed to the peasants, Luther quotes 13:1–2 and alludes to 13:4 as well, in a strong statement that the peasants must obey. The section concludes with Luther's words that the Peasants' Revolt is not only against the law of Christ and the gospel, but also against natural law and all reasonableness.[41]

While we might wish that Luther himself had practiced the "associate with the lowly" command of 12:16, instead he quotes 12:19 in a statement to the peasants to desist from taking vengeance into their own hands.[42] His later advice to nobility to go ahead and massacre the peasants continues in this vein as well. Luther's circumstances of joining his prince in a break from Rome, and then receiving protection from his prince, thus lead him consistently to exegete Romans 13 from the top of the social hierarchy, not from the bottom.

Luther thus uses 13:1–7 to empower secular authorities and encourage their independence from the Vatican. But he shows no evidence of interpreting this paragraph in Romans in a manner that would highlight the moral responsibility of the secular authorities (e.g., 13:4—"For it is a minister of God to you *for good*") and allow for civil disobedience when this responsibility was broken.

This locus, like the first one we encountered in this book, is a locus today largely because of how it was seized and used by Luther. As one protected by the state, Luther's exegesis sided with the state. The rule of God that comes through the secular authorities in Luther's two-kingdoms doctrine is the medium through which the first use of the law operates. Luther interprets this locus in a more straightforward, less suspicious manner than Origen.

BARTH

As in Luther's case, so also for Barth, the interpretation of 13:1–7 is heavily influenced by the commentator's political context and theologically informed self-perception in relation to that context.[43] Barth's exegesis of this locus arises out of two conscious breaks he made with his political context. Barth left the camp of German liberal theology when he heard his teachers use their theology to legitimize the German war effort. When he broke with theological liberalism in 1915, Barth was very invested in the Swiss form of religious socialism. But by the time he was revising the draft of *Romans I*, he had become disillusioned with the religious socialism of Leonhard Ragaz, and in this commentary he reacts directly against this party. Barth's exegesis of these seven contested verses in Romans drives toward his assertion that no political organization or ideology can be equated with the kingdom of God. This means then that believers should grant no legitimacy to the existing state, nor should they entertain the possibility of political revolution, for such revolution uses the same evil, power-oriented methods as the regimes it seeks to oust.[44] The church should starve the state of the legitimacy it craves.[45]

In *Romans I* Barth could not get past his idealistic ethics, because he did not want simply to Christianize political life by use of a divine-command theory. In *Romans I* therefore two different things are going on ethically. There is first of all a critique of idealistic ethics, but in his treatment of politics in Romans 13 he lapses back into such idealism.[46]

In *Romans II* Barth focuses on the theological deficiencies behind political revolution, because the political climate had now become dominated by the quest for revolution. In continuity with *Romans I*, he emphasizes that in essence the state is evil. Since he recognizes how the quest for political revolution could readily emerge from the recognition of the state's nature, he goes on in *Romans II* to make clear that revolution is not the way for the Christian to respond to government. The political revolutionary still uses evil to be rid of evil and thus cannot escape from the snares endemic to the state. Barth leaves the only option for the Christian to be one of theologically informed inactivity. To avoid fighting the state is to avoid granting it the passion-filled legitimacy it seeks.[47]

From *Romans I* Barth maintains his exegesis of the state as evil by redrawing the boundaries of Paul's treatment of the political sphere. In both editions he treats this section of the believer's political posture as beginning at 12:21 ("Do not be conquered by evil, but conquer evil with good"). When this is viewed as the beginning of the section, it throws a new light on the commands for civil obedience that follow. For Barth, to be conquered by evil (12:21a) would be to follow one's political idealism, however theologically motivated it might be, into politically revolutionary behavior. This would entail being conquered by evil because one would use the world's evil methods of power wielding to effect political change.[48] But to conquer evil with good (12:21b) is to live as a witness to a divinely orchestrated revolution. One witnesses to such a revolution by refusing to legitimize or use the methods of politics.

Barth begins his section on Paul's treatment of the political sphere in *Romans II* with an insistence that it is mistaken to respond to the powers that seek to order our existence, whether church or state, with either legitimism or revolution. Barth takes the essence of Paul's instructions to be a prohibition against civil disobedience.[49] This negative approach to the paragraph, what he calls the "Great Negative Possibility," is grounded by him in 12:16, where believers are commanded not to think on lofty things but to associate with the lowly.[50] Why then does he choose to emphasize that political revolution is not what Paul is teaching? He tells us that one who reads Romans would more likely be led to political revolt than to political legitimation, so he chooses to focus his energy on showing how this section of Romans does not teach revolution.[51]

What is wrong with the state, according to Barth, is that it claims for those who rule a transcendence that only God can rightfully have: "This whole pseudo-transcendence of an altogether immanent order is the wound that is inflicted by every existing government—even by the best—upon those who are most delicately conscious of what is good and right."[52] On 13:1 he says, "To *be in subjection* is, when it is rightly understood, an action void of purpose, an action, that is to say, which can spring only from obedience to God. Its meaning is that men have encountered God, and are thereby compelled to leave the judgment to Him."[53] Where Paul writes that "the powers that be are ordained of God," Barth comments that this means that all existing government is under God's judgment: "He of whom the power is and by whom every existing authority is ordained is God the Lord, the Unknown, Hidden God, Creator and Redeemer, the God who elects and rejects. This means that the mighty powers that be are measured by reference to God, as are all human, temporal, concrete things. God is their beginning and their end, their justification and their condemnation, their 'Yes' and their 'No.'"[54] This is in direct continuity with the negative evaluation of the state on which Barth waxes eloquently in *Romans I*: "These powers in their contemporary pattern of existence are not God's creation and foundation; they are still to be understood as degenerations of divine intentions within his general oversight."[55] The nature of political activity makes government evil: "All political activity is a struggle for power, the diabolical art of outvoting, filthy dirt. Even the most noble, the most pure conviction of its proponents does not change the anti-God status of its essence a hairsbreadth."[56]

Though a later editor of *Romans I* attests to a handwritten quotation of Luther in the manuscript that attributes government to the line of Cain, it seems that Barth in his detestation of the state is actually far beyond Luther's two-kingdoms viewpoint.[57] It was of course the religious socialists that Barth was opposing in *Romans I*, though such opposition survives in *Romans II* as well: "We, therefore, have to remember that it is not for us to arm ourselves for action with the standard of the measurement of God—as though He acted through us!"[58] The problem with the revolutionary is that the revolutionary is trying to do something that only God can do: "If God be the Judge, who can share in His judgment?" Barth says that the existing order is a witness to the order that only God can bring.[59] With a reference back to 12:19 ("Vengeance is mine"), he writes, "Our subjection means, therefore, no more than that vengeance is not our affair."[60] At the same time that he claims that the text forbids revolution, he also thinks the text forbids those who fight against revolution, captured by his term the "White Guard."[61] This is because they are taking judgment that belongs only to God into their own hands; they make the same mistake as the revolutionary and condemn themselves when judging others (2:1).[62]

Paul's command to do what is good in 13:3 is interpreted by Barth to mean that the believer should do nothing, in order to testify to the divine condemnation and justification under which the world exists.[63] In response "the rulers . . . are, in fact, rejoicing over one whose behaviour means 'only' the judgment of God, who has so much to say against them that he no longer complains of them."[64] The good of existing government and human attempts at reform are to be accepted "as shadows preserving the lineaments of that which is contrasted with them." Barth shocks us by applying the statement of 13:4 ("If you do evil . . .") to every reader of Romans, for he writes that we all participate in evil: "Our whole visible behaviour is either an acceptance of the present order or a denial of it; and in both cases we do wrong. We can do right only in the 'not-doing' of our relationship to God."[65] Barth thinks that this section of Romans asserts God's sovereignty over both existing authorities and revolutionaries: "Whether we attempt to build up some positive human thing or to demolish what others have erected, all our endeavours to justify ourselves are in one way or another shattered in pieces. We must now assert that all these endeavours of ours not merely cannot be successful, but ought not to be so."[66] Paul commands people to pay taxes to the government officials, who are ministers of good, because the order that human government, however evil, provides is a testimony to the order that only God can bring.[67]

Barth thus reconfigures this locus, as we have seen in previous loci, around his radical insistence on starting with God. While most commentators on this locus start with the human citizen, and spend all their exegetical energy describing the circumstances in which the human citizen should obey the state, Barth starts with God's relationship to the state. God's condemnation and justification of the world, including the state, overshadows any authoritarian relationship that the state holds over the individual citizen in Barth's exegesis of this paragraph. Indeed, the terror that Paul says the ruling authorities are to the evildoer (13:3) is explained by Barth as ultimately the terror of God's judgment of evil.[68] God is thus the power that rises above the typically binary reading of government and individual in this paragraph, and this divine power reconfigures the entire locus so that the believer's position before the governing authorities must always reflect the coming judgment of God over all evil, including that evil inherent in human government and in those who wish to overthrow or reform unjust governments.

This God-centered orientation would keep Barth unswayed by such a letter as the one he received from Gerhard Kittel in 1934: "Even the church in the state of the antichrist, even the church under Nero in Romans 13 is bound, insofar as it knows, that even in this historical situation the hand of God is ruling over it, even here 'God works.'"[69]

What behavior does Barth suggest will best point to the coming judgment of God over existing rulers and potential revolutionaries? For Barth it is not doing, not taking action, that would either legitimate or overthrow a given government. While he does admit in his exegesis of 13:3–4a that the one who does good will not be threatened by government, his emphasis even here is on "not-doing." He describes the believer in whom God works the good as follows: "And what is his *good work* but his standing upon the eternal ground of judgment and of righteousness? To him, the *good work* is the dissolution of the man of this world and the establishing of the individual in God. The good work is the 'not-doing' by which all action is related to its Primal Origin. To such good work, since it has no temporal existence, rulers—or anarchy!—have no *terror*."[70]

In this locus as well we see a swing away from Luther and toward Origen. Like Origen, Barth articulates a theologically informed suspicion of human government. Like Origen, Barth finds exegetical space in the locus for the believer's essential disconnection from government. Against Luther, who invoked 13:1–7 as decisive against the peasants' scripturally informed grievances, Origen and Barth view this paragraph as only one of a number of texts that speak to the Christian's relationship to government.

What then of the impact of both editions of Barth's *Romans* on Christian ethics? When composing these two Romans commentaries, Barth is not yet so Reformed that he has a robust third use of the law that will introduce a decisively ethical focus to the exegesis. These two Romans commentaries of Barth thus are still on the ethical trajectory of Luther and Melanchthon, who evacuated Romans of the ethical significance it held for one and a half millennia of readers. Barth's break with the liberalism of his past in favor of a theology that always starts with God makes it difficult for him even to ask the starting question of any ethicist, "What shall we do?" for this question belongs in Barth's mind to a realm of law and religion that God's new order would overturn.[71]

It is true that Barth frames 12:21–13:7 as "The Great Negative Possibility" alongside 13:8–14, which he calls "The Great Positive Possibility." Love of neighbor, in which that which participates in God recognizes and loves that which participates in God that is found within the human other, is this great possibility. Love of neighbor is the fulfillment of the law, Barth says. But even in this section, he refuses to define love as a movement of human will or thinking. Love is always encountered beyond the law and religion, he says, though it fulfills the law.[72] The concretely ethical implications of this paragraph are further muted by Barth's insistence that the possibility of love can only arise when one knows the time (13:11a) in the sense that one sees each moment of time as a moment that is between time and eternity.[73] Barth is very brief on "being clothed with the Lord Jesus Christ," saying that ours is the possibility of being clothed with the offensive and defensive armor of God, a possibility from which no one is to be excluded.[74]

John Webster can find statements in *Romans II* that take seriously the moral agency of humans, and affirm that "Barth is at the beginning of a process of reconstituting human action on grounds quite other from those to which appeal was made in the dominant Protestant tradition of his day. Barth's goal is scarcely visible, essentially because the reconstitution proceeds by a fierce iconoclasm which Barth judged the only means of reattaching consideration of ethics to consideration of the being and action of God."[75] Webster's detection of some positive appreciation of human agency in *Romans II* notwithstanding, the ethical turns in Paul's letter are exegeted in both *Romans I* and *II* through the din of that "fierce iconoclasm" he himself admits. In essence, then, Barth mutes the ethical appeal that interpreters such as Origen and Augustine heard in this letter by enclosing human existence in a temporal world from which God is absent. If one only encounters love outside law and religion, one will not spend energy learning how exactly to fulfill the law. If one can perform love only when recognizing each moment of existentially experienced time as a moment between that time and eternity, one would be less ready to pull a neighbor's ox from a ditch.

The theological revolution that Barth's early commentaries on Romans sparked was thus effected without a clear voice given to the ethical appeal that readers before Luther had heard in Romans. This is not to say that Barth's theology as a whole should be judged as impoverished in the category of ethics. In his later commentary on Romans, published in English in 1959, there is no mention of "not-doing" in Barth's exegesis of Romans 13, and there is a much more robust call, grounded in more explicitly christological and ecclesiological terms, for the Christian to live in love toward the neighbor.[76]

A NARRATIVE-BASED APPROACH

Katherine Grieb sees how 13:1–7 contains a subtle warning for vulnerable Jews and Christian *ethnē* within the Roman Empire. Paul contradicts Roman propaganda regarding Nero's idle sword to warn readers that the Roman sword is still dangerous. The earlier reference to "sword" in Romans comes as the last of the threats to God's people listed within the hymn on God's love (8:35).[77] Grieb's narrative-based approach here involves not simply finding the story in Paul's Scriptures that lies beneath his letter, but finding the story in the lives of Paul and his readers that make his locus understandable. Grieb is right to emphasize Paul's status as a Roman prisoner within this story.[78] Wright finds Jewish precedent in Paul's position toward government in the Pharisaic School of Hillel. He then moves more to the narrative—as best as can be reconstructed—of the first-century followers of Jesus who strove first to obey the God of Israel while living under Roman power.[79]

Close attention to the context also helps us understand how this locus works in Romans, which in turn helps us understand what the locus is really saying. The preceding context includes the prohibition against vengeance. This is found in the first part of the "love your neighbor as yourself" verse (Lev. 19:18) quoted in Romans 13:9. The reference to vengeance in 12:19 is followed by the paragraph enjoining subjection to the authorities that avenge the evildoer (note the verbal link of *ekdikeō* in 12:19 with *ekdikos* in 13:4). This paragraph is then followed by the love command, which immediately follows a prohibition of vengeance in its original context, and renders Grieb's title a sensible introduction to what Paul is communicating in Romans 13: "Be Subject for the Sake of the Neighbor."[80] A consideration of the number of synagogues in first-century Rome and the circumstances of the Jews' expulsion from Rome in 49 is also often added to this story.[81] The implications of this reading are that we do not consider this locus as Paul's textbook presentation of his theology of the state. Rather, Paul the Roman prisoner is writing to other vulnerable people under Rome's imperial power with advice on how best to love one's neighbor while exposed to Rome's violent rule.

As Romans continues to move in its full circle among the nations, believers living under imperial regimes still read this text. There are some breakthroughs, like the Japanese people's acceptance on May 3, 1947, of a constitution that was not based on the absolute authority and divinity of the emperor.[82] But there are still challenges, almost wherever one looks on the globe, to the unquestioning allegiance demanded by sovereign states, and the church needs therefore to understand the contingent nature of this locus.

CONCLUSION

This locus is a latecomer to the list of controversial texts in Romans, since it really came into its own only in the early sixteenth century when Luther debated the peasants. While Origen found exegetical space in this locus by close attention to Paul's diction, some interpreters today create similar space by linking the locus to events facing the first-century churches and dangers facing both Jews and Christians then. As the church continues to spread among *ethnē* under political or religious oppression, there may be more opportunities to explore and understand how this locus sounds when read by believers who cannot be completely subject to their authorities.

Conclusion

After [Paul] had been seven times in chains, had been driven into exile, had been stoned, and had preached in the East and in the West, he won the genuine glory for his faith, having taught righteousness to the whole world and having reached the farthest limits of the West.

1 Clement 5:6–7[1]

Lest there be any doubt, this book is not a claim that Romans is the most important book in the Christian's Bible, or that Romans has been the most formative biblical book for Western civilization. Such a claim is easily proven false by a simple examination of biblically related art, whether visual, musical, or theatrical. The Gospels without question provide the font of imagery and theological stimuli for the Bible's engagement with Western civilization. Michael Goldberg is right to identify the gospel story as the master story of the church.[2]

Still we may wonder how one book could generate such differing interpretations. I suggest that the variety in interpretations in Romans results from the vistas it opens and the tensions within each locus.

VISTAS OF ROMANS

While not theologically complete, Romans is theologically ambitious in the vistas it opens. Of all Paul's letters, in Romans Paul is most comprehensive in a self-conscious and theological attempt to construct a model for understanding God's dealings with humanity. More can be said: of all the New Testament books,

143

Romans deals most directly with the relationship of the human person to a divinely created and sustained world, considered in this letter both in its spatial and temporal dimensions. Romans deals most directly with the relationships of followers of Jesus to Judaism and society in general, and the relationship between the Jesus-follower and the Jewish Scriptures.

THE TENSIONS OF ROMANS

Paul's letter to the Romans, like other great pieces of literature, contains tensions. As we are drawn to people with profound tensions, so texts with tensions in them have a more lasting impact on us. The *Odyssey* is a more compelling read than the *Aeneid* because complex Odysseus, both "crafty" and yet noble, attracts us in ways with which the more flat hero, "pious Aeneas," simply cannot compete. So Paul's Romans is especially compelling because it is driven by a number of tensions.[3] Robert Morgan's characterization of Romans as a "powerfully ambiguous text" illustrates how the uncertainties in this text are often the departure points for influential theological turns.[4] The "warring laws" locus of Romans 7 and the "not running or willing" locus of 9:16–19 exemplify tensions generated within single loci in Romans. As Origen would tell us, some of these tensions within a single locus (e.g. 1:16–17 or 11:25–27) simply conduct out to the reader in a specific way the basic Jew-Gentile tension that drives the whole book.

DIACHRONIC SURVEY

This book has progressed through Romans locus by locus so that students can listen in on past conversations about the letter while reading through the letter themselves. A diachronic survey of how Romans as Scripture has functioned for the nations who have been reading this letter seems appropriate here. I have endeavored to let students hear conversations with few evaluative reflections from me. But now, in this concluding diachronic summary, some evaluation will be inevitable. I am aware of how particular and idiosyncratic this evaluation might be and how limited my perspective is in relation to the giants' conversations we have been hearing in the last twelve chapters. With a bow to Adrasteia, then, I begin.

Origen

Origen is the hero of this book. His opinions on questions that relate to Greek usage, as well as the opinions of a Greek theologian in his line of influence, John Chrysostom, deserve careful attention. Both figures spoke and wrote within worlds much closer to Paul's language than we can enter today. Origen is also worth reading because he respected the whole letter of Romans and made use of it both for building theological constructs and for calling readers to holy lives. To some extent, we owe the possibility of reading Romans to Origen. For it was he, following Irenaeus's first attempts, who brought this letter into prominence for orthodox Christianity, wresting it from the second-century Gnostics who were using it as a key text in their argument that people are born with fixed natures. I recognize that some readers have no desire to know what anyone thought or wrote about Romans before the Reformation, but for those who recognize the diversity of theological tendencies that occurred in the sixteenth century, some recognition of one of their primary sources is useful. Origen remains the unacknowledged ancestor in the two millennia of conversations that have occurred over Romans interpretation.

This book is using the metaphor of the full circle of Paul's gospel (Rom. 15:19) to say that the way the *ethnē* are reading Romans has come full circle, so that it now approximates Origen's reading. By this I mean that people are much more ready to see the whole letter as explicitly concerned with steering between and accounting for both the Jews (including those who do not follow Jesus and those who do) and the church of the *ethnē*.

Under this broad rubric, Romans readers beginning with Barth are moving in the direction of specific approaches that Origen pioneered. These approaches include reading both Christ's faithfulness and faithfulness in Christ as in view in Romans 3, a willingness to discuss the universal scope of Christ's obedience at the end of Romans 5, reading the *egō* of Romans 7 as someone who is not fully in Christ, insisting on a human will whose free choices have real consequences in the order of salvation (8:28–30; 9:16–23), viewing ethnic Israel as God's chosen people (Romans 9–11), and reading 13:1–7 with deconstructive strategies that emphasize how believers must not always be subject to the government.

I am not claiming that all commentaries written today employ all of these approaches. There are still commentators who are wary of Origen and avoid him. In that sense I cannot chart patterns of interpretation on Romans as if they are scientific revolutions in which one paradigm completely replaces another. Biblical interpretation and the theologies that result from it do not work that way. My claim is only that approaches that Origen pioneered are returning into our discourse about Romans, whether or not today's exegetes are aware of their debt to him.

Augustine

Augustine used Romans to fight against the Manichees and Pelagians. As master of the battlefield of Romans he called special attention to chapters 5 (humans all sinned in Adam), 7 (first against the Manichees it was the unbeliever who was the *egō*, then against the Pelagians it was the believer speaking as the *egō*), and 9 (God's grace triumphs over the human will).

By focusing attention on Romans as a guide for the individual's entrance into salvation, Augustine effectively removed physical Israel as a live factor in the letter.

Romans was now only about the *ethnē*. The agenda of the scribe who had added 16:25–27 would now remain firmly established for over fourteen hundred years.

Some readers of my book will insist that Augustine remains the primary ancestor of Romans interpretation in the Western church. While he is named more in all later commentaries on the letter than Origen is, Augustine's influence is confined to a limited section of the letter. His emphasis on grace has certainly been fruitful for all readers of the letter. But Augustine's picture of grace pulling individuals among the *ethnē* to salvation is an incomplete reading of the letter, for it ignores the ethical challenge that the letter provides and its open window onto the people of Israel. Augustine's approach to Romans is thus somewhat limited, while Origen's repeated recognition that in Romans Paul serves as an arbiter between Jews and the *ethnē* allows a more complete use of the letter today, without detracting from a recognition of the profound debt humanity owes to divine grace.

So I remain insistent that Origen retain his place as the unacknowledged ancestor of Romans interpretation for the two millennia that this book surveys. But Augustine was blessed to read Romans with others in a garden rather than alone in a tower.

Pelagius

Pelagius correctly saw that Romans contains significant grist for the call to discipleship. He used Origen to emphasize the ethical calling of the letter on humans who can make real choices to follow Christ. His commentaries on the Pauline letters, including Romans, were credited to Jerome's authorship and recopied for a millennium by monks who found them useful for living out the Christian life. Medieval exegetes such as Cassiodorus, Sedulius Scottus, and Abelard used both Augustine and Pelagius in exegeting the letter. However strong the Augustinian current was to read the letter as all about divine grace sovereignly pulling souls into salvation, the ethical call of the letter found real traction in the exegesis of Pelagius and the use of this exegesis through the Middle Ages.

Abelard

Abelard used both Origen and Augustine in his attempt to write an academic commentary on the letter to the Romans. He fits into the medieval pattern of exegetes who refused to see the letter as only charting how divine grace pulls an elect individual into salvation. While Abelard certainly heeded Augustine's indication of divine grace in the letter, he also remained open to the letter's call on the wills of its readers.

Aquinas

While Aquinas is famous for using Aristotle, he remained also dependent on Augustine. What results is a mixture of an emphasis on cultivating righteousness by habitual practice and an expectation of divine grace that will bring healing to the soul. Aquinas represents a stage in which he considers all fourteen of the letters regarded as Pauline to form a systematic theology, with each letter covering a distinct topos within that theology. His sense for interpreting Romans allowed him to find Israel, at least in locus 11, with ease.

Luther

In the modern period, the influence of Luther's Romans interpretation is without peer. It is difficult to do justice to such a far-reaching reading of the letter; I only invoke someone's encouragement, "Pecca fortiter!" as I begin.

Luther and Melanchthon were the ones who first read Romans as a theologically complete treatise. (Luther considered Romans the purest presentation of the gospel, and Melanchthon based his systematic theology, the popular *Loci Communes*, on Romans.) This raised the stakes for Romans interpretation from Aquinas's recognition that Paul's letters taken together formed a complete theology. While the Lutheran concentration on Romans has helped the church plumb the depths of this letter, it also presents challenges to the church's construction of balanced theological models.

Luther's legacy on Romans is the forensic justification of individual sinners. His emphasis on the total incapacity of the human will is in basic continuity with one aspect of Augustine's teaching. Luther hated Aristotle and the scholastics, for he considered that they still retained a place for an active righteousness that humans could cultivate on their own. Instead, Luther coined the phrase "passive righteousness" for his new idea that righteousness comes only from one's faith in Christ while attempting no good works.

Luther is also significant for crediting his reading of Romans with prompting him to read the Bible nonallegorically. He sought to read the Bible as literally telling one story, how God in his mercy sends God's Son to save sinners by giving them the righteousness that comes by faith alone. While he did not abandon allegory completely, Luther's hermeneutical move was a key step in the process, already underway, that resulted in the historical-critical reading of Scripture.

Luther's emphasis on grace met a psychological need by refocusing attention on the sufficiency of divine grace. When combined with his idea of passive righteousness and some Lutherans' rejection of Melanchthon's later openness to the third use of the law, a theology based on the first eight chapters of Romans resulted that was perceived by some to be deficient in ethics.

Erasmus

While Luther lectured on Romans 9 in 1516, he received the first published edition of a complete Greek New Testament. This New Testament was edited and published by Erasmus, who thus made the Greek text of Romans available to a number of avid Romans readers of the sixteenth century. With regard to the thesis of this book, Erasmus is the voice through whom Origen's ideas were carried into Renaissance biblical interpretation. As André Godin has shown so well, Erasmus was the premier reader of Origen in the sixteenth century. Erasmus carried an awareness of Paul's context along with a robust insistence on the capability of the human will to make choices with real consequences.

Calvin

This Reformation leader is always worth reading on Romans. His approach to Romans was generally in continuity with Augustine. Calvin is significant for his attention to hear and follow God's Word wherever it led him. "The second turn of the Reformation," for which Calvin was largely responsible, is understood in the context of this book as the use of Scripture in ethics, which was so necessary in the sixteenth century but is only now beginning to slip into the interpretation of Romans.[5] In that sense Calvin's input is still significant as this letter gets lived out in full circle among the *ethnē*.

Barth

The God-centered wake-up call to modernity that sounds from Barth's *Romans II* ensures that this book will long remain in print. For its ability to hold both the individual and corporate dimensions of humanity in view and for its prophetic stance against idolatry, this commentary is a classic. While this commentary does not carry Origen's sense of the Jew-Gentile pairing in the letter, Barth invested this topos with prophetic urgency in his writings beginning in the 1930s.

The New Perspective

The new perspective, pioneered by W. D. Davies, E. P. Sanders, and J. D. G. Dunn, takes first-century Judaism very seriously and looks at it as a grace-conscious rather than legalistic religion. This emphasis has moved Romans interpreters closer to Origen's sense of the Jew-Gentile conversations in the letter and away from the justification-by-faith-alone center that some have claimed for it. The new perspective has not yet fully explained the antitheses of faith versus works of the law in 3:27–28 and 9:30–10:13. Nor has it assimilated Paul's complex view of "law," for example, Paul's assertion that "the law of the Spirit of life" has delivered him from the law of sin and death (8:2,4). Origen rightly saw that the historical Paul was capable of viewing the law as an instrument of deliverance, while modern interpreters continue to resist this point of view.

Narrative-Based Approaches

Exegesis of a Pauline letter based on an underlying narrative, an approach pioneered by Richard Hays on Galatians and applied to Romans in different ways by

N. T. Wright and A. Katherine Grieb, is open to viewing Christ as the successor to Israel. Since it is so sensitive to Israel's story in its Scriptures and in the experience of Paul, it has the advantage of reading everything Paul says about the Jews and the *ethnē* in Romans as of primary importance. It has not proven to all observers that it has the necessary controls for determining when a narrative panel should be included as part of the substructure of Romans. Still, it comes closest to a sensitivity to the layers in the text that the church held for its first fifteen hundred years of reading Romans and to Origen's useful Jew-Gentile lens for this letter.

NOT A FULL CIRCLE

Romans interpretation among the *ethnē* has moved generally in a full circle from Origen to some features of narrative-based approaches. Once more the privileges and challenges of reading Romans and viewing Christian existence through a Jew-Gentile lens are in full view. The secondary points of faith in Christ and faith of Christ, openness to universalism, viewing the *egō* of Romans 7 as unregenerate, the insistence of the exercise of a human will that can make real choices, the emphasis on the salvation of ethnic Israel, and a hermeneutics of suspicion on Romans 13 are all back in view.

But in another sense the circle is not full. The Western church is moving to Africa, Asia, and Latin America. As it does so, new approaches to Romans will gain visibility and more loci from Romans 12–16 will appear on the table. Romans is a wonderful text for this centrifugal movement away from Europe and North America. This letter, with its sights on the geographical and temporal ends of the world, is an excellent companion for a church crossing cultural and ideological thresholds. Still, as Origen observed, Paul's letter to the Romans balances its attention between this universal horizon and the particular focus that remains one of the church's central theological riddles today—the election of Israel.

Notes

Introduction

1. Ulrich Wilckens, *Der Brief an die Römer*, EKK 6.1–3 (Neukirchen-Vluyn: Neukirchener Verlag, 1978–82) passim; Robert Morgan, *Romans* (Sheffield: Sheffield Academic Press, 1995), 128–51; idem, "Romans, Letter to the," in *Dictionary of Biblical Interpretation*, ed. J. H. Hayes (Nashville: Abingdon, 1999), 411–22.
2. Application of this theory onto Romans has already been made by Gertrud Yde Iversen, *Epistoloarität und Heilsgeschichte: Eine rezeptionsästhetische Auslegung des Römerbriefs*, TI 2 (Münster: LIT, 2003), 46–53, on "Leerstellen." For English equivalents, Iversen offers "blank," "vacancy," and "gap" (46 n. 71). The loci offered below are my own, not Iversen's.
3. I follow here James Barr, *The Semantics of Biblical Language* (Oxford: Oxford University Press, 1961), 233.
4. E. P. Sanders uses "righteous" as a verb (*Paul: A Very Short Introduction* [Oxford: Oxford University Press, 1991], 53–57, 78–81), but this is a neologism that is not catching on, so I just use "make/made righteous" so that it is clear what I mean.
5. Ludwig Wittgenstein, *The Blue and Brown Books* (1958; repr., New York: Harper & Row, 1965), 44.
6. I am indebted to Thomas Scheck for emphasizing this to me on November 21, 2004, and for the index of his translation of Origen's commentary. See Origen, *Commentary on the Epistle to the Romans*, trans. Thomas Scheck, 2 vols., FC103–4 (Washington, D.C.: Catholic University Press of America, 2001–2002). The references in this and the following two footnotes are based on Scheck's division of the text. See *ComRm* 2.14.1–5 (on Rom. 3:1–4; Scheck 1:165–67); 3.9.1 (on Rom. 3:27–28; Scheck 1:225); 8.1.2 (on Rom. 10:1–3; Scheck 2:13.2); 8.10.2 (on Rom. 11:13–15; Scheck 2:171); 10.11.2 (on Rom. 15:15–16; Scheck 2:277).
7. Paul arbitrates between Jewish and Gentile believers in Jesus: *ComRm* 3.2.2 (on Rom. 3:9–18; Scheck 1:188); 10.8.2 (on Rom. 15:8–12; Scheck 2:272).
8. Paul arbitrates between unbelieving Israel and believing Gentiles: *ComRm* 3.1.2–3 (on Rom. 3:5–8; Scheck 1:178–79); 8.6.9 (on Rom. 10:16–21; Scheck 2:153).

9. He does not use Romans directly in the Donatist controversy.
10. Henri de Lubac, *Medieval Exegesis*, vol. 1: *The Four Senses of Scripture*, trans. Mark Sebanc (Grand Rapids: Eerdmans, 1998), 161–211; Thomas P. Scheck, "The Reception of Origen's Exegesis of Romans in the Latin West" (Ph. D. diss., University of Iowa, 2004).
11. E-mail correspondence from A. Katherine Grieb and N. T. Wright, January 6–18, 2005.
12. E-mail communication, January 7, 2005.
13. E-mail communication, January 15, 2005.

Locus 1: To the Jew First and to the Greek

1. Origen, *ComRm*, Preface (Scheck 1:57; Hammond Bammel 41.92–100).
2. Ibid., 1.16 (Scheck 1:86; Hammond Bammel 79.16–20).
3. Ibid., 1.17 (Scheck 1:86–87; Hammond Bammel 79.1–11). Scheck cites *CCels* 4.21; 5.42–44; Josephus, *Contra Apionem* 2.151ff. on such ethnic distinctions.
4. Origen, *ComRm* 2.7 (Scheck 1:123; Hammond Bammel 125.252–56).
5. Ibid., 1.18 (Scheck 1:87; Hammond Bammel 79.1–80.11). Scheck directs us to Origen's *Homilae in Genesim* 10.5 and Tertullian, *Contra Marcion* 5.13.2 here.
6. Origen, *ComRm* frag. 12, in Origen, *Comentarii in Epistulam ad Romanos: Fragmenta*, ed. and trans. Theresia Heither, O.S.B., Fontes Christiani 2/6 (Freiburg im Breisgau: Herder, 1999), 52.16–20.
7. Ibid., frag. 12 (Heither 54.1–3).
8. Augustine, *gr. et lib. arb.* 20 (*Basic Writings of Saint Augustine*, ed. Whitney J. Oates, trans. P. Holmes, 2 vols. [New York: Random House, 1948], as quoted in Wayne Meeks, ed., *The Writings of St. Paul* [New York: Norton, 1972], 221).
9. Abelard on Rom. 1:16 in *Expositio in Epistolam ad Romanos*, ed. and trans. Rolf Peppermüller, Fontes Christiani 26/1 (Freiburg im Breisgau: Herder, 2000), 138.8–15.
10. Abelard, *Expositio* on 1:17 (Peppermüller 138.16–140.17).
11. Thomas Aquinas, *Super Epistolas S. Pauli Lectura*, ed. P. Raphael Cai, O.P. (Turin: Marietti, 1953), no. 107, pp. 20–21.
12. Ibid., 104 (Cai 20). He cites Rom. 4:2–3 to support his understanding of "my [God's] just one," and Gal. 2:20 to support "the just shall live by his faith."
13. An example of someone solidly within Luther's legacy on the "righteousness of God" is Adolf Schlatter, *Romans: The Righteousness of God*, trans. Siegfried S. Schatzmann (Peabody, MA: Hendrickson, 1995); an example of someone who rejects "righteousness" as the theme of Romans but still uses this locus to outline the letter's argument is Steven E. Enderlein, "The Gospel Is Not Shameful: The Argumentative Structure of Romans in the Light of Classical Rhetoric" (Ph.D. diss., Marquettte, 1998).
14. David Steinmetz, *Luther and Staupitz* (Durham, NC: Duke University Press, 1980), 113, draws attention to this, citing *WA* 56:172.8–15 (on Rom. 1:17; *LW* 25.152.); 349.23–26 (on Rom. 7:17; *LW* 25:338).
15. *WA* 56:172.3–11/*LW* 25:151–52, quoting *spir. et litt.* 11.18; 9.15 against *NE* 3.7 (1114a); 5.9 (1134a); 5.10 (1136a).
16. For autobiographical reflection see *WA* 34:336–37; for identification of Rom. 1:17 as "whole conclusion" of the letter, *WA* 3:174.13–16; *LW* 29:188.
17. Erasmus, *Annotations* on Rom. 1:14, 16 (CWE 56.39–40, 42).
18. Ibid., on Rom. 1:17 (CWE 56.42–44).
19. Karl Barth, *Der Römerbrief (Erster Fassung) 1919*, ed. Hermann Schmidt, Karl Barth Gesamtausgabe: Akademische Werke 2 (Zürich: Theologischer Verlag, 1985), 9.

20. Ulrich Wilckens, *Der Brief an die Römer*, EKK 6/1–3 (Neukirchen-Vluyn: Neukirchener Verlag, 1978–82), 1.230–31. On the ethical outworking of Barth's idea of the righteousness of God, Wilckens cites Karl Barth, *Church Dogmatics* Vol. II/1: The Doctrine of God, trans. T. H. L. Parker, et al. (New York: Charles Scribner's Sons, 1957), 386–87, as well as Barth's *Church and State*, trans. G. Ronald Howe (Greenville, South Carolina: Smyth & Helwys, 1991).

21. Bruce McCormack, *Karl Barth's Critically Realistic Dialectical Theology: Its Genesis and Development 1909–1936* (Oxford: Clarendon, 1995), 154.

22. Karl Barth, *The Epistle to the Romans*, trans. Edwyn C. Hoskyns (London: Oxford University Press, 1933), 102.

23. J. T. Beck, *Erklärung des Briefes Pauli an die Römer*, vol. 1 (Gütersloh: Bertelsmann, 1884), 79.

24. *Römerbrief 1919*, 18 n. 12.

25. Barth provides no documentation, but see Rudolf Liechtenhan's two articles in the same issue of *Kirchenblatt für die reformierte Schweiz* 34 (1919): "Der Römerbrief in neuer Beleuchtung" (163–64, 167–69); "Zur Frage nach der Treue Gottes" (192–93).

26. *Romans*, 14; *Der Römerbrief* (Munich: Chr. Kaiser, 1922), xviii.

27. *Romans*, 41; *Römerbrief 1922*, 16.

28. *Romans*, 40; "Übereinstimmung Gottes mit sich selbst," *Römerbrief 1922*, 15. Cf. to "God deals with consistency to his very self, when he extends his saving hand to this whole world" (*Römerbrief 1919*, 9).

29. *Romans*, 42.

30. Rudolf Bultmann, "DIKAIOSUNĒ THEOU," in his *Exegetica: Aufsätze zur Erforschung des Neuen Testaments* (Tübingen: J. C. B. Mohr [Paul Siebeck], 1967), 470–75.

31. Ernst Käsemann, "'The Righteousness of God' in Paul," in *New Testament Questions of Today*, translated by W. J. Montague (Philadelphia: Fortress, 1969), 168–82.

32. Arland Hultgren, *Paul's Gospel and Mission* (Philadelphia: Fortress, 1985), 12–34.

33. The quoted phrase is from R. Barry Matlock, "Almost Cultural Studies? Reflections on the 'New Perspective' on Paul," in *Biblical Studies/Cultural Studies*, ed. J. Cheryl Exum and Stephen D. Moore, Journal for the Study of the Old Testament Supplement 266 (Sheffield: Sheffield Academic Press, 1998), 435.

34. E. P. Sanders, *Paul and Palestinian Judaism* (Philadelphia: Fortress, 1977), 488.

35. Ibid., 491.

36. Ibid., 491–95.

37. Richard Hays, *The Faith of Jesus Christ: The Narrative Substructure of Galatians 3:1–4:11*, 2nd ed. (Grand Rapids: Eerdmans, 2002).

38. A. Katherine Grieb, *The Story of Romans: A Narrative Defense of God's Righteousness* (Louisville: Westminster John Knox, 2002), 24–25.

39. N. T. Wright, "The Letter to the Romans," in *The New Interpreter's Bible* Vol. 10 (Nashville, Abingdon: 2002), 423–24.

40. Ibid., 425.

41. Revelation Enriquez Velunta, "'*Ek Pisteôs Eis Pistin*' and the Filipinos' Sense of Indebtedness (*Utang Na Loob*)," in *Navigating Romans through Cultures*, ed. Yeo Khiok-khng (New York: T. & T. Clark, 2004), 234–55.

Locus 2: Natural Theology

1. Karl Barth, *Theology and Church: Shorter Writings 1920–1928*, trans. Louise Pettibone Smith (New York: Harper & Row, 1962), 243, as quoted in Stanley Hauerwas, *With the Grain of the Universe* (Grand Rapids: Brazos, 1999), 149–50.

2. Origen, *ComRm* 1.16.1 (trans. Scheck 1:88); Hammond Bammel 1.19; 81.9–10.

3. Origen, *ComRm* 1.16.5–6 (Hammond Bammel 1.19; 83.56–84.83); *mikroteros* in frag. 4 of the Tura Papyrus on Rom. 3:21–24 (Heither, 96.11).

4. Origen, *ComRm* frag. 4 (of the Tura Papyrus; Heither 94.3–11).

5. *Natural Theology: Comprising "Nature and Grace" by Professor Dr. Emil Brunner and the Reply "No!" by Karl Barth*, trans. Peter Fraenkel (London: Geoffrey Bles, 1946).

6. These are the last six lines of A. Ramsbotham's fragment 5 ("The Commentary of Origen on the Epistle to the Romans," *JTS* 13 [1912]: 215, lines 16–21) that Heither has inserted after Staab frag. 13 on Rom. 1:18 (Heither 56.4–10).

7. *ComRm*, 1.16.2 (Scheck 1:88; Hammond Bammel 1.19; 81.24–82.30).

8. Origen, *ComRm* 1.17.1–2 (Scheck 1:91–92; Hammond Bammel 1.20; 85.1–86.32).

9. Origen, *ComRm* 7.18.7 (Scheck 2:125; Hammond Bammel 7.16; 633.102–9).

10. Augustine, *s.* 241.1 (WSA III/7:70).

11. Augustine, *s.* 241.7 (WSA III/7:74 n. 17).

12. Augustine, *s.* 241.2 (WSA III/7:71).

13. Augustine, *s.* 241.7 (WSA III/7:74–75).

14. Augustine, *s.* 241.8 (WSA III/7:75–76), citing 1 Cor. 15:40–42 and Plato, *Timaeus* 38c–41b.

15. Augustine, *civ. Dei* 8.1; *The City of God against the Pagans*, ed. and trans. R. W. Dyson (Cambridge: Cambridge University Press, 1998), 312.

16. Augustine, *civ. Dei* 8.6 (Dyson 322).

17. Augustine, *spir. et litt.* 12.19 (translation from WSA I/23:162).

18. Augustine, *spir. et litt.* 26.43–44 (WSA I/23:177–78).

19. Pelagius's *Commentary on St. Paul's Epistle to the Romans*, trans. Theodore de Bruyn (Oxford: Clarendon, 1993), 65 on 1:19b–20.

20. See Pelagius on Rom. 3:2–4 and de Bruyn's comment (*Pelagius's Commentary*, 77 n. 2).

21. Hauerwas, *With the Grain*, 36. He cites *Summa contra Gentiles* 1.4 and *Summa theologica* 1–2.94.1 and 95.1 as places where Aquinas discusses natural law.

22. Aquinas, *Lectura* nos. 114–15 (Cai 21–22).

23. *LW* 25:157; *WA* 56:176.26–32.

24. *LW* 25:154, 156; *WA* 56:174.12–25, 176.10.

25. *WA* 56:358.17–20, my translation; cf. *LW* 25:347–48.

26. *WA* 56:405.6–7, quoting Augustine, *ench.* 98.

27. CWE 56:47–48 ("what is known of God"), 48 (on philosophers), 49–50 (on "invisible things").

28. John Calvin, *The Epistles of Paul the Apostle to the Romans and to the Thessalonians*, trans. Ross Mackenzie (Grand Rapids: Eerdmans, 1960), 31, on Rom. 1:19.

29. Ibid., 31–32.

30. Alvin C. Plantinga, "The Reformed Objection to Natural Theology," in *Major Themes in the Reformed Tradition*, ed. Donald K. McKim (Grand Rapids: Eerdmans, 1992), 67–69, cites *Institutes* 1.3.1, 3; 1.5.1–2; and 1.7.4.

31. Barth, *Römerbrief 1919*, 14.

32. Hauerwas, *With the Grain*, 149–50.

33. Barth, *Römerbrief 1919*, 16.

34. Ibid., 129.

35. Barth, *Romans*, 44. Mention is also made twice elsewhere of eternity in this section (ibid., 43, 48).

36. Barth, *CD* I/2:306.

37. Barth, *CD* II/1, chap. 5: "The Knowledge of God," §§25–27, pp. 3–254.

38. Barth, *CD* II/1:121.

39. Cf. Origen, *ComRm* 1.16–1.17.2 (Scheck 1:87–92; Hammond Bammel 1.19–1.20; 80.1–86.32).

40. John Hesselink "Karl Barth and Emil Brunner—A Tangled Tale with a Happy Ending (or, The Story of a Relationship)," in *How Karl Barth Changed My Mind*, ed. Donald K. McKim (Grand Rapids: Eerdmans, 1986), 134.

41. Letter 207 from *Karl Barth: Letters 1961–1968*, trans. Geoffrey W. Bromiley (Grand Rapids: Eerdmans, 1981), 202 as quoted in Hesselink, "Karl Barth and Emil Brunner—A Tangled Tale with a Happy Ending," 141.

42. Philipp Vielhauer, "On the 'Paulinism' of Acts" in *Studies in Luke-Acts: Essays Presented in Honor of Paul Schubert*, ed. L. E. Keck and J. L. Martyn (Nashville: Abingdon, 1966), 36–37.

43. James D. G. Dunn, *Romans*, 2 vols., Word Biblical Commentary (Dallas: Word, 1988), 1:56–57.

44. Ibid., 58.

45. See, e.g., Milton Steinberg, *Basic Judaism* (New York: Harcourt, Brace & World, 1947), 39–41.

46. Dunn, *Romans*, 1:58.

47. N. T. Wright, *Paul for Everyone, Romans: Parts 1–2* (Louisville: Westminster John Knox, 2004), 1:18.

48. Wright, "Romans," 429.

49. C. K. Barrett, *A Commentary on the Epistle to the Romans*, BNTC (London: Adam & Charles Black, 1957), 35; and on his general debt to Barth, see vi.

50. Plantinga, "Reformed Objection to Natural Theology," 75 n. 8.

Locus 3: Made Righteous by Christ

1. Adolf Schlatter, *Der Glaube im Neuen Testament*, 5th ed. (Stuttgart: Calwer, 1963), 352.

2. *ComRm* 3.6.1–9 on Rom. 3:20 (Scheck 1:202–8; Hammond Bammel 3.3; 221.1–227.149).

3. Ibid., 3.7.2–10 on Rom. 3:21 (Scheck 1:208–14; Hammond Bammel 3.4; 227.5–233.129).

4. Ibid., frag. 4 of book 5 and 3:21–24 (Heither 96.29, 98.1–2). Heither's translation is: "und die an Jesus Christus glauben oder den Glauben an den Vater empfangen, den ihnen Jesus Christus eingegeben hat" (ibid., 97, 99). Roy A. Harrisville III labels this as an ambiguous case, "*Pistis Christou*: Witness of the Fathers," *NovT* 36 (1994): 235.

5. *ComRm* frag. 5 of book 5 on Rom. 3:25–26 (Heither 102.30–31, 104.1–6; my emphasis). Cf. Harrisville, who takes this same selection and focuses only on the "believe(s) in [*eis*] Jesus" phrases to argue that Origen understands Paul's "*ek pisteōs Iēsou*" phrase in 3:26 to mean the objective genitive in "*Pistis Christou*," 238.

6. Michael J. Gorman, *Cruciformity: Paul's Narrative Spirituality of the Cross* (Grand Rapids: Eerdmans, 2001), 110–11, as quoted in Douglas Harink, *Paul among the Postliberals* (Grand Rapids: Brazos, 2003), 41.

7. Origen, *ComRm* 3.8.3–4 on Rom. 3:25 (Scheck 1:218–19; Hammond Bammel 3.5; 238.54–239.95). The exegetical strategy of taking the dimensions of the tabernacle or temple and its components as indicative of spiritual reality has a long history, including Guillaume Dufay's use of temple dimensions in composing his motet *Nuper rosarum flores* for the dedication of the cathedral in Florence (Craig Wright, "Dufay's *Nuper rosarum flores*, King Solomon's Temple, and the Veneration of the Virgin," *Journal of the American Musicological Society* 47/3 (1994): 395–427; 429–41.

8. *ComRm* 3.8.9 (trans. Scheck, 1:222; Hammond Bammel 3.5; 243.158–59).

9. Ibid., 3.8.2–3 (Scheck 1:218; Hammond Bammel 3.5; 237.49–238.66).

10. Ibid., 3.8.11–12 (trans. Scheck 1:223; Hammond Bammel 3.5; 245.200–202).
11. This is the extreme position of T. Heither, *Translation Religionis: Die Paulusdeutung des Origenes in seinem Kommentar zum Römerbrief,* BBK 16 (Cologne: Böhlau, 1990), who makes Origen into a direct precursor of Luther.
12. *ComRm* on 3:27–28 (Jean Scherer, *Le commentaire d'Origène sur Rom. III.5–V.7,* IFAO 27 (Cairo: Institut Français d'Archéologie Orientale, 1957), 164.8. Heither 104.24; Scheck 3.93; 1:226; Hammond Bammel 3.6; 248.25–27).
13. R. Roukema, "Origenes visie op de rechtvaardiging volgens zijn Commentaar op Romeinen," *Gereformeerd theologisch tijdschrift* 89 (1989): 100–101, citing the Greek text of Origen's commentary on 4:2, 5, 7, 16 (Scherer 178–86, 206). See also *ComRm* frag. 1 of book 6 (Heither 120.29–122.23).
14. Maurice Wiles, *The Divine Apostle: The Interpretation of St. Paul's Epistles in the Early Church* (London: Cambridge University Press, 1967), 114. I am indebted to Thomas P. Scheck, "Justification by Faith Alone in Origen's *Commentary on Romans* and Its Reception during the Reformation Era," in *Origeniana Octava: Origen and the Alexandrian Tradition,* Papers of the 8th International Origen Congress, Pisa, 27–31 August 2001, ed. L. Perrone (Leuven: Leuven University Press, 2003), vol. II: 1282, for this reference.
15. *ComRm* 8.7.6 on 11:6 (Scheck 2:159; Hammond Bammel 8.6; 672.111–15).
16. Scheck, "Justification," 1284.
17. Roukema, "Origenes visie op de rechtvaardiging," 104–5.
18. *ComRm* 3.9.3 (Scheck 1:226–27; Hammond Bammel 3.6; 248.25–39); note abbreviated reference in Greek fragment (Scherer 164.9; Heither 104.25).
19. *ComRm* 4.1.16 (Scheck 1:244; Hammond Bammel 4.1; 279.191–97); missing from the Greek fragment on 4:1–8 (Heither 118–26).
20. *ComRm* 5.9.7 (Scheck 1:364; Hammond Bammel 5.9; 435.83–436.90); missing from the Greek fragment on 6:5 (Ramsbotham frag. 29; Heither 172).
21. *ComRm* 3.10.5 (Scheck 1:233; Hammond Bammel 3.8; 256.73–82).
22. Camille Verfaillie, *La doctrine de la justification dans Origène d'après son commentaire de l'Épître aux Romains* (Strasbourg: Université de Strasbourg, 1926), 105–6.
23. Augustine, *ex. prop. Rm.* 13–18 (Paula Fredriksen Landes, *Augustine on Romans: Propositions from the Epistle to the Romans, Unfinished Commentary on the Epistle to the Romans* (Chico, California: Scholars Press, 1982), 4–7.
24. Augustine, *spir. et litt.* 9.15 (trans. WSA I/23:158).
25. Ibid., 10.16 (WSA I/23:159–60).
26. Ibid., 9.15; 11.18 (WSA I/23:158, 161).
27. Cf. Harink, *Paul among the Postliberals,* 26. The German phrase is from the 1546 version of Luther's Bible, *D. Martin Luthers Deutsche Bibel: 1522–1546,* vol. 7, ed. Ulrich Köpf (Weimar: Hermann Böhlaus, 1931), 39.
28. Augustine, *spir. et litt.* 26.44–45 (WSA I/23:178).
29. Abelard, *Expositio* at 3:21 (Peppermüller 274.10–12). I have altered Peppermüller's text by designating "Sed nunc" as part of the lemma. Even though it is different from the Vulgate's "Nunc autem" with which the paragraph begins, Abelard is clearly offering a paraphrase of the Vulgate's phrase.
30. Augustine, *f. et op.* 16.27; Rolf Peppermüller, *Abaelards Auslegung des Römerbriefes,* BGPTM n.s. 10 (Münster: Aschendorff, 1972), 80.
31. Abelard, *Expositio* on 3:22 (Peppermüller 274.16–276.12).
32. Ibid., on 3:23 (Peppermüller 276.13–15).
33. Ibid., on 3:24 (Peppermüller 276.16–20).
34. Ibid., on 3:25 (Peppermüller 276.21–278.6); cf. Origen, *ComRm* 3.8.1; 3.9.4 (Scheck 1:216, 228; Hammond Bammel 3.5; 236.15–16 and 3.6; 249.59–60).
35. Abelard, *Expositio* on 3:26 (Peppermüller 278.7–27).
36. Ibid., on 3:27 (Peppermüller 290.26–298.12).

37. Ibid., on 3:28 (Peppermüller 298.18–19).
38. Anselm, *Cur Deus Homo* I, chaps. 19–23; II, chaps. 18–19.
39. Ibid., I, chap. 23; citation and explanation by Charles P. Carlson Jr., *Justification in Earlier Medieval Theology* (The Hague: Nijhoff, 1975), 91.
40. Peppermüller, *Abaelards Auslegung des Römerbriefes*, 91–92; idem, "Einleitung," in *Expositio* 35 n. 148.
41. Abelard, *Expositio* at 3:26 (Peppermüller 280.16–284.21); Luke 16:19–31; 8:2; Matt. 9:2.
42. Abelard, *Expositio* at 3:26 (Peppermüller 286.12–288.16).
43. Ibid., at 3:26 (Peppermüller 288.18–25).
44. Carlson, *Justification*, 47–48.
45. Abelard, *Expositio* at 3:26 (Peppermüller 278.12, 14–15).
46. Aquinas, *Lectura* no. 300 (Cai 53).
47. Giorgio Agamben, *Il tempo che resta: Un commento alla Lettera ai Romani* (Turin: Bollati Boringhieri, 2000), 62–84.
48. Aquinas, *Lectura* nos. 302–3 (Cai 53).
49. Ibid., 302 (Cai 53).
50. Carlson, *Justification*, 59, on Rom. 1:17.
51. Aquinas, *Lectura* no. 307 (Cai 54). Texts from Origen that are closest to Aquinas here are at *CmRom* 5.6.65–74 (Hammond Bammel 415; Scheck 1:347); 5.10.186–92 (Hammond Bammel 450–51; Scheck 1.375–76).
52. Aquinas, *Lectura* nos. 309–10 (Cai 54).
53. Ibid., 311 (Cai 54).
54. Aquinas, *Lectura* no. 312 (Cai 54–55).
55. Aquinas, *Lectura* nos. 315–16 (Cai 55).
56. Aquinas, *Lectura* no. 317 (Cai 56). See also Carlson, *Justification*, 60.
57. Mary Daly, "The Notion of Justification in the Commentary of St. Thomas Aquinas on the Epistle to the Romans" (Ph.D. diss., Marquette, 1971), 81, on the "law of faith" in Rom. 3:27 in relation to 1:17.
58. *Summa theologica* I-II q. 113, art. 1–6, as summarized in Carlson, *Justification*, 118–22.
59. The German title of the hymn is "Aus Tiefer Not." *Liturgy and Hymns*, ed. Ulrich S. Leupold, *LW* 53 (Philadelphia: Fortress, 1965), 224; *WA* 35.419.19–20.
60. Harink, *Paul among the Postliberals*, 30.
61. Richard Hays, "PISTIS and Pauline Christology: What Is at Stake?" in *Pauline Theology*, vol. 4: *Looking Back, Pressing On*, ed. Elizabeth Johnson and David M. Hay (Atlanta: Scholars Press, 1997), 39.
62. *WA* 56:37.11–13.
63. *WA* 56:41.7–8 (gloss on 4:4).
64. *LW* 25:39; *WA* 56:45.7–8.
65. Hultgren, *Paul's Gospel and Mission*, 47–50.
66. *WA* 56:1.6–11.
67. Stephen Westerholm, *Perspectives Old and New on Paul: The "Lutheran" Paul and His Critics* (Grand Rapids: Eerdmans, 2004), 444.
68. *LW* 54:46–47; *WA Tischreden* 1:136–37 (no. 335).
69. de Lubac, *Medieval Exegesis*, 75.
70. J. A. Fitzmyer, *Romans*, AB 33 (New York: Doubleday, 1993), xiv. See also Marie-Joseph Lagrange, *Saint Paul: Epître aux Romains* (Paris: J. Gabalda, 1950); Franz J. Leenhardt, *The Epistle to the Romans: A Commentary*, trans. Harold Knight (London: Lutterworth, 1961); Otto Kuss, *Der Römerbrief*, 2 vols., 2nd ed. (Regensburg: F. Pustet, 1963); Heinrich Schlier, *Der Römerbrief: Kommentar* (Freiburg im Breisgau: Herder, 1977); Brendan Byrne, *Romans,* ed. Daniel J. Harrington, Sacra Pagina 6 (Collegeville, Minnesota: Liturgical Press, 1996); Luke

Timothy Johnson, *Reading Romans: A Literary and Theological Commentary* (New York: Crossroad, 1997); Romano Penna, *Lettera ai Romani*: Vol. 1: *Romans 1–5*, Scritti delle origini cristiane 6 (Bologna: EDB, 2004).

71. Alain Gignac's Romans commentary is scheduled to be published by the Paris publisher le Cerf around the year 2008.

72. John Henry Newman, *An Essay on the Development of Christian Doctrine*, rev. ed. (London: Longmans, Green, 1878), 8.

73. Cf. William Sanday and A. C. Headlam, *A Critical and Exegetical Commentary on the Epistle to the Romans*, 2nd ed., ICC (New York: Charles Scribner's Sons, 1896), cix, on Schaefer's Catholic commentary and on Theophanes's Russian Orthodox commentary, though they later admit one negative result of the Reformers' ideas of the imputation of Christ's merits (152).

74. Fyodor Dostoyevsky, *The Brothers Karamazov*, trans. Constance Garnett (New York: Signet, 1957), 291.

75. Heiko Oberman, *Luther: Man between God and the Devil*, trans. Eileen Walliser-Schaarzbart (New Haven: Yale University Press, 1989), 152–53.

76. See Luther's sermon "Two Kinds of Righteousness," in *LW* 31:297–306; *WA* 2:145–52.

77. Heiko Oberman, *The Dawn of the Reformation: Essays in Late Medieval and Early Reformation Thought* (Edinburgh: T. & T. Clark, 1986), 124.

78. *LW* 25:33; *WA* 56:39.10–11.

79. The best survey of "faith alone" at 3:28 may be found in Fitzmyer, *Romans*, 360–62. I am indebted to Fitzmyer for the references that follow. Alexander Souter, *Expositions of Thirteen Epistles of St. Paul* (Cambridge: Cambridge University Press, 1922–31) 2:34.

80. Augustine, *f. et op.* 22.40 (CSEL 41.84–85); Pelagius, *Expositio* at 3:28 (Souter ed. 34; de Bruyn 83; Aquinas, *Lectura* no. 317 (Cai 56).

81. Carlson, *Justification*, 130–32, citing *WA* 56:273–76 (*LW* 25:259–64) on Rom. 4:7. The nominalist teaching that one should take responsibility for first steps toward God is summarized in the phrase "facere quod in se est" (to do what lies in oneself). E. Jane Dempsey Douglas, *Justification in Late Medieval Preaching*, 2nd ed., SMRT 1 (Leiden: Brill, 1989), 207–8, credits the pastoral rigor in the preaching of John Geiler with preparing Strasbourg for the Reformation that so quickly took hold in that city. Perhaps nominalism exerted a similar influence on Luther, heightening a tension that was finally resolved by the passive righteousness in the justification by faith he discovered in Romans.

82. We can now call this "an innovation"; the Reformers and Counter-Reformers never claimed to be making an innovation. Their reforms were all explicitly based on recognizing the proper precedents (Douglas, *Justification*, 208).

83. *Romans*, 283.

84. McCormack, *Karl Barth's Dialectical Theology*, 258–61.

85. *Romans*, 281–82.

86. Ibid., 234.

87. Ibid., 195.

88. Ibid., 206.

89. *Römerbrief 1919*, 71 (102).

90. *Romans*, 107–9; *Römerbrief 1922*, 82–83.

91. *Romans*, 96–97.

92. Sanders, *Paul and Palestinian Judaism*, 487; idem, *Paul*, 88.

93. Sanders, *Paul*, 87–88.

94. Sanders, *Paul, the Law, and the Jewish People*, 42.

95. Ibid., 4.

96. A. Andrew Das, *Paul and the Jews* (Peabody, MA: Hendrickson, 2003), 12, 17.

97. Westerholm, *Perspectives*, 441.
98. Harink, *Paul among the Postliberals*, 32–38. Cf. Seyoon Kim, *Paul and the New Perspective* (Grand Rapids: Eerdmans, 2002), 85–100, for an imaginative but futile attempt to find "Justification by Grace and through Faith in 1 Thessalonians."
99. Simon Gathercole, *Where Is Boasting? Early Jewish Soteriology and Paul's Reponse in Romans 1–5* (Grand Rapids: Eerdmans, 2002), 135; Kari Kuula, *The Law, the Covenant and God's Plan*, vol. 2: *Paul's Treatment of the Law and Israel in Romans*, FES 85 (Göttingen: Vandenhoeck & Ruprecht, 2003), 5.
100. Grieb, *Story*, 38–42.
101. Ibid., 40–41.
102. Ibid., 37–38, 41.
103. Wright, "Romans," 470.
104. Ibid., 471–75.
105. Wright, *Paul for Everyone*, 1:61–63.
106. R. Barry Matlock, "Detheologizing the *Pistis Christou* Debate," *NovT* 42 (2000): 20–23.
107. Anders Nygren, *Commentary on Romans*, trans. Carl C. Rasmussen (Philadelphia: Muhlenberg, 1949), 68, 71, as cited in Hultgren, *Paul's Gospel and Mission*, 39–40.
108. Arland J. Hultgren, "The *Pistis Christou* Formulation in Paul," *NovT* 22 (1980): 253–58, and comments on *pistis Christou* in his forthcoming Romans commentary, due from Eerdmans by 2008.
109. Matlock, "Detheologizing," 17–20, following Barr, *Semantics of Biblical Language*, 201–3.
110. C. E. B. Cranfield, "On the *Pistis Christou* Question," in *On Romans* (Edinburgh: T. & T. Clark, 1998), 81–97.
111. Hultgren, "*Pistis Christou* Formulation," 256–57, 263 (quotations).
112. Morna D. Hooker, "*PISTIS CHRISTOU*," *NTS* 35 (1989): 336, 339–40; Sam K. Williams, "Again *Pistis Christou*," *CBQ* 49 (1987): 431–37. Hooker also exegetes ancillary texts (2 Cor. 1:17–22; 4:13; Gal. 4:19) to show that Paul's logic demands both objective and subjective senses behind the phrase ("*PISTIS CHRISTOU*," 334–35, 342).
113. Hooker, "*PISTIS CHRISTOU*," 341–42.
114. Grieb, *Story*, 25.
115. Hultgren, *Paul's Gospel and Mission*, 52–72, and conversation with Daniel Bailey on December 17, 2004.
116. Vielhauer, "On the 'Paulinism' of Acts," 41–42.

Locus 4: All Sinned

1. Augustine, *mor.* 22.40, as quoted in Henri Blocher, *Original Sin*, NSBT (Grand Rapids: Eerdmans, 1997), 15.
2. Hays, *Echoes*, 54–55. See also the discussion in Fitzmyer, *Romans*, 369–72.
3. Sanders, *Paul and Palestinian Judaism*, 485–86 has been helpful for me in seeing chap. 5 as a "swing vote" in how one understands the first half of Romans.
4. Dunn, *Romans,* 1:242–44.
5. Origen, *ComRm* 5.1.20–21 (Scheck 1:313–15; Hammond Bammel 5.1; 372.262–373.296).
6. Pelagius's comments immediately after his quotation of Rom. 5:12 (de Bruyn 92). This is much different from the organic transmission of sin from human generation to generation that Origen sees here.
7. Scheck, *ComRm* 1:303 n. 1.

8. Origen, *ComRm* 5.4.3 (Scheck 1:341; Hammond Bammel 407.27–32) on Rom. 5:18. See also *PArch* 2.8.5.
9. Cf. John Chryssavgis, "Original Sin—An Orthodox Perspective," appendix in Neil Ormerod, *Grace and Disgrace* (Newton, New South Wales: E. J. Dwyer, 1992), 197–206.
10. *ComRm* 5.3–4 on 5:12–14 (Scheck 1:304–5; Hammond Bammel 5.1.20–55 [359–61]).
11. Ibid., 5.1.1 (Scheck 1:303; Hammond Bammel 5.1; 359.6). 5.1.6 (Hammond Bammel 359; Scheck 5.1; 359.20–361.55). The omission of "not" is found also in the first hand of a significant manuscript related in Romans to Origen's lemma, 1739. Most manuscripts of this commentary do not contain the "not." Only K and the original scribe of Y, according to Hammond Bammel's apparatus, read Rom. 5:14 as saying (with the Nestle-Aland critical edition of the New Testament and all contemporary translations) that "death reigned over those who sinned and those who did not sin in the likeness of Adam's transgression."
12. Origen, *ComRm* 5.1.32–36 (Scheck 1:322–24; Hammond Bammel 5.1; 382.482–386.548).
13. Ibid., 5.1.37 (Scheck 1:324–25; Hammond Bammel 5.1; 386.549–387.574).
14. Ibid., 5.1.27 (Scheck 1:318–19; Hammond Bammel 5.1; 378.392–379.406).
15. *pecc. mer.* 1.12.15 (PL 44:117).
16. On Augustine's response to Pelagius in this book, see Delaroche, *Saint Augustin*, 292–300.
17. *pecc. mer.* 3.4.9 (CSEL 60:134–35).
18. Rom. 5:20; *pecc. mer.* 3.11.20 (CSEL 60:148).
19. De Bruyn, *Pelagius's Commentary*, 37–39.
20. *ex prop. Rm.* 13 (on Rom. 3:20); *pecc. mer.* 1.10.12; 3.11.20 (PL 44:116, 198).
21. *pecc. mer.* 1.4.4 (PL 44:111).
22. *ep.* 157.11–12 (CSEL 44:457–59).
23. Ibid., 6, 9, 16, 17 (CSEL 44:452, 455, 464–65).
24. Ibid., 10 (CSEL 44:456).
25. Ibid., 15 (CSEL 44:462).
26. Abelard, *Expositio* on 5:12 (Peppermüller 390.1–25).
27. Ibid., on 5:19 (Peppermüller 406.16–408.24).
28. Ibid., on 5:19 (Peppermüller 410.1–412.3), citing Augustine, *div. qu.* 24.
29. Abelard, *Expositio* on 5:19 (Peppermüller 412.5–418.20), citing Augustine, *div. qu.* 24, and Boethius, *In Aristotelis de Interpretatione commentarius* 3.9.
30. Abelard, *Expositio* on 5:19 (Peppermüller 424.28–426.6). The earlier quotation is at 5:16 (Peppermüller 398.6–12).
31. Ibid., on 5:19 (Peppermüller 428.1–438.10), following Augustine, *ench.* 46.
32. *LW* 25:45–46; *WA* 56:51.19–52.7.
33. *LW* 25:296–302; *WA* 56:309.20–315.12; see Augustine, *pecc. mer.* 1.10–11.
34. Carlson, *Justification*, 130–32.
35. *LW* 25:301–2; *WA* 56:314.25–315.12.
36. Erasmus, CWE 56.137–38, quotation from 138.
37. Ibid., 139–41 and 153 n. 7.
38. Ibid., 142 (quotation of Pelagius), 145–46 (context before and after points to individuals' sins), 146 (Chrysostom quote from *Homilae in epistulam ad Romanos* 10.1).
39. *Römerbrief 1919*, 128 (177).
40. Ibid., 128–29 (178).
41. Ibid., 131–32 (182–84).
42. *Romans*, 168.
43. Ibid., 167.

44. Ibid., 169; cf. *Römerbrief 1919*, 130 (180–81).
45. *Romans*, 166; cf. *Römerbrief 1919*, 127–28 (175–78). Barth is clearer in *Romans I* that death does not belong in God's primal world (127 [176]).
46. Rom. 1:32; 5:6–8, 12–21; 6:3–23; 7:2–24; 8:2, 6, 36, 38; 14:7–9.
47. *Romans*, 171.
48. Ibid.
49. See also *CD* II/2:92–93.
50. E. P. Sanders, *Paul and Palestinian Judaism* (Philadelphia: Fortress, 1977), 442–47. J. Louis Martyn, who follows Barth and Sanders on the law, draws the connection between the two in *Theological Issues in the Letters of Paul* (Nashville: Abingdon, 1997), 170 n. 23; idem, *Galatians*, AB 33A (New York: Doubleday, 1997), 95 n. 43, 266 n. 163. Against Sanders, cf. Frank Thielman, *From Plight to Solution: A Jewish Framework for Understanding Paul's View of the Law in Galatians and Romans* (Leiden: Brill, 1989); Thomas R. Schreiner, *The Law and Its Fulfillment: A Pauline Theology of Law* (Grand Rapids: Baker, 1993).
51. Sanders, *Paul and Palestinian Judaism*, 474.
52. Ibid., 474–75 n. 2.
53. Sanders, *Paul*, 44–46.
54. Dunn, *Romans,* 1:290.
55. Ibid., 292.
56. Grieb, *Story*, 64–66.
57. Wright, "Romans," 522–27.
58. Blocher, *Original Sin*, 76–78 (quotation from 78).
59. Ibid., 80.
60. Ibid., 122–23.

Locus 5: The All and the Many

1. Nicolas von Zinzendorf, "Jesus, Thy Blood and Righteousness," trans. John Wesley, in *The Methodist Hymnal* (New York: The Methodist Publishing House, 1939), no. 205.
2. Sanders, *Paul*, 146–47. Sanders also lists 1 Cor. 15:21–22.
3. Origen, *ComRm* 5.5.2–4 (Scheck 1:342–43; Hammond Bammel 5.5; 408.18–409.44).
4. Ibid., 5.5.2 (Scheck 1:342; Hammond Bammel 5.5; 408.15–18).
5. Ibid., 8.13.3–4 (Scheck 2:186–87; Hammond Bammel 8.12; 705.28–707.63). Peter Gorday also emphasizes the goodness of God as a theme in Origen's Romans exegesis (*Principles of Patristic Exegesis* [New York: Mellen, 1983], 88–89).
6. Gorday, *Principles*, 86–88.
7. Origen, *PArch* 1.6; discussion and not definition (ibid., 1.6.1; see *On First Principles*, trans. G. W. Butterworth [New York: Harper & Row, 1966], 52).
8. Origen, *ComRm* 3.8.13 (Scheck 1:224; Hammond Bammel 3.5; 245.204–212). Origen uses 1 John 2:2 to inform his exegesis here.
9. Origen, *PArch* 2.10; *CCels* 6.26.
10. Origen, *PArch* 1.6.3 (Butterworth 56 n. 4).
11. Augustine, *ex. prop. Rm.* 29.9–10 (Fredriksen 11).
12. Idem, *civ. Dei* 20.1.
13. Ibid., 21.9.
14. Ibid., 21.10–27.
15. Abelard, *Expositio* on Rom. 5:18 (Peppermüller 400).
16. Ibid., on Rom. 5:19 (Peppermüller 402).
17. Aquinas, *Lectura* nos. 443, first quotation; 444, second and third quotations (all on Cai 81).

18. *LW* 25:48 n. 26; *WA* 56:55 n. 3; Augustine, *pecc. mer.* 1.15.

19. *LW* 25:48 n. 27; *WA* 56:55 n. 4.

20. J. W. Colenso, *St. Paul's Epistle to the Romans: Newly Translated and Explained from a Missionary Point of View* (New York: Appleton, 1863), 114, as quoted in Jonathan A. Draper, "A 'Frontier' Reading of Romans," in *Navigating Romans through Cultures*, 73. On the legacy of Colenso, see also Jonathan A. Draper, *The Eye of the Storm: Bishop John William Colenso and the Crisis of Biblical Interpretation* (Edinburgh: T. & T. Clark, 2004); Jeff Guy, *The View Across the River: Harriette Colenso and the Zulu Struggle against Imperialism* (Charlottesville, VA: University of Virginia Press, 2002).

21. Barth, *Römerbrief 1919*, 124 (172).

22. Webster, *Barth's Moral Theology*, 3, 11–39.

23. Barth, *Römerbrief 1919*, 142–43 (197–98).

24. Barth, *Romans*, 98–99.

25. Ibid., 182.

26. Ibid., 183.

27. Barth, *CD* II/2:502; cf. Matt. 26:24/Mark 14:21; Dante, *Inferno*, canto 34.

28. Christian T. Collins Winn, "Barth and Pietism," paper presented at the Karl Barth Society of North America, San Antonio, Texas, November 20, 2004; the following works are cited in Collins Winn's paper. On Barth's relationships to pietists: F. Gärtner, *Karl Barth und Zinzendorf: Die bleibende Bedeutung Zinzendorfs auf Grund der Beurteilung des Pietismus durch Karl Barth* (Munich: Kaiser, 1953); Claudia Hake, *Der Bedeutung der Theologie Johann Tobias Beck für die Entwicklung der Theologie Karl Barths* (Frankfurt am Main: Peter Lang, 1999). On Württemberg pietism: Friedhelm Groth, *Die 'Wiederbringung Aller Dinge' im Württembergischen Pietismus: theologiegeschichtliche Studien zum eschatologischen Heilsuniversalismus Württembergisher Pietisten des 18. Jahrhunderts* (Göttingen: Vandenhoeck & Ruprecht, 1984); idem, "Chiliasmus und Apokatastasishoffnung in der Reich-Gottes-Verkündigung der beiden Blumhardts," *Pietismus und Neuzeit* 9 (1983): 56–116; Hartmut Lehmann, *Pietismus und weltliche Ordnung in Württenberg, vom 17. bis zum 20. Jahrhundert* (Stuttgart: Kohlhammer, 1969).

29. Karl Barth, *Christ and Adam: Man and Humanity in Romans 5*, trans. T. A. Smail (New York: Collier, 1956), 74–75.

30. Ibid., 109–10.

31. Ibid., 91–92, 100.

32. Ibid., 113. There is some movement on the dialectic of corporate humanity and individual humans between *Romans I* and *Romans II* that is partially explained by Barth's use of Overbeck and Kierkegaard in the latter work.

33. Karl Barth, "The Humanity of God," trans. J. S. McNab, in *Karl Barth: Theologian of Freedom*, ed. Clifford Green (Minneapolis: Fortress, 1991), 63–64.

34. Barth, "All!" in *Deliverance to the Captives*, trans. Marguerite Wieser (New York: Harper & Brothers, 1961), 86.

35. Ibid., 91.

36. Ibid., 88.

37. G. B. Caird, "Predestination—Romans ix–xi," *ExpT* 68 (1957): 324–27.

38. Sanders, *Paul and Palestinian Judaism*, 446–47.

39. Sanders, *Paul*, 148–49.

40. George Hunsinger, "Hellfire and Damnation: Four Ancient and Modern Views," in *Disruptive Grace* (Grand Rapids: Eerdmans, 2000), 226–49; on "reverent agnosticism" see 242–48.

41. Richard John Neuhaus, *Death on a Friday Afternoon* (New York: Basic, 2000), 65.

42. Brendan Byrne, *Romans*, Sacra Pagina (Collegeville, MN: Liturgical Press, 1996), 182 (on 5:12–21), 353 (on 11:30–21); and similarly Lagrange, *Romains*, 289.

43. Richard Bell, "Romans 5.18–19 and Universal Salvation," *NTS* 48 (2002): 418–25, 427.
44. Ibid., 430.
45. Cf. Thomas R. Schreiner, *Romans*, BECNT 6 (Grand Rapids: Baker, 1998), 292, 629.
46. Bell, "Romans 5.18–19 and Universal Salvation," 430–42.
47. Wright, *Romans*, 529.
48. Alain Badiou, *Saint Paul: The Foundation of Universalism*, trans. Ray Brassier (Stanford: Stanford University Press, 2003), ix (Brassier's note), 36, 62.
49. Ibid., 96 (both quotations).
50. See "Apocatastasis" and "Constantinople, Second Council of," in *ODCC*, 83, 407.

Locus 6: Warring Laws

1. *LW* 25:328; *WA* 56:340.5–7.
2. Sanders, *Paul and Palestinian Judaism*, 466–69; idem, *Paul*, 94.
3. Heinrich Schlier, *Der Römerbrief*, HTKNT 6 (Freiburg im Breisgau: Herder, 1977), 192–98.
4. Karl Barth, "Death—But Life!" in *Deliverance to the Captives*, 149–50.
5. Cf. *Philocalia* 9 (Heither 190.1–194.21) to *ComRm* 6.8.2 (Scheck 2:29; Hammond Bammel 6.8; 497.14–17) on Rom. 7:7.
6. *ComRm* 6.2–7 (Scheck 2:29–33).
7. Ibid., 6.5–6 (Scheck 2:31–32).
8. Hermann Lichtenberger, *Das Ich Adams und das Ich der Menschheit: Studien zum Menschenbild in Römer 7*, WUNT 164 (Tübingen: Mohr Siebeck, 2004), 133. Cf. Stanley K. Stowers, "Romans 7.7–25 as a Speech-in-Character," in *Paul in His Hellenistic Context*, ed. Troels Engberg-Pedersen (Minneapolis: Fortress, 1995), 180–202, who thinks that both paragraphs are spoken to an implied audience of *ethnē*.
9. Origen, *ComRm* 6.9.3, 6 (Scheck 2:37, 38; Hammond Bammel 6.9; 508.40–42; 510.75–78).
10. Ibid., 6.9.10 (Scheck 2:41; Hammond Bammel 6.9; 514.154–515.162).
11. Ibid., 6.9.9, 11 (Scheck 2:40, 42; Hammond Bammel 513.127–31; 515.177–79).
12. Ibid., 6.9.10 (Scheck 2:41; Hammond Bammel 6.9; 514.158–515.162).
13. Ibid., 6.9.11 (Scheck 2:42; Hammond Bammel 516.181–184).
14. Ibid., 6.11.2 (Scheck 2:45–46; Hammond Bammel 6.11; 520.6–521.39).
15. Ibid., 6.11.3 (Scheck 2:46–47; Hammond Bammel 6.11; 521.40–523.64). See 2 Cor. 3:6.
16. Ibid., 6.12.2–3 (Scheck 2:48–49; Hammond Bammel 6.12; 523.17–525.43).
17. Ibid., 6.12.4–5 (Scheck 2:49–50; Hammond Bammel 6.12; 525.47–526.78).
18. Cf. frag. 45 (Heither 206.18–208.1) with *ComRm* 6.12.5 (Scheck 2:49; Hammond Bammel 6.12; 526.59–69).
19. Augustine*, ex prop. Rm.* 37–48 (on Rom. 7:8–8:3; Fredriksen 14–21); *div. qu.* 66.4–5 (Mosher, *Augustine: Eighty-three Different Questions*, trans. David L. Mosher (Washington, D.C.: Catholic University of America Press, 1982), 142–44); *Simp.* 1.1, 7 (this and all other translations of *Ad Simplicianum* are from John H. S. Burleigh, trans. and ed., *Augustine: Earlier Writings*, LCC 6 [Philadelphia: Westminster, 1953]; here, 376, 379).
20. *pecc. mer.* 1.27.43 (PL 44:133–34). By identifying the position of *De peccatorum meritis et remissione* on Romans 7 as transitional, I am in agreement with Marie-François Berrouard, "L'exégèse augustinienne de Rom., 7, 7–25 entre 396 et 418

avec des remarques sur les deux premières périodes de la crise 'pélagienne,'" *Recherches augustiniennes* 16 (1981): 127–49, who places this text into the middle phase ("La polémique contre Célestius") of Augustine's evolving exegesis of Romans 7.

21. *pecc. mer.* 2.12.17 (PL 44:161–62). This is also noticed by Frederick Van Fleteren, "Augustine's Evolving Exegesis of Romans 7:22–23 in Its Pauline Context," *Augustinian Studies* 32 (2001): 102, where he also describes book 2 of the *On the Merits* as "the first absolutely clear intimation in Augustine's theological writings regarding man's occasional submission to concupiscence *sub gratia* with explicit mention of Romans 7:22–23."

22. *ep.* 6*, lines 138–55 (BA 46B:136–38).

23. *Retract.* 1.23.1.

24. Berrouard, "Exégèse augustinienne de Rom., 7, 7–25," 192.

25. See Peter Brown, "Pelagius and His Supporters: Aims and Environment," *JTS* 19 (April 1968): 111–14, for an analysis of how conflicting ideas on the church form the motivating basis of Augustine's opposition to the Pelagian revolution. J. Patout Burns, "The Interpretation of Romans in the Pelagian Controversy," *Augustinian Studies* 10 (1979): 46–47, argues that Augustine's change on Rom. 7 and his opposition to Caelestius and Pelagius stems from Augustine's high Christology. He seems to equate Augustine's arguments with his motives for opposing Pelagianism.

26. *spir. et litt.* 4–5, trans. by R. J. Teske, S.J., in WSA I/23:151 (CSEL 60: 156–57).

27. *pecc. mer.* 1.65–66 (CSEL 60:65–66). I learned of this point on which Augustine depends on Origen's commentary, which had recently become available to Augustine via Rufinus's translation of 406, in Caroline Hammond Bammel, "Rufinus' Translation of Origen's Commentary on Romans and the Pelagian Controversy," in *Storia ed Esegesi in Rufino di Concordia*, Antichità Altoadriatiche 39 (Udine: Arti Grafiche Friulane, 1992), 137.

28. *spir. et litt.* 14–16, 50–51.

29. Ibid., 27–42.

30. Ibid., 54. Augustine and Paul follow Western civilization's tendency to defend its gods from the charge of causing evil (see Plato, *Republic* 3.391d-e; Rom. 3:26; 9:6a).

31. The quotation is from *spir. et litt.* 52; see also 54, 58. Cf. Rom. 3:31.

32. This sermon, also known as Dolbeau 30, may be found in François Dolbeau, "Le sermon 348A de saint Augustin contre Pélage: Édition du texte intégral," *Recherches augustiniennes* 28 (1995): 37–63. It dates from late May or early June 416 (ibid., 50).

33. Dolbeau 30, lines 1–16.

34. Ibid., lines 24–30.

35. Ibid., lines 50–56: "Et hoc ipsum quod mori pro nobis uoluit, medicina nostra fuit. Magna illa misericordia est, fraters, medici nostri curare nos eum uoluisse non de narthecio suo, sed de sanguine suo. 'Multo magis,' inquit, 'nunc iustificati.' Unde? 'In sanguine ipsius,' non in uiribus nostris, non in meritis nostris, sed 'in sanguine ipsius, salui erimus ab ira per ipsum,' non per nos, sed 'per ipsum.' Constrinxit nos ad crucem: prorsus si uiuere uolumus, morti adhaereamus."

36. This is the Synod of Diospolis that met on December 20, 415. See Dolbeau 30.6.76–80; 7.93–108; and see Peter Brown, *Augustine of Hippo: A Biography* (Berkeley: University of California Press, 1967), 357–58, 463.

37. Dolbeau 30.5.63–75; 8.109–22.

38. *s.* 169.3.

39. *s.* 169.9.

40. *C. duas ep. pelag.* 1.5–7; cf. *div. qu.* 66.150–56 (Mutzenbecher, CCL 44A:157); *Simp.* 2, 15–16.
41. Serge Lancelet, *Saint Augustin* (Paris: Fayard, 1999), 744, dates the composition of these letters to 420–421.
42. *C. duas ep. pelag.* 1.10.22. Those who commented on Romans before Stephen Langton (ca. 1150–1228) placed our chapter divisions on the New Testament text were likely to make associations that we who read the sixteen-chapter version of Romans now are not likely to make. We tend to think that Romans 7 describes one sort of person and Romans 8 another, because of the chapter division. Augustine did not have the chapter division and so used Romans 8 to exegete Romans 7. *Div. qu.* 66 also illustrates this, since it concerns 7:1–8:11.
43. Robert Morgan, "Romans, Letter to the," in *Dictionary of Biblical Interpretation*, 413.
44. Trans. R. J. Teske, S.J., WSA I/23:391.
45. Abelard, *Expositio* on 7:13 (Peppermüller 514.1–516.11).
46. Ibid. (516.13–526.19).
47. See the section on Augustine and Pelagius on Rom. 5:12 above.
48. Abelard, *Expositio* on 7:21–23 (Peppermüller 538.1–4, 20–29).
49. Ibid. (544.1–5).
50. See the Origen section on Rom. 3:25 above.
51. Abelard, *Expositio* on 8:4 (Peppermüller 546.13–20).
52. Aquinas, *Lectura* no. 537 (Cai 98).
53. Ibid., 558 (Cai 101), citing *div. qu.* 66 and *Contra Julianum* 2.3.
54. Aquinas, *Lectura* no. 571 (Cai 103).
55. Ibid., 576 (Cai 104).
56. Ibid., 580 (Cai 104).
57. Ibid., 575, 579 (Cai 104).
58. Ibid., 592, 593 (Cai 106).
59. Ibid., 602 (Cai 110), referring to Aristotle, *NE* 2.1 (1103b).
60. Aquinas, *Lectura* no. 604 (Cai 110–11).
61. Ibid., 611 (Cai 112).
62. See the references to Aristotle in ibid., nos. 616–17 (referring to *NE* 3.12 (1119a–b on temperance); 6.7 (1141a–b on prudence), besides the text already mentioned in Aquinas, *Lectura* no. 602.
63. Hans Hübner, *Rechtfertigung und Heiligung in Luthers Römerbriefvorlesung* (Witten: Luther-Verlag, 1965), 117–29.
64. Demmer, *Lutherus Interpres,* 235–36, identifies the scholastics against which Luther is directing his *simul iustus et peccator* teaching: Lombard (*Sentences* 3.23.5 [PL 192:805–6] and Biel (*Sentences* 2.28.1 n. 4; 3.37.3 dub. 1).
65. *LW* 25:332; *WA* 56:343.13–16.
66. *WA* 56:343.3–6.
67. *LW* 25:333; *WA* 56:344.13–15.
68. *LW* 25:336; *WA* 56:347.2–6.
69. Steinmetz, *Luther and Staupitz,* 113–19. Steinmetz does not mention the connection between Luther's use of human sinfulness as a starting theologoumenon and Augustine.
70. *Collected Works of Erasmus*: Vol. 56: *Annotations on Romans*, ed. Robert D. Sider, trans. and notes by John B. Payne, Albert Rabil Jr., and Warren S. Smith Jr. (Toronto: University of Toronto Press, 1974), 196–97 (on Rom. 7:25).
71. See Fitzmyer's eloquent rebuttal of attempts to read Rom. 7 on "an individual, historical level" and his espousal of the "historical and corporate point of view," *Romans*, 465.

72. John Wesley, *s.* 29 in *Wesley's Standard Sermons*, vol. 2, ed. E. H. Sugden, 7th ed. (London: Epworth, 1968), 37–57.

73. *Römerbrief 1919*, 213 (287–88).

74. Ibid., 207 (279).

75. Ibid., 212–13 (286–88).

76. Ibid., 214 (289): "Die Eigengesetzlichkeit des Stoffes, des äußeren, materiellen Lebens, der natürlichen und geschichtlichen Welt . . . die Ordnung der von Gott abgefallenen Welt."

77. McCormack, *Karl Barth's Dialectical Theology*, 136; Schmidt's edition of *Romans I* only mentions Barth's reading of Tholuck (290 n. 54). Schmidt also provides explanatory notes for Barth's references to Tholuck's dream (292 n. 58) and Spener (286 n. 46) that occur in this section on Rom. 7.

78. *Romans*, 260.

79. The section on 7:1–6 he changed from "The New Existence" to "The Boundary of Religion" (Hoskyns has "frontier" for Barth's *Grenze*); the section on 7:7–13 from "The Law and Romanticism" to "The Meaning of Religion"; the section on 7:14–25 from "The Law and Pietism" to "The Actualization of Religion" (Hoskyns has "reality" for Barth's *Wirklichkeit*).

80. *Romans*, 261–62.

81. Ibid., 230.

82. Ibid., 270.

83. Ibid.

84. Cf. the association between God and religion that Barth makes in a comment on 7:21–23: "Apart from God, [religion] is the most dangerous enemy a man has on this side of the grave" (ibid., 268).

85. M.-J. Lagrange, *Saint Paul, Épitre aux Romains* (Paris: Gabalda, 1916), 176, 188; Dunn, *Romans*, 1:376–77, 385–86, 403; Fitzmyer, *Romans*, 463; Byrne, *Romans*, 220, 229.

86. *Romans*, 241; *Römerbrief 1922*, 223.

87. *Romans*, 242; *Römerbrief 1922*, 224.

88. *Romans*, 244.

89. McCormack, *Karl Barth's Dialectical Theology*, 237.

90. Rudolf Bultmann, *The New Testament and Mythology and Other Basic Writings*, ed. and trans. Schubert Ogden (Philadelphia: Fortress, 1984).

91. Origen, *ComRm* 6.9.12 (Scheck 2:42–43; Hammond Bammel 6:9; 516.188–518.223).

92. Ibid., 6.10.1–3 (Scheck 2:44; Hammond Bammel 6:10; 518.1–519.25).

93. Sanders, *Paul and Palestinian Judaism*, 475.

94. Dunn, *Romans*, 1:394. See also 395–96, 398–99.

95. Ibid., 417.

96. Wright, *Paul for Everyone*, 1:132.

97. Lichtenberger, *Ich Adams*, 105, lists A. Vergote, "Der Beitrag der Psychoanalyse zur Exegese: Leben, Gesetz und Ichspaltung im 7. Kapitel des Römerbriefs," in *Exegese im Methodenkonflikt*, ed. X. Léon-Dufour (Munich: Kösel-Verlag, 1973), 73–116; G. Theissen, *Psychological Aspects of Pauline Theology*, trans. John P. Calvin (Philadelphia: Fortress, 1987); and M. Reichardt, *Psychologische Erklärung der paulinischechen Damaskusvision? Ein Beitrag zum interdisziplinären Gespräch zwischen Exegese und Psychologie seit dem 18. Jahrhundert* (Stuttgart: Katholisches Bibelwerk, 1999), as psychological studies of Rom. 7, before also listing sociological, ethical, and philosophical approaches. See Jean-Noël Aletti, "Rm 7.7–25 encore une fois: enjeux et propositions," *NTS* 48 (2002): 358–76.

98. Lichtenberger, *Ich Adams*, 149–50.

99. Ibid., 190–91, against H. Hübner, *Law in Paul's Thought,* trans. John C. G. Gerig, ed. John Riches (Edinburgh: T. & T. Clark, 1984), and Dunn, *Romans* 1:416–19.

100. Lichtenberger, *Ich Adams,* 269, quoting Barth, *CD* IV/1:591.

101. Aletti, "Rm 7.7–25 encore une fois," 362–72.

101. W. G. Kümmel, *Römer 7 und das Bild des Menschen im Neuen Testament,* TB 53 (Munich: Kaiser, 1974), 104–11.

103. H. D. Betz, "The Concept of the 'Inner Human Being' in Paul's Anthropology," *NTS* 46 (2000): 321–22, following Christoph Markschies, "Innerer Mensch," *RAC* 18 (1997): 267–80.

104. Betz, "Concept," 335–41.

105. Ibid., 337.

106. Ibid., 338 n. 98, 340–41. See Kümmel, *Römer 7,* 138.

107. Yeo Khiok-khng, *What Has Jerusalem to Do with Beijing?* (Harrisburg: Trinity Press International, 1998), 152–61, quotation 152.

Locus 7: Calling, Foreknowledge, Predestination

1. Origen, *ComRm* 1.1.1 (Scheck 1:53; Hammond Bammel 37.1–9).

2. *ComRm* 7.7.2 (Scheck's trans. 2:83; Hammond Bammel 7.5; 583.11–12).

3. Ibid., 7.5.10 (Scheck 2:77; Hammond Bammel 7.3; 575.126–576.128).

4. Frag. 1 (Heither 34.22–36.8).

5. *ComRm* 7.8.1–2 (Scheck 2:87–89; Hammond Bammel 7.6; 587.1–590.60).

6. Ibid., 7.8.7 (Scheck 2:91; Hammond Bammel 7.6; 592.110–11).

7. *ComRm* 7.7.5 (Scheck trans. 2:86; Hammond Bammel 7.5; 586.78–81).

8. *ComRm* 7.7.7 (Scheck trans. 2.87; Hammond Bammel 7.5; 587.103–4).

9. *ComRm* 7.8.5 (Scheck 2:90; Hammond Bammel 7.6; 591.85–88).

10. Ibid., 7.8.6 (Scheck 2.91; Hammond Bammel 7.6; 592.102–5).

11. Ibid., 7.8.4 (Scheck 2.89–90; Hammond Bammel 7.6; 590.60–591.79). See also frag. 2 (Heither 28.1–9), where Origen on 1:2 distinguishes between the called and chosen apostle Paul and the called apostle Judas. See also Chrysostom, *Homilae in epistulam ad Romanos* 15.

12. Origen, *ComRm* 7.8.2 (Scheck 2:88; Hammond Bammel 7.6; 588.21–589.34).

13. Augustine, *ep.* 131.

14. The English titles and dates for these works are according to the usage in *Augustine through the Ages,* ed. Allan D. Fitzgerald, O.S.A. (Grand Rapids: Eerdmans, 1999).

15. Augustine, *div. qu.* 24 (Mosher 50–51).

16. Augustine, *ex. prop. Rm.* 55–56 (Fredriksen 26–29).

17. Augustine, *ep.* 102.15; *Retract.* 2.31.

18. Abelard, *Expositio* on 8:28 (Peppermüller 576.15–25).

19. Ibid., on 8:29 (Peppermüller 578.1–9).

20. Ibid., on 8:29 (Peppermüller 578.4–6).

21. Ibid., on 8:29 (Peppermüller 578.16–20).

22. Ibid., on 8:30 (Peppermüller 578.26–580.7).

23. Ibid., on 8:30 (Peppermüller 580.9–582.7), referring to *Theologia Scholarium* 3.96–111 (Corpus Continuatio mediaevalis 13:539–46).

24. *LW* 25:75; *WA* 56:83.11–13, 27–29.

25. *LW* 25:373–76; *WA* 56:383.25–386.22.

26. *LW* 25:371, 378; *WA* 56:381.12–20; 388.10–28.

27. André Godin, *Érasme, Lecteur d'Origène* (Geneva: Librairie Droz, 1982), 179–82.

28. CWE 56:226–27.

29. Schelkle, *Paulus, Lehrer der Väter*, 310–12.
30. Erasmus letter 844 to Johann Maier von Eck in 1518, CWE 6:35. I am indebted to Thomas Scheck for locating this reference.
31. CWE 56:227.
32. *Romans*, 321.
33. Ibid.
34. Ibid., 323.
35. Ibid., 324. My use of the verb "demythologizes" takes its cue from Barth, who says on this page that "Augustine and the Reformers represented [predestination to blessedness] in *mythological* form as though it were a scheme of cause and effect, thereby robbing it of its significance" (my emphasis). In the first edition he similarly seeks to reposition the "absolute decree" of Reformed theology to an "eternal, heavenly, next-worldly, divine ground of life, which is made known in Christ" (*Römerbrief 1919*, 256 [346]).
36. Aquinas, *Lectura* no. 702 (Cai 126).
37. Immanuel Kant, *The Critique of Pure Reason*, trans. Norman Kemp Smith (1929; reprint ed. New York: St. Martin's Press, 1963), 464–79 (A 533–58; B 561–86).
38. See Barth, *CD* II/2:114, for a thorough grounding of the election of Christ in the Reformed tradition, with reference to Rom. 8:29.
39. Sanders, *Paul and Palestinian Judaism*, 446.
40. Sanders, *Paul*, 50.
41. Ibid., 446–47.
42. Dunn, *Romans*, 1:480–82, 494.
43. Ibid., 480.
44. Ibid., 486; see also 495.
45. Grieb, *Story*, 80.
46. N. T. Wright, *The Climax of the Covenant* (Minneapolis: Fortress, 1991), 32 n. 57 (image), 127 n. 19 (*Shema*).
47. Yeo Khiok-khng, "Messianic Predestination in Romans 8 and Classical Confucianism," in *Navigating Romans through Cultures*, 268.
48. Ibid., 271.
49. Ibid., 283.

Locus 8: Not Willing or Running

1. *LW* 25:389; *WA* 56:400.5–6.
2. Conversation on November 30, 2004, in St. Paul, Minnesota.
3. Jürgen Becker, *Paul: Apostle to the Gentiles* (Louisville: Westminster John Knox, 1993), 351.
4. Hermas, *Similitude* 8.6.2 (God gives repentance only to those God foreknows will repent; Karl Hermann Schelkle, *Paulus, Lehrer der Väter* (Düsseldorf: Patmos, 1956), 18 n. 2, 310–12.
5. Origen, *ComRm* 7.16.1–4 (Scheck 2:113–15; Hammond Bammel 7.14; 619.1–621.58).
6. Origen *ComRm* 7.16.5 (Scheck trans. 2:116; Hammond Bammel 7.14; 622.69–71).
7. Origen, *ComRm* 7.16.8 (Scheck trans. 2:118; Hammond Bammel 7.14; 625.135–37).
8. Augustine, *div. qu.* 68.4 (Mosher 163).
9. *ex. prop. Rm.* 62.8: "sed quia dignum se praebuit, cui cor obduraretur, priore infidelitate."
10. *div. qu.* 68.126–29 (CCL 44A:180). He then quotes Rom. 1:28 in support of his explanation.

11. *div. qu.* 68. 153 (CCL 44A:181). Augustine goes on in the last paragraph of this work to quote texts that describe God's choice of people before their birth (Jer. 1:5; Mal. 1:2–3 as quoted in Rom. 9:13).

12. *Simp.* 2.12.

13. *Conf.* 7.12.18.

14. Cf. Michael Wyschogrod, "Sin and Atonement in Judaism," in *The Human Condition in the Jewish and Christian Traditions*, ed. Frederick E. Greenspahn (Hoboken, NJ: KTAV, 1986), 115, who rejects the example of Pharaoh as theologically foundational. God's special purpose of multiplying signs (Exod. 7:3), announced in the same verse in which the hardening of Pharaoh's heart is mentioned, signals for Wyschogrod that the case of Pharaoh cannot be considered normative.

15. *Simp.* 2.15–16.

16. Cf. *ex. prop. Rm.* 62.5–13.

17. Augustine, *Confessions*, trans. Henry Chadwick (Oxford: Oxford University Press, 1991), 293 n. 29.

18. Frank A. James III, *Peter Martyr Vermigli and Predestination: The Augustinian Inheritance of an Italian Reformer* (Oxford: Clarendon, 1998), 95.

19. Pierre-Marie Hombert, *Gloria Gratiae: Se glorifier en Dieu, principe et fin de la théologie augustinienne de la grace* (Paris: Institut d'Études Augustiniennes, 1996), 489–97.

20. Ibid., 495, citing *Contra Julianum* 4.58–60 (PL 45:1373–75).

21. Brown, *Augustine of Hippo*, 216–17.

22. Ibid., 348–49; Brown, "Pelagius and His Supporters," 112–13; against William S. Babcock, "Augustine's Interpretation of Romans (A.D. 394–396)," *Augustinian Studies* 10 (1979): 55–74, who argues that it is primarily Augustine's exegesis of Romans that accounts for Augustine's move toward a rigidly predestinarian position by 396.

23. *Simp.* 2.10.

24. Origen, *ComRm* 7.16.1–8 (Scheck 2:113–18; Hammond Bammel 7.14; 619.1–625.137).

25. *On the Hardening of Pharaoh's Heart* ¶ 30 (de Plinval 169). Georges de Plinval dates the anonymous work to 397–398 and suggests a forerunner of Pelagius, a contemporary of Pelagius or perhaps Pelagius himself as author, *Essai sur le style et la langue de Pélage suivi du traité inédit De Induratione Cordis Pharaonis*, CF n.s. 31 (Fribourg: Librairie de l'Université Fribourg en Suisse, 1947), 131–34.

26. Pelagius's commentary must have been completed by 410, for he fled Rome as Alaric's army approached (de Bruyn, *Pelagius's Commentary*, 11).

27. Brown, *Augustine of Hippo*, 348.

28. Ibid., 345–46, 355–56.

29. *ep.* 4*, lines 16–86 (BA 46B:108–14).

30. Augustine, *Retract.* 2.1.1: "laboratum est quidem pro libero arbitrio uoluntatis humanae, sed uicit dei gratia." See Burleigh, *Augustine*, 370.

31. Abelard, *Expositio* 9:16–18 (Peppermüller 626–30).

32. Ibid., 9:17 (Peppermüller 628.11–14).

33. A. Andrew Das, *Paul and the Jews* (Peabody, MA: Hendrickson, 2003), 23.

34. *LW* 25:81; *WA* 56:90.6–7.

35. *LW* 25:82; *WA* 56:91.16–17.

36. *LW* 25:388–89.

37. *LW* 25:392–94.

38. *WA* 56:92.30–93.19.

39. Ibid., 261. CWE 56:261.

40. Robert Wilken, "Free Choice and the Divine Will in Greek Christian Commentaries," in *Paul and the Legacies of Paul*, ed. William S. Babcock (Dallas: Southern Methodist University Press, 1990), 124–27. On Erasmus's use of Origen on

this locus in his *Paraphrases on Romans*, see Godin, *Érasme, Lecteur d'Origène*, 387–88.

41. Erasmus, "On the Freedom of the Will, Part II," in *Luther and Erasmus: Free Will and Salvation*, trans. and ed. E. Gordon Rupp et al., LCC 17 (Philadelphia: Westminster, 1969), 66.
42. *Römerbrief 1919*, 280–81 (375–78).
43. Ibid., 281 (377).
44. Ibid., 283 (379–80).
45. See George Hunsinger, *How To Read Karl Barth* (New York: Oxford University Press, 1991), 185–224.
46. *Romans*, 351; cf. *Römerbrief 1919*, 281 (377–78).
47. *Romans*, 352.
48. *Romans*, 355; *Römerbrief 1922*, 340. This difference is noted by Nico Tjepko Bakker, *In der Krisis der Offenbarung*, trans. Wolfgang Bunte (Neukirchen-Vluyn: Neukirchener Verlag, 1974), 46.
49. Dunn, *Romans,* 2:562, citing Rom. 1:5; 6:12–23; 8:13.
50. Dunn, *Romans,* 2:555.
51. This is also in his commentary; see Schreiner, *Romans*, 506, 514.
52. Cf. Schreiner, *Romans*, 506–8.
53. See Juan Escarfuller, "Repudiating Assimilation in Reading Romans 9–11," and Elsa Tamez, "Our Struggle as *Mestizios*," in *Navigating Romans through Cultures*, 137–67, 168–70.

Locus 9: Potter and Clay

1. Lagrange, *Romains*, 238, on Rom. 9:21.
2. Origen, *ComRm* 7.17.1–7 (Scheck 2:118–21; Hammond Bammel 7.15; 625.1–628.86).
3. Ibid., 7.18.2 (Scheck 2:122; Hammond Bammel 7.16; 629.8–11).
4. Ibid., 7.18.2 (Scheck 2:122; Hammond Bammel 7.16; 629.12–630.28).
5. Augustine, *div. qu.* 68.4 (Mosher 162–63); Rom. 1:28.
6. Ibid., 68.5 (Mosher 164).
7. Augustine, *Simp.* 2.20 (Burleigh 403).
8. Ibid., 2.21 (Burleigh 404–5).
9. Ibid., 2.18 (Burleigh 400–401).
10. Augustine, *s.* 27.3–4, 6.6, 7.7.
11. Abelard, *Expositio* at 9:20 (Peppermüller 632.3–18).
12. Ibid., at 9:21 (Peppermüller 632.19–634.23). The quotation is from Calcidius's Latin translation of Plato's *Timaeus,* 28a.
13. Ibid., at 9:21 (Peppermüller 634.24–636.12).
14. Ibid., at 9:21 (Peppermüller 636.14–638.14).
15. Ibid., at 9:22 (Peppermüller 642.23–644.27).
16. *LW* 25:84; *WA* 56:1–7.
17. *LW* 25:394–95; *WA* 56:404.20–405.12; Augustine, *ench.* 99.
18. *Institutes* 3.23.5; *Calvin: Institutes of the Christian Religion*, 2 vols., ed. John T. McNeill, trans. Ford Lewis Battles, LCL 20–21 (Philadelphia: Westminster, 1960), 2:953, citing Augustine, *s.* 27.
19. Calvin, *Institutes*, 3.23.6 (Battles 2:953–55).
20. Calvin, *Romans*, 210.
21. Ibid., 211.
22. Ibid.
23. I. John Hesselink, "Calvin's Theology," in *The Cambridge Companion to John Calvin*, ed. Donald K. McKim (Cambridge: Cambridge University Press, 2004), 83–84.

24. *Römerbrief 1919*, 284 (381–82).
25. *Romans*, 357.
26. Bakker, *In der Krisis*, 64, 166–67.
27. Barth, *Romans*, 359.
28. What Origen said about the Gnostics can equally apply to the route of mechanistic determinism taken by the late Augustine and Luther: they focus on this text to the neglect of the rest of Scripture.
29. See Barth, *CD* II/2:94–194; C. K. Barrett, *A Commentary on the Epistle to the Romans*, BNTC (London: Adam & Charles Black, 1957), 183, for why it is not arbitrary; and Grieb, *Story* 96–97, for how the election of Christ includes both destruction and salvation.
30. Sanders, *Paul and Palestinian Judaism*, 446; idem, *Paul*, 50.
31. Dunn, *Romans*, 2:557, citing Deut. 32:6; Isa. 43:1, 7; 44:2, 21, 24.
32. Ibid.
33. Ibid., 558–60.
34. A. Katherine Grieb, e-mail to me on January 6, 2005.
35. Grieb, *Story*, 95.
36. Grieb, e-mail, January 6, 2005. Cf. Nils Alstrup Dahl, *Studies in Paul* (Minneapolis: Augsburg, 1977), 131–32, 171, 172 n. 20; Barth *CD* II/2:306–506.

Locus 10: Christ the *Telos* of the Law

1. Trans. *LW* 25:405; *WA* 56:414.18–19: "quod hoc verbum alienissimum a Christo, tamen Christum significat."
2. Origen, *ComRm* 8.2.2 (Scheck 2:135–36; Hammond Bammel 8.2; 645.12–646.34).
3. Reimer Roukema, *The Diversity of Laws in Origen's Commentary on Romans* (Amsterdan: Free University, 1988), 80–81.
4. Origen, *ComRm* 4.3.2; 4.4.2 (Scheck 1:253–54; Hammond Bammel 4.3, 4; 292.25–28; 293.21–28).
5. Origen, *ComRm* frag. 35 (Heither 188).
6. Origen, *ComRm* 1.10.2 (Scheck 1:79–80; Hammond Bammel 1.12; 69.21–70.33).
7. Roukema, *Diversity of Laws*, 18.
8. *ex. prop. Rm.* 13–18. Fredriksen's "The Law was introduced" (5) or "the Law entered in" (11) does not do justice to Augustine's "Lex subintravit" or the Greek text's *nomos de pareisēlthen*. See also *Simp.* 1.6, 12 for a "Lutheran" or "second use" presentation of the law.
9. See Goulven Madec, "*De libero arbitrio*" in *Agostino d'Ippona* (Palermo: Edizioni Augustinus, 1990), 30, on eternal law in *De libero arbitrio*. C. P. Hammond Bammel, "Augustine, Origen and the Exegesis of St. Paul," *Augustinianum* 32 (1992): 353–54, discusses Augustine's simplistic treatment of "law" in his early works on Romans, *Commentary on Statements* and *Unfinished Commentary*. Hammond Bammel describes how in his later commentary on Galatians Augustine is much more sensitive to distinguishing between types of law, a strategy she traces to his use of Jerome, who was himself using Origen's works. She also mentions that Augustine would later fault the Manichees for distinguishing between the law of Christ and the law of the Jews in Rom. 7 (*Simp.* 1, 16). I would suggest that a desire to avoid the Manichean tendency to say there were two laws might have contributed toward his early, monolithic exegesis of "law."
10. *Simp.* 1, 7.
11. *C. duas ep. pelag.* 3.2; besides texts from Rom. 2, 7, 8, and 10, he also quotes 2 Cor. 3:6 and 1 Cor. 15:56 in this context.

12. Aquinas, *Lectura* no. 819 (Cai 152).
13. *LW* 25:89; *WA* 56:99.5–7.
14. But cf. Gerhard Forde, "Lex semper accusat?" in *A More Radical Gospel*, ed. Mark C. Mattes and Steven D. Paulson (Grand Rapids: Eerdmans, 2004), 48–49, for a positive reclamation of the law in its "civil use."
15. *LW* 25:307; *WA* 56:319.28–32.
16. *LW* 25:317; *WA* 56:329.13–14.
17. Dorothea Demmer, *Lutherus Interpres: Der theologische Neuansatz in seiner Römerbriefexegese* (Witten: Luther-Verlag, 1968), 238.
18. Johann von Staupitz, "Libellus de Exsecutione Aeternae Praedestinationis," in *Samtliche Schriften: Abhandlungen, Predigten, Zeugnisse*, vol. 2, eds. Lothar Graf zu Dohna and Richard Wetzel (Berlin: de Gruyter, 1979), ¶122–123 (pages 198–99).
19. This is his gloss on Rom. 6:14; *LW* 25:53; *WA* 56:61.2–4.
20. Calvin, *Institutes* 2.8.1–59 (Battles 367–423).
21. Wesley, *s.* 29 in *Wesley's Standard Sermons*, 2:53–54.
22. *Römerbrief 1919*, 73 (105) on 3:31. He parenthetically refers to Rom. 7 here when describing this sense of the law that has disappeared.
23. He does admit that when we realize that God is the only source of righteousness for humanity, "a critical attitude to the law" becomes possible (*Romans*, 107), but this is in regard to using the law as a means for righteousness. He still retains a high view of the law, since it shows the chasm between human and divine righteousness.
24. *Romans*, 71.
25. Ibid., 116; *Römerbrief 1922*, 91 (quotation), 92 (equation of "law" with Bible and religion).
26. *Romans*, 116, 42 (on 1:17).
27. Ibid., 375.
28. Ibid., 184.
29. Dunn, *Romans*, 2:596.
30. Philip Alexander, review of E. P. Sanders, *Jesus and Judaism*, *JJS* 37 (1986): 103–6, as cited in Matlock, "Almost Cultural Studies?" 444–45.
31. Simon J. Gathercole, *Where Is Boasting?* (Grand Rapids: Eerdmans, 2002) 67, no. 110–11, 134–35; 263–64.
32. Francis Watson, *Paul and the Hermeneutics of Faith* (New York: T. & T. Clark, 2004), 332–33 (quotation from 333).
33. See nn. 6, 7, 8 in the Introduction above.

Locus 11: Israel's Salvation

1. CSEL 81:383; trans. from *Romans*, ed. Gerald Bray, Ancient Christian Commentary on Scripture 6 (Downers Grove, IL: InterVarsity Press, 1998), 298.
2. Standard topoi include *ComRm* 8.1.2; 8.2.2 (on Rom. 10:2, 4–11; Scheck 2:133, 136; Hammond Bammel 8.1, 2; 641.27–28; 645.30–646.34).
3. Ibid., 8.1.2 (Scheck 2:132; Hammond Bammel 8.1; 640.5–641.7).
4. Ibid., 2.13.35 (Scheck 1:164; Hammond Bammel 2.9; 175.586–92).
5. Ibid., 8.9.3 (Scheck 2:167; Hammond Bammel 8.8; 682.24–26).
6. Gorday, *Principles*, 298 n. 156.
7. Caroline P. Bammel, "Die Juden im Römerbriefkommentar des Origenes," in *Christlicher Antijudaismus und jüdischer Antipaganismus: Ihre Motive und Hintergründe in den ersten drei Jahrhunderten*, ed. Herbert Frohnhofen, Hamburger theologische Studien 3 (Hamburg: Steinmann & Steinmann, 1990), 145–46.
8. *ComRm* 2.14.1 (Scheck 1:165; Hammond Bammel 2.10; 176.7–11).

9. Ibid., 8.12.2–3 (Scheck 2:181–82; Hammond Bammel 8.11; 699.6–18).
10. Ibid., 8.12.3 (Scheck 2:182–83; Hammond Bammel 8.11; 700.40–701.45). On these earlier quotations in Rom. 9:25–27 see Richard B. Hays, *Echoes of Scripture in the Letters of Paul* (New Haven: Yale University Press, 1989), 66–68.
11. *ComRm* 8.12.4 (Scheck 2:183; Hammond Bammel 8.11; 701.48–50).
12. Ibid., 8.12.6–7 (Scheck 2:183-84; Hammond Bammel 8.11; 702.68–703.95).
13. Ibid., 8.12.8 (Scheck 2:185; Hammond Bammel 8.11; 703.100–704.111); 1 Tim. 2:4.
14. *ComRm* 8.12.8 (Scheck 2:185; Hammond Bammel 8.11; 704.112–17); Tob. 12:7.
15. *Simp.* 2.19. Later in this same section he emphasizes that not all Jews are under God's condemnation.
16. Ibid., 2.2.
17. Philip D. Krey, "Martin Luther," in *Augustine through the Ages*, 516–18.
18. *ex. prop. Rom.* 66 (on 10:1); 70 (on 11:11); 82 (on 15:8).
19. *Simp.* 2, 20; trans. Burleigh.
20. Abelard, *Expositio* at 11:26 (Peppermüller 702.9–11).
21. Ibid., at 11:26 (Peppermüller 702.14–26).
22. Ibid., at 11:26 (Peppermüller 704.24–706.3).
23. Ibid., at 11:26 (Peppermüller 706.18–27).
24. Aquinas, *Lectura* nos. 915–20 (quotation from no. 915; Cai 170).
25. Clyde Leonard Manschreck, *Melanchthon: The Quiet Reformer* (New York: Abingdon, 1958), 21.
26. *LW* 25:80; *WA* 56:88.13–89.1. "New law" for Luther means the law of Christ.
27. *LW* 25:80; *WA* 56:89.19–23.
28. *WA* 11:315.25–31.
29. Oberman, *Luther*, 292–97.
30. *WA* 53:419.22–27.
31. *WA* 53:448.3–10.
32. *WA* 53:511.3–12; 522.23–28.
33. *WA* 53:522.23–526.6.
34. *WA* 51:195.31; 196.1–3.
35. *WA* 51:195.28–31: "Anders wird nicht draus, denn sie machens zu gros, Sie sind unsere öffentliche Feinde, hören nicht auff unsern Herrn Christum zu lestern, Heissen die Jungfrau Maria eine Hure, Christum ein Hurenkind, Uns heissen sie Wechselbelge oder mahlkelber."
36. *WA* 51:195.10–15, 39–41.
37. Katherine Sonderegger, *That Jesus Christ Was Born a Jew: Karl Barth's "Doctrine of Israel"* (University Park, PA: Pennsylvania State University Press, 1992), 13.
38. *Romans*, 88.
39. Other places where the "empty canal" metaphor is used are in ibid., 65, 339.
40. Ibid., 88, 90.
41. Ibid., 90–91.
42. Sonderegger, *Christ Was Born a Jew*, 42. Her reference to the circle and the line is of course from Barth, *Romans*, 29–30.
43. *Römerbrief 1919*, 339 (453).
44. *Romans*, 416.
45. Ibid., 417. It is a fairly well attested textual variant that Barth follows.
46. Karl Barth, *Against the Stream: Shorter Post-War Writings 1946–52* (New York: Philosophical Library, 1954), 200, as quoted in Grieb, *Story*, xi n. 7.
47. The sermon is *Die Kirche Jesu Christi*, Theologische Existenz heute 5 (Munich: Chr. Kaiser, 1933). Barth's letter to Hitler is available in Klaus Scholder, *The Churches and the Third Reich*: Vol. 2: *The Year of Disillusionment 1934, Barmen and Rome*, trans. John Bowden (Philadelphia: Fortress, 1988), 54. I received these

descriptions and references from Eberhard Busch, "Indissoluble Unity: Barth's Position on the Jews during the Hitler Era," in *For the Sake of the World: Karl Barth and the Future of Ecclesial Theology*, ed. George Hunsinger (Grand Rapids: Eerdmans, 2004), 55.

48. Dunn, *Romans,* 2:681; cf. F. Refoulé, *". . . Et ainsi tout Israel sera sauvés": Romains 11:25–32* (Paris: Cerf, 1984).

49. Wright, *Climax of the Covenant,* 250 (Paul transfers the identity of Israel onto the Messiah and the Messiah's people); idem, "Romans and the Theology of Paul," in *Pauline Theology,* vol. 3: *Romans,* ed. David Hay and E. Elizabeth Johnson (Minneapolis: Fortress, 1995), 61 (Paul transfers identity of Israel onto Jesus the Messiah).

50. Wright, "Romans and the Theology of Paul," 60–61.

51. Wright, "Romans," 693.

52. Harink, *Paul among the Postliberals,* 153–84.

Locus 12: Let Every *Psychē* Be Subject to Authorities

1. *Address by President P. W. Botha on the Occasion of the Award of the Freedom of Moria,* April 7, 1985 (Cape Town: Office of the State President), 1985, as quoted in Jan Botha, *Subject to Whose Authority? Multiple Readings of Romans 13,* ESEC 4 (Atlanta: Scholars Press, 1994), 1–2.

2. Yeo Khiok-khng, *What Has Jerusalem to Do with Beijing?* (Harrisburg, PA: Trinity Press International, 1988), 161.

3. N. T. Wright, *The Climax of the Covenant* (Minneapolis: Fortress, 1991), 259.

4. *ComRm* 9.25.1–2 (Scheck 2:222–23; Hammond Bammel 9.25; 748.1–749.26).

5. Ibid., 9.26 (Scheck 2:223; Hammond Bammel 9.26; 749.1–750.14).

6. Ibid., 9.28.2 (Scheck 2:224–25; Hammond Bammel 9.28; 750.5–752.37).

7. Ibid., 9.28.3 (Scheck 2:225; Hammond Bammel 9.28; 752.37–51).

8. Ibid., 9.29 (Scheck 2:226; Hammond Bammel 9.29; 752.1–753.13).

9. *Exhortation to Martyrdom* 42, trans. by Rowan A. Greer, *Origen,* Classics of Western Spirituality (New York: Paulist Press, 1979), 73.

10. Antonin Scalia, "A Call for Reckoning: Religion and the Death Penalty," address at University of Chicago Divinity School, January 25, 2002; reprinted as "God's Justice and Ours," *First Things* 123 (May 2002): 17–21.

11. *ComRm* 9.30.3–4 (Scheck 2:227–28; Hammond Bammel 9.30; 754.31–755.50).

12. Mark Reasoner, "Ancient and Modern Exegesis of Romans 13 under Unfriendly Governments," *Society of Biblical Literature 1999 Seminar Papers* (Atlanta: Society of Biblical Literature, 1999), 359–74.

13. *ex. prop. Rm.* 72.

14. Ibid., 73.

15. Ibid., 74.

16. Brown, *Augustine of Hippo,* 459–61.

17. *De unico baptismo* 1.4.5; 1.7.8; 2.4.9; 2.15.35; 3.36.42; 3.42.51; 3.49.59; 3.50.62; 3.54.66; *ep.* 185 (= *De correctione Donatistarum*) 9.37.

18. Augustine, *s.* 359B, also known as Mainz *s.* 5 and Dolbeau *s.* 2, available in Augustine, *Vingt-six Sermons au Peuple d'Afrique,* retrouvés à Mayence, ed. François Dolbeau, Collection des Études Augustiniennes Ancient Series 147 (Paris: Institut d'Études Augustiniennes, 1996), no. 2, quotes Rom. 13:1 in section 13 of the sermon, but the exegesis is qualified by reference to the highest authority—"I don't call anyone obedient who complies with the emperor's wishes against those of God" (WAS III/11:344).

19. Abelard, *Expositio* at 13:2 (Peppermüller 752.2–5).

20. Ibid., at 13:7 (Peppermüller 754.9–10).

21. Aquinas, *Lectura* no. 1028 (Cai 191).
22. Ibid., 1034 (Cai 192).
23. Machiavelli wrote *The Prince* three years earlier, but it was not published till decades later.
24. Rom. 13:8; Erasmus, *The Education of a Christian Prince*, trans. Neil M. Cheshire and Michael J. Heath (Cambridge: Cambridge University Press, 1997), 40–42.
25. Oberman's translation (*Luther*, 29) from *Reichstagakten* 2.595, 23–25, 34–35. Erasmus's vision for a harmoniously Christian Europe—shown by the dedications of his commentaries on the four Gospels to the monarchs of the new nation-states England, Austria, France, and Spain—was also not to come true, due in large part to the religious strife that the Reformation fomented (Roland H. Bainton, *Here I Stand: A Life of Martin Luther* [New York: Abingdon-Cokesbury, 1950], 98).
26. Oberman, *Luther*, 17–18.
27. Ibid., 20.
28. Bainton, *Here I Stand*, 301; *WA Tischreden* 3:40.25–26 (no. 2867b).
29. *WA* 8:680.22–27.
30. Oberman, *Luther*, 66–74.
31. I am indebted to Richard Nysse for this clarification, made in conversation, July 31, 2004. See also U. Duchrow, *Christenheit und Weltverantwortung: Traditionsgeschichte und systematische Struktur der Zweireichelehre*, FBES 25 (Stuttgart: Klett, 1970), 437–575.
32. Luther, *Admonition to Peace* (published April 19, 1525); *Against the Robbing and Murdering Hordes* (published May 5, 1525).
33. *WA* 56:476.4.
34. *WA* 56:480–82; cf. Origen, *ComRm* 9.25.1–2 (Scheck 2:222–23; Hammond Bammel 9.25; 748.1–749.26).
35. *LW* 25:474–75; *WA* 56:482.16–18.
36. *WA* 56:478.26–479.10
37. *WA* 6:409.34–35.
38. Martin Luther, *On Governmental Authority*, in *The Christian in Society*, vol. 2, ed. Walther I. Bandt, *LW* 45 (Philadelphia: Fortress, 1962), 99–103; *D. Martin Luthers Werke: Kritische Gesamtausgabe*, ed. Paul Pietsch, *WA* 11 (Weimar: Hermann Böhlaus, 1900), 257.16–261.24.
39. *LW* 25:109; *WA* 56:123.16–124.14 (quotation from 123.20–21).
40. Bainton, *Here I Stand*, 268–70.
41. "Ermahnung zum Frieden auf die zwölf Artikel der Bauerschaft in Schwaben" was written in 1525; the section summarized above is found in *WA* 18:303.18–304.26.
42. *WA* 18:309.33–34.
43. Among Romans literature, other politically charged interpretations of 13:1–7 include Elsa Tamez, *The Amnesty of Grace: Justification by Faith from a Latin American Perspective*, trans. Sharon H. Ringe (Nashville: Abingdon, 1993); Neil Elliott, *Liberating Paul: The Justice of God and the Politics of the Apostle* (Maryknoll, NY: Orbis, 1994).
44. Barth, "Letter to Eberhard Bethge," in *Fragments Grave and Gay*, ed. Martin Rumscheidt, trans. Eric Mosbacher (London: Fontana, 1971), 120; McCormack, *Karl Barth's Dialectical Theology*, 86–92, 117–25, 173–79.
45. *Römerbrief 1919*, 388 (517).
46. McCormack, *Karl Barth's Dialectical Theology*, 165–66.
47. For this summary I am indebted to ibid., 280–82.
48. *Romans*, 480–81: "Far more than the conservative, the revolutionary is overcome of evil, because with his 'No' he stands so strangely near to God. This is the tragedy of revolution. Evil is not the true answer to evil. The sense of right which

has been wounded by the existing order is not restored to health when that order is broken."

49. Ibid., 477.
50. Ibid.
51. Ibid., 478.
52. Ibid., 479.
53. Ibid., 483–84.
54. Ibid., 484.
55. *Römerbrief 1919*, 376 (501); he goes on to cite Pharaoh in Rom. 9:17 as an example.
56. Ibid., 377 (502).
57. Ibid., 376 (501 n. 44 in Hermann Schmidt's 1985 edition of *Romans I*, citing Martin Luther, *In Genesin Declamationes*, *WA* 24:143.1–3).
58. *Romans*, 484.
59. Ibid., 485.
60. Ibid.
61. Ibid., 486.
62. Ibid.
63. Ibid., 487.
64. Ibid., 488.
65. Ibid., 489.
66. Ibid., 490.
67. Ibid., 491.
68. Ibid. 487.
69. Gerhard Kittel, letter to Karl Barth dated June 28, 1934, in Karl Barth and Gerhard Kittel, *Ein theologischer Briefwechsel* (Stuttgart: Kohlhammer, 1934), 34.
70. *Romans*, 487; *Römerbrief 1922*, 471.
71. McCormack, *Karl Barth's Dialectical Theology*, 124, citing Barth's letter to Martin Rade, 19 June 1915, *Karl Barth—Martin Rade: Ein Briefwechsel*, ed. Christoph Schwöbel (Gutersloh: Gerd Mohn, 1981), 134.
72. *Romans*, 493–94.
73. Ibid., 497–501.
74. Ibid., 502.
75. John Webster, *Barth's Moral Theology: Human Action in Barth's Thought* (Grand Rapids: Eerdmans, 1998), 27; see his complete section on moral agency in *Romans II* in ibid., 27–31. The places Webster cites as evidence of a positive appreciation of human agency in *Romans II* are at *Romans*, 216, 434–35, 451, 461.
76. Karl Barth, *A Shorter Commentary on Romans* (Richmond: John Knox, 1959), 157–61.
77. Grieb, *Story*, 125, following Neil Elliott, "Romans 13:1–7 in the Context of Imperial Propaganda," in *Paul and Empire: Religion and Power in Roman Imperial Society*, ed. Richard A. Horsley (Harrisburg: Trinity Press International, 1997), 184–204.
78. Grieb, *Story*, 125–26.
79. Wright, "Romans," 718–21.
80. Grieb, *Story*, 122–26.
81. Peter Lampe, *From Paul to Valentinus: Christians at Rome in the First Two Centuries* (Minneapolis: Fortress, 2003), 11–16, 431–32.
82. Kosuke Koyama, *Mount Fuji and Mount Sinai: A Critique of Idols* (Maryknoll, NY: Orbis, 1992), 198–99.

Conclusion

1. *The Apostolic Fathers*, trans. J. B. Lightfoot and J. R. Harmer, ed. and rev. Michael W. Holmes, 2nd ed. (Grand Rapids: Baker, 1989), 31.

2. Michael Goldberg, *Jews and Christians: Getting Our Stories Straight* (Philadelphia: Trinity Press International, 1991), 135–43.
3. I am indebted to Beverly Roberts Gaventa, whose address at Princeton Theological Seminary in June 1998, "The Tensions in Luke-Acts," prompted me to think about Romans in this way.
4. The quoted phrase comes from Robert Morgan, "Romans, Letter to the," in *Dictionary of Biblical Interpretation*, ed. John H. Hayes (Nashville: Abingdon, 1999), 420. In his *Romans*, New Testament Guides (Sheffield: Sheffield Academic Press, 1995), 147, Morgan mentions "the dialectical structure of Paul's thought and the antithetical formulation of his argument."
5. The phrase is from Karl Barth, *Theology of John Calvin*, trans. Geoffrey W. Bromiley (Grand Rapids: Eerdmans, 1995), 49.

Index of Ancient Sources

Boldfaced page numbers in this index indicate where this book's twelve loci of Romans are most explicitly addressed.

Index of Names

Abelard, Peter, xxv, xxvii, 3–4, 27–29, 47–48, 57–58, 73–74, 87, 89–90, 100–101, 107–8, 123–24, 132, 146
Abraham, 101
Achtemeier, Paul, 38
Adam/Eve, 46–47, 49–51, 53, 62, 68, 72, 84
Agamben, Giorgio, 29
Akedah, 111
Alaric, 99
Aletti, Jean-Noël, xi, 82–83
Alexander of Aphrodisias, 101
Alexander, Donald, xi
Alexander, Philip, 119
Alston, Wallace, Jr., xi
Ambrosiaster, 16, 121
Anderson, Gary, xi
Anderson, Joseph, xi
Anselm, 28
Aquinas, Thomas. *See* Thomas Aquinas
Aristotle, 4, 13, 20, 63, 75–76, 82, 146–47
Arndt, Johann, 77–78
Arnobius, 64

Augustine, xxiii, xxv, xxvii, 3, 12–14, 21, 26–27, 45–47, 54, 57, 64, 70–73, 81–82, 88–89, 94, 97–102, 106–7, 114–15, 123, 131–32, 145–46

Babcock, William S., 169 n.22
Bach, Johann Sebastian, xxiv, 83
Badiou, Alain, 65–66
Bailey, Daniel, xi, 159 n.115
Bainton, Roland, 175 nn.25, 28, 40
Bakker, Nico Tjepko, 110, 170 n.48
Balthasar, Hans Urs von, 64
Barnes, Jay, xi
Barr, James, 39
Barrett, C. K., 20, 171 n.29
Barth, Karl, xxvi–xxvii, 5–7, 12, 17–20, 35–37, 50–51, 54, 59–64, 67–68, 77–82, 87, 92–94, 96, 102–3, 109–11, 117–18, 126–27, 136–41, 148
Basilides, 45
Beck, J. T., 6, 79
Becker, Jürgen, 95
Bede, xvii
Bell, Richard, 64–65

Index of Subjects